40.00

D1517787

Diversity Across the Curriculum

Diversity Across the Curriculum

A Guide for Faculty in Higher Education

Edited by

Jerome Branche
John W. Mullennix
Ellen R. Cohn
University of Pittsburgh

ANKER PUBLISHING COMPANY, INC.
Bolton, Massachusetts

Diversity Across the Curriculum
A Guide for Faculty in Higher Education

Copyright © 2007 by Anker Publishing Company, Inc. All rights reserved. Printed in the United States of America. No part of this publication may be reproduced or distributed in any form or by any means, electronic or mechanical, including photocopying, recording, or by any information storage or retrieval system, without the prior written consent of the publisher.

ISBN 978-1-933371-28-3

Composition by Deerfoot Studios
Cover design by Dutton & Sherman Design

Anker Publishing Company, Inc.
563 Main Street
P.O. Box 249
Bolton, MA 01740-0249 USA

www.ankerpub.com

Library of Congress Cataloging-in-Publication Data

Diversity across the curriculum : a guide for faculty in higher education / edited by Jerome Branche, John W. Mullennix, Ellen R. Cohn.
    p. cm.
  Includes bibliographical references and index.
  ISBN 978-1-933371-28-3
  1. Multicultural education—Curricula—United States. 2. Education, Higher—Curricula—United States. 3. Minorities—Education (Higher)—United States. I. Branche, Jerome. II. Mullennix, John W. III. Cohn, Ellen R., Ph. D.

  LC3727.D538 2007
  378.1'99—dc22

                            2007010510

Table of Contents

About the Authors

About the Editors

Jerome Branche, Ph.D., Dip. Ed.; John W. Mullennix, Ph.D.; and Ellen Cohn, Ph.D., were nominated as 2005 Provost's Diversity Fellows at the University of Pittsburgh and met as members of a two-week faculty diversity seminar. The coeditors fervently believe that every faculty member who stands before a class has the responsibility to incorporate both content and methods that meet the needs of a multicultural student body. They thus decided to assemble, as a guide for others, the work of exceptional teachers and scholars who actively incorporate diversity into their teaching.

Jerome Branche is associate professor and director of graduate studies in the Department of Hispanic Languages and Literatures at the University of Pittsburgh. His teaching and research interests are in literature and society in Latin America, with a special emphasis on race and national formation. He has published several articles on the Hispanic Caribbean and on Afro-Latino literature.

He wrote *Colonialism and Race in Luso-Hispanic Literature* (University of Missouri Press, 2006) and edited *Lo que teníamos que tener: Raza y revolución en Nicolás Guillén* (Instituto Internacional de Literatura Iberoamericana, 2003). He is a member of several professional organizations, including the Modern Language Association of America, the Latin American Studies Association, and the Instituto Internacional de Literatura Iberoamericana.

John W. Mullennix is professor in the Department of Psychology at the University of Pittsburgh–Johnstown. An expert in the areas of psycholinguistics, speech perception, and speech technology, he has published a number of research articles in major journals in the areas of psychology and speech communication; a number of chapters in edited volumes; and a coauthored/edited book with Keith Johnson, titled *Talker Variability in Speech Processing* (Academic Press, 1997). In addition to basic research on human speech perception, he has conducted and published research on the perception and comprehension of computer-generated speech and is an expert in the area of human-machine interaction (human factors).

Dr. Mullennix also has a strong interest in teaching and pedagogy. He has extensive experience teaching psychology at both undergraduate and graduate levels. He received teaching awards from both Wayne State University and the University of Pittsburgh–Johnstown and is a member of Project Kaleidoscope, a national alliance of colleges and universities devoted to building strong learning environments for undergraduate students in mathematics, engineering, and the sciences. He was one of the first faculty members at the University of Pittsburgh to test electronic distance learning systems for courses and has given talks on the use of electronic discussion groups for college classes.

Dr. Mullennix's participation in this book was funded in part by a 2006 University of Pittsburgh–Johnstown Faculty Scholarship Grant.

 *Ellen R. Cohn* is assistant dean for instruction at the University of Pittsburgh's School of Health and Rehabilitation Sciences and associate professor in the Department of Communication Science and Disorders. She has a secondary faculty appointment in the School of Pharmacy and is a faculty member of the McGowan Institute for Regenerative Medicine. Dr. Cohn's academic activities span multiple disciplines. She teaches in the areas of cleft palate and craniofacial disorders, pharmacy and therapeutics, orthodontics, and rhetoric and communication. Previously, she served as a speech-language pathologist and research associate at the University of Pittsburgh Cleft-Palate Craniofacial Center and was director of the University of Pittsburgh Speech and Hearing Clinic. In 2003, she coauthored a proposal at the University of Pittsburgh's School of Law to create a master's of law concentration in disability law.

Dr. Cohn has authored multiple distance education manuals and web-based course developments. She coauthored *Videofluoroscopic Studies of Speech in Patients with Cleft Palate* (Springer-Verlag, 1989, with M. Leon Skolnick) and is a member of numerous professional organizations, including the American Speech-Language-Hearing Association and the American Cleft Palate-Craniofacial Association. She has contributed to *Educause Quarterly, Cleft Palate-Craniofacial Journal, Plastic and Reconstructive Surgery, Journal of Speech-Language and Hearing Disorders,* and *Radiology.* Dr. Cohn currently serves as a co-investigator on the Rehabilitation Engineering Research Center on Telerehabilitation at the University of Pittsburgh, funded by the U.S. Department of Education's National Institute on Disability Research and Rehabilitation.

About the Contributors

Susan A. Albrecht is associate professor and associate dean for academic affairs at the University of Pittsburgh's School of Nursing. Her area of expertise and research is smoking cessation in pregnant women. She teaches in the master's and doctoral programs at the School of Nursing.

Lorin Basden Arnold is associate professor of communication at Rowan University. Her area of research is interpersonal communication, with a specific focus on family communication. Most recently, her presented and published work has concentrated on non-normative families and family issues, such as large families and mothers with eating disorders.

Lisa Marie Bernardo is associate professor at the University of Pittsburgh's School of Nursing and director of continuing education. Her area of expertise is wellness and fitness. She teaches in the RN Options program at the School of Nursing.

David Bogen is associate professor of sociology and executive director of the Institute for Liberal Arts and Interdisciplinary Studies at Emerson College. His research and publications focus on the relationships between contemporary media, discourse, and the philosophy of language, and, more recently, on the development of interactive technologies in education.

Helen Bond has a doctorate in human development and is professor of education in the graduate school at the University of Maryland University College in Adelphi, Maryland. Her area of research is multicultural education, human rights, and genocide. Dr. Bond's research on human rights in cross-cultural contexts has taken her to West Africa, Cuba, and Europe. Currently, she is working on a book about genocide and African-Americans.

Jean Ferguson Carr is associate professor of English and Women's Studies at the University of Pittsburgh. She teaches and writes on 19th-century American literature and literacy, composition, and women's studies. She is coauthor of *Archives of Instruction: Nineteenth-Century Rhetorics, Readers, and Composition Books in the United States* (Southern Illinois University Press, 2005), which won the MLA's Mina P. Shaughnessy Prize. She was co-director of the University of Pittsburgh's faculty seminar on diversity 1996–1999. She also won the Chancellor's Diversity Award from the University of Pittsburgh.

Shelly S. Chabon is executive director and CEO of Children's TLC Easter Seals. She served as the first chair and a former professor of the Department of Communication Sciences and Disorders at Rockhurst University. Her areas of interest are diversity education, health care ethics, and language-learning disabilities. She has published and presented several papers on these topics. Dr.

Chabon is a fellow of the American Speech-Language-Hearing Association (ASHA) and currently serves as the chair of the ASHA Board of Ethics.

Denise Chisholm is assistant professor in the Department of Occupational Therapy at the University of Pittsburgh. Her area of research is mental health, evidence-based practice, and outcome assessment. She is coauthor of a book on occupation-based practice and past recipient of the Pennsylvania Occupational Therapy Association's Academic Educator Award and OTR (occupational therapist, registered) Award of Recognition.

Fred W. Clothey is professor of Religious Studies at the University of Pittsburgh. He is the author or editor of seven books, the cofounder of the *Journal of Ritual Studies*, and the producer and director of six documentary films on festivals in India and Pittsburgh. Most of his research has been done in South Asia or on émigrés of South Asian descent in Southeast Asia and the United States. In addition to South Asian religions, he specializes in the study of myth and ritual and on issues of religion and identity.

Mindy L. Columbus is director of student services and registrar at the University of Pittsburgh's School of Health and Rehabilitation Sciences. She earned her Bachelor of Science degree in information sciences from Robert Morris University and Master of Science degree in health and rehabilitation sciences with a concentration in Health Information Systems from the University of Pittsburgh. She is currently pursuing a doctoral program in epidemiology from the University of Pittsburgh and serves as secretary on the Pennsylvania division board of directors of the International Association of Administrative Professionals.

Valire Carr Copeland is associate professor in the School of Social Work and in the Graduate School of Public Health's Department of Community and Behavioral Health Sciences, associate director of the Public Health Social Work Training Program, and faculty affiliate in the Center for Minority Health at the University of Pittsburgh's Graduate School of Public Health. Dr. Copeland is the co-director of the University of Pittsburgh's provost diversity seminar, and her current scholarship focuses on culturally competent engagement and intervention strategies and their impact on mental health disparities.

Lydia B. Daniels is a lecturer and the director of undergraduate programs for the Department of Biological Sciences at the University of Pittsburgh. She regularly teaches Biochemistry and Writing in the Biological Sciences. She oversees all aspects of undergraduate education for the department—including course offerings, judicial affairs, curricular review, and advising—and serves as a resource on teaching-related issues for the faculty.

James Davis is chair and professor of Spanish and foreign language education in the Department of Modern Languages and Literatures at Howard University, in Washington, DC. He earned his doctorate from the University of Michigan. His research interests include African-Americans and second language learning, and Dominican literature.

Lynne Degitz serves as communications specialist for diversity and multicultural affairs, an administrative unit under the executive vice chancellor and Office of the Provost at the University of North Carolina–Chapel Hill.

Dan P. Dewey is assistant professor of Foreign Language Education at the University of Pittsburgh. He conducts research on Second Language Acquisition during study abroad and intensive domestic immersion. He also teaches courses for language teachers on teaching methods, classroom assessment, and technology in the classroom.

Teresa E. Donegan is assistant professor in the University of Pittsburgh's School of Pharmacy. Her training and education are in clinical psychology. Along with her primary role of teaching the human dimensions of pharmaceutical care in the curriculum, she is a coordinator for community outreach efforts to underserved and minority populations. Her research expertise is in evaluating behavioral and health care programs as well as in curriculum assessment.

Kris English is associate professor at the University of Akron. Her areas of interest include improving patient counseling in audiology and improving auditory perception of children who have hearing loss. She has authored 5 books and 11 chapters and has published research in several scientific journals.

Barbara A. Frey is a senior instructional designer in the Center for Instructional Development and Distance Education at the University of Pittsburgh, where she provides support and training to faculty on a variety of teaching and learning projects. In addition, she teaches as an adjunct assistant professor in the Department of Learning and Performance Systems at the Pennsylvania State University's World Campus. Her research interests include web-based distance education, program evaluation, instructional design and technology, and human resource development.

Monica Frölander-Ulf, a citizen of Finland, is associate professor of anthropology at the University of Pittsburgh–Johnstown. She teaches courses on the anthropology of women, the history and contemporary cultures of North American indigenous societies, and the cultures of the African diaspora. She has organized field trips in Jamaica for several groups of students and has directed two service-learning courses in Jamaica and the Navajo Nation. Her research interests include women's status and roles in Finland and cooperative development and grassroots organizing in Jamaica.

John W. Gareis directs undergraduate advising and is an instructor in the University of Pittsburgh's communication department. An award-winning instructor, he teaches courses including organizational communication, introduction to the communication process, freshman studies, and rhetoric and culture: civil religion.

Shelome Gooden has been assistant professor of linguistics at the University of Pittsburgh since 2003. Her research areas include sociolinguistics, language variation, language contact, phonology, and phonetics/phonology interface. She does research on pidgin and Creole languages and has published her research in journals and monographs in her field. Dr. Gooden is currently the undergraduate student advisor.

Robert M. Goodman is professor and chair of the Graduate School of Public Health at the University of Pittsburgh. His interests are in the areas of community-based participatory research, evaluation research, social ecology intervention research, community capacity development, and qualitative methods. He teaches a course in community public health development and has taught courses in evaluation methods and social issues in public health. Dr. Goodman is a past president (1999) of the Society for Public Health Education.

Meredith Guthrie is a lecturer in communication at the University of Pittsburgh. Her area of research includes charting the development of marketing demographics aimed at preteen children. She also has forthcoming articles on depictions of disability in children's literature and the use of "trash" cinema as a tool for teaching film theory.

Roberta Hatcher is assistant professor of French at the University of Pittsburgh. Her teaching and research interests focus on French language literatures of sub-Saharan Africa and the Caribbean, African cinema, and postcolonial studies. In addition to research articles on African literature and film, she has published on pedagogical issues, including the use of maps and visual texts to introduce the history of colonialism in the intermediate-level language classroom.

Daqing He is assistant professor at the School of Information Sciences at the University of Pittsburgh. His main research interests are in the areas of information retrieval and natural language processing, especially in the area of applying natural language processing techniques to improve users' ability to access relevant information. Dr. He has published more than 30 journal and conference papers. He has been teaching courses related to digital library, information retrieval, and databases for several years.

Reinhard Heinisch is professor of political science and director of international studies at the University of Pittsburgh–Johnstown. He has been at the school since 1994, specializing in comparative politics and international political economy. He is the author of *Populism, Proporz, Pariah: Austria Turns Right* (Nova Science, 2002) as well as of numerous other publications. His most recent article is forthcoming in *Twenty-First Century Populism: Structure and Agency of the Unwelcome Guest of Western European Democracy* (Palgrave).

Ako Inuzuka is assistant professor of communication at the University of Pittsburgh at Johnstown. Her area of research is intercultural/international communication, rhetorical criticism, media studies, gender studies, and postcolonial studies. Her recent projects include the collective memory of the Pacific War in Japan and the cultural representation of Lafcadio Hearn in Japan and the United States.

Kenneth J. Jaros is assistant professor and associate department chair of the Graduate School of Public Health at the University of Pittsburgh, where he serves as the director of the Center for Maternal and Child Health Leadership in Public Health Social Work. His research focuses on applied community-based research, helping organizations translate ideas into effective intervention programs. His primary areas of interest include children and youth services, community organizing, and issues of health disparities.

Raymond Jones is assistant professor of business administration at the University of Pittsburgh, where he teaches introductory undergraduate and graduate courses in business ethics and organizational behavior, as well as advanced undergraduate courses on gender and diversity in management and on governance and management. For the past two years, he has served as coordinator of the Certificate Program in Leadership and Ethics.

Susan Gillis Kruman is instructor of dance and yoga at the University of Pittsburgh. Her area of research is dance performance, education, technology, and history. She has received numerous grants for choreography and has presented workshops in dance both nationally and internationally.

Dorian Lee-Wilkerson is coordinator of graduate studies in the Department of Communicative Sciences and Disorders at Hampton University. She has published and presented papers on diversity education, test/evaluation bias, and language development.

Linda Lindroth is adjunct assistant professor of Fine Arts, Women's Studies, and Interactive Digital Design at Quinnipiac University. Her recent fellowships include the Connecticut Commission on the Arts, the National Endowment for the Arts, and the John Anson Kittredge Foundation. She has exhibited her photographs and mixed media artwork in over 100 solo and group shows and is represented in public and private collections, including the Museum of Modern Art and the Metropolitan Museum of Art.

Dennis Looney is associate professor of Italian in the Department of French and Italian at the University of Pittsburgh, where he also currently serves as assistant dean in the humanities. He teaches courses and conducts research on the classical tradition in European literary culture, with a focus on the relationship between Italian vernacular culture and classical culture as articulated through Renaissance humanism.

Sarah McGaughey is lecturer and German language program coordinator at the University of Massachusetts Amherst. Her areas of research are 19th- and 20th-century culture, architectural history, visual and aesthetic theory, and foreign language pedagogy. She has recently received funding to develop black German studies curriculum content for incorporation throughout the German language curriculum at the university.

Jack Meacham is SUNY Distinguished Teaching Professor at the University at Buffalo–The State University of New York and a member of the Department of Psychology. He is currently teaching World Civilizations, an undergraduate general education course, and his interests include the influence of student diversity on teaching and learning and the pedagogy for, and assessment of, teaching and learning.

Jaime P. Muñoz is assistant professor in the Department of Occupational Therapy at Duquesne University. His area of research is culturally responsive caring and multicultural education in the health professions and outcomes measurement of programs for people who are homeless or formerly incarcerated.

Audrey J. Murrell is associate professor of Business Administration at the University of Pittsburgh and serves as the director of the Program on Women and the Workforce at the University Center for Social and Urban Research. Dr. Murrell has conducted research on the effects of career mobility and transition, with a special emphasis on factors that can impact the careers of women in management. Dr. Murrell is coauthor of *Mentoring Dilemmas: Developmental Relationships Within Multicultural Organizations* (Lawrence Erlbaum & Associates, 1999).

Diane Pisacreta is professor of psychology at St. Louis Community College. She teaches a variety of psychology courses, including general psychology, human sexuality, and introduction to women's studies. Ms. Pisacreta has completed an M.A. in psychology from the University of Michigan and an M.A. in women's studies from the University of Cincinnati. Areas of research interest include heterosexuality, feminist pedagogy, and the relationship between systems of oppression and identity formation.

Deborah E. Polk is assistant professor of Dental Public Health at the University of Pittsburgh's School of Dental Medicine. Her area of research is socioeconomic health disparities in oral health.

Michael Pramuka is assistant professor of Rehabilitation Science and Technology in the School of Health and Rehabilitation Sciences at the University of Pittsburgh. He teaches in the M.S. program in rehabilitation counseling and conducts research in psychosocial aspects of epilepsy, in telerehabilitation, and in vocational rehabilitation of cognitive disability. He is a licensed psychologist and a certified rehabilitation counselor.

Xaé Alicia Reyes is associate professor in Curriculum and Instruction at the University of Connecticut, where she holds a joint appointment in Puerto Rican and Latino studies. Her publications in journals such as the *Journal of Latina/os and Education, Journal of Latino Studies,* and *Journal of Hispanic Higher Education* reflect her concerns for social justice and her commitment to equity and access. Dr. Reyes's areas of expertise include critical ethnography, teacher preparation for linguistically and culturally diverse communities, media representations, and migration issues as they affect schooling, civic engagement, and political participation.

Richard W. Rubin is assistant professor of Dental Public Health at the University of Pittsburgh's School of Dental Medicine. He is currently the director of the Student Community Outreach Program and Education.

Kathryn Russell teaches courses in modern philosophy, philosophy of science, and political philosophy and interdisciplinary general education courses in science and society as well as prejudice and discrimination. She has been active in the State University of New York College–Cortland's Multicultural and Gender Studies Council, chaired the college's general education committee, and was team leader for a campus-wide two-year faculty development project on diversifying the curriculum.

María Cristina Saavedra is assistant professor in the Department of Modern Languages at Susquehanna University. She writes on Cuban film and on Cuban and Cuban-American literary, artistic, and cultural issues.

Katherine Seelman is associate dean for disability programs and professor of rehabilitation science and technology at the University of Pittsburgh and former director of the U.S. National Institute on Disability and Rehabilitation Research. Her research interests are in disability studies and science, technology, and public policy. She is the recipient of many awards and is widely published.

Ravi K. Sharma is assistant professor in the Graduate School of Public Health at the University of Pittsburgh, where he serves as chair of the Graduate School of Public Health's faculty diversity committee and where he teaches spatial data analysis, demographic techniques, and social inequalities and health. His research is directed at understanding the community and environmental determinants of health and illness. Additionally, he is studying the determinants of physical activity, obesity, and maternal smoking by neighborhoods.

Bonnie Shulman is associate professor of mathematics at Bates College in Lewiston, Maine, where she has taught since 1991. Her research interests include mathematical modeling, history and philosophy of mathematics, and feminist science studies. She has published articles on all of these topics and has received funding to facilitate campus-wide faculty development seminars on women and scientific literacy.

Gerald R. Shuster recently retired as associate professor of communications at Robert Morris University and is now a full-time lecturer with the Department of Communication at the University of Pittsburgh, where he served as an adjunct professor for more than 20 years. His primary teaching area is political communication and presidential rhetoric. He regularly provides political analysis for local and regional media—printed and electronic—on local, state, and national political events and personalities.

Anita Silvers is professor of philosophy at San Francisco State University and a member of the ethics committee at San Francisco General Hospital. She has published 8 books and more than 150 articles on ethics, political and social philosophy, medical ethics, feminist philosophy, aesthetics, and disability studies. She is a polio survivor with a severe disability.

Janet Skupien teaches in the Department of Communication at the University of Pittsburgh. Her research interests include interpersonal relationships within a social and historical perspective, methodology in the human sciences, and communication theory.

Dereece Smither is assistant professor of psychology at the University of Pittsburgh–Johnstown. She is interested in various aspects of cognitive and social development. In particular, her current research activities involve the cognitive benefits of computer learning, understanding and use of gender and sexual information, and the relationship between language usage and cognitive dissonance.

Jeannette E. South-Paul joined the Department of Family Medicine at the University of Pittsburgh in July 2001, after serving for 22 years as a family physician in the U.S. Army. She currently serves as Andrew W. Mathieson Professor and chair of the Department of Family Medicine at the University of Pittsburgh, and maintains an active family medicine practice. Her research interests include maternal child health and fitness and evaluating cultural competence in clinicians and trainees.

Gary P. Stoehr is associate professor in the Department of Pharmacy and Therapeutics at the University of Pittsburgh School of Pharmacy. His area of research is drug use in the elderly and the scholarship of teaching. He teaches two introductory courses in the professional pharmacy curriculum that introduce student pharmacists to the responsibilities of the professional pharmacist and the clinical skills needed to deliver pharmaceutical care.

Martha Ann Terry is a senior research associate and director of the Master of Public Health Program at the University of Pittsburgh's Graduate School of Public Health. Her research interests include sociocultural aspects of human sexuality, reproductive decision-making, HIV/AIDS and women's health, community-based participatory research, and implementation and evaluation of community-based interventions. Her areas of expertise include process evaluation, focus group facilitation and analysis, stage-based outreach training, and role model story development training.

Valerie J. M. Watzlaf is associate professor of Health Information Management at the University of Pittsburgh and holds a secondary appointment in the Graduate School of Public Health. She has published extensively in the field of health information management and is the recipient of the American Health Information Management Association's Research Award. Dr. Watzlaf has chaired the association's Coding, Policy, and Strategy Committee and its Council on Accreditation, and she is currently serving on its Foundation of Research and Education.

Laurel Willingham-McLain directs the Center for Teaching Excellence (CTE) at Duquesne University, where she supports faculty and teaching assistants in their teaching and professional development campus wide. She leads the academic learning outcomes assessment initiative, oversees teaching awards, promotes cross-cultural understanding through CTE programming, and teaches a seminar for students returning from study abroad.

Flore Zéphir has been teaching at the University of Missouri–Columbia since 1988 in the Department of Romance Languages and Literatures. She is currently professor of French, director of undergraduate studies, coordinator of the Master's program in Foreign Language Teaching, and chair of the linguistics program. She has published numerous articles and review essays, and her books include *Haitian Immigrants in Black America: A Sociological and Sociolinguistic Portrait, Trends in Ethnic Identification Among Second-Generation Haitian Immigrants in New York City,* and *The Haitian Americans* (Greenwood, 2004).

Part I

Introduction

1

An Overview

John W. Mullennix

In today's academic environment faculty members at colleges and universities must often excel in three domains: teaching, professional development, and service. At times faculty can find the demands of maintaining proficiency in these three areas overwhelming, considering their limited time and resources. As faculty we view ourselves as simultaneously filling several roles in academe, including that of teacher, mentor, scholar, university citizen, local community citizen, and member of national or international scholarly communities. In this book we focus on the role of teacher. More specifically, we are concerned with the role of a teacher in an increasingly multicultural world. In the United States, as Frederick (1995) stated:

> Multiculturalism is not a new but rather a familiar issue in American culture and history, as old as the recurring question of what it means to be an American. This redefinition occurs in every era of demographic change, as new immigrants come to the United States. (p. 84)

Certainly, when looking at demographic trends in the United States, major changes have occurred recently in immigration patterns. And as technology makes it easier to communicate to people around the world, even people in relatively isolated areas, there is no question that we are becoming a more global society. In light of these recent developments, we believe that every faculty member who stands before a class has a responsibility to incorporate both content and methods that meet the needs of multicultural students and that prepare all students to enter a multicultural, globalized society when they complete their education.

Overall, the book provides a practical guide for college and university faculty members and staff to efficiently and effectively create culturally inclusive courses and learning environments across many different disciplines. We present the work of a number of exceptional teachers and scholars who have actively incorporated diversity into their teaching.

In the first part of the book, we present a number of chapters that provide an overarching discussion of theoretical and pragmatic issues that one should keep in mind when incorporating diversity into college courses. In the first contribution in this section, Jerome Branche discusses barriers that impede the accomplishment of this goal and how to overcome such barriers. Next, Ellen Cohn and I present a view of diversity within the context of a curricular initiative. The third contribution consists of Ellen Cohn and John Gareis covering some structural design issues—such as syllabi, readings, assignments, and participation norms—that one must take into account when redesigning a course to be more inclusive. This is followed by Barbara Frey's chapter examining the issues surrounding principles of inclusive assessment in the classroom environment, with a special focus on the use of rubrics. And finally, the first section of the book concludes with Jean Carr discussing how, in the larger view of diversity and the curriculum, disciplinary traditions can frame discussions of curricular change with respect to diversity.

In the second part of the book, we feature the efforts of several institutions of higher education to promote diversity across the curriculum. Each institution provides a description of the programs, resources, and/or systems that support faculty's efforts to incorporate diversity into the curriculum.

The third, fourth, and fifth parts of the book consist of a collection of concise essays written by faculty members at institutions of higher learning. Each essay features a discussion of a particular course, cluster of courses, or program of approach in a discipline where the authors have made significant attempts to incorporate culturally responsive elements and/or awareness into their teaching. Some of these vignettes focus on the practical issues of implementation and the mechanics by which instructors have transformed their teaching in a discipline to address diversity. In these cases one will find descriptions of specific courses with reports on student responses, outcomes, results, improvements and/or changes made over time, and lessons learned during the process of transformation. Other vignettes focus on more general issues that must be considered when modifying curricula to address issues of diversity. Upon perusing these vignettes, one will find that the authors present an astonishing array of advanced pedagogical techniques used to enhance cultural sensitivity and awareness and that these educators rely on an innovative use of techniques, such as interpersonal dialogues, experiential learning situations, audience analysis, film, self-reflection, peer tutoring, student coinstructors, and collaborative learning. In addition, some authors discuss barriers to emphasizing diversity in their classes, along with problem-solving techniques designed to address classroom tensions and conflicts that may crop up.

The faculty-authored vignettes are grouped according to three different academic areas: Humanities, Health Sciences, and Natural and Social Sciences. In the Humanities section authors discuss how they handle teaching courses that lend themselves to an infusion of diversity in a more overt manner, because of their intrinsic content (e.g., Francophone studies, Hispanic studies, fine arts, etc.). In the Health Sciences section, the contributions span a wide range of clinical and health-related services, including audiology, speech pathology, dentistry, occupational therapy, nursing, rehabilitation counseling, pharmacy, and medicine. Across these areas, there is a strong focus on educating students about the diverse populations that they will encounter in their professions; for these students, cultural awareness and diversity is an important and necessary component to their education. In the Natural and Social Sciences section, a variety of disciplines is represented. Some chapters deal with students' perceptions of other cultures, particularly those across the geopolitical spectrum. Certain topics (e.g., religion and India, Islam and the *Qur'an*, etc.) are entertained that are of particular interest given the current world political situation. There is also a special focus on communication across different environments, including communication within families, communication across cultures, and communication within politics. This section also includes essays on hard sciences and technology, areas that some may believe are more difficult to incorporate diversity into. Authors here describe their experiences and provide models that could eventually apply to a broad range of scientific disciplines and areas that have a focus on technology, such as engineering, information science, and library science.

In conclusion, the chapters that follow present valuable information and practical advice on diversity and curricular issues from experts in instruction and pedagogy, from staff at colleges and universities where diversity-related initiatives operate, and from faculty instructors who have transformed their courses with diversity in mind. Our book functions primarily as a practical guide for faculty and administrators interested in curricular change. In particular, the contributions from faculty who are in the trenches—who explain how they approach diversity, coursework, and the curriculum in their individual disciplines—are an invaluable aid to other faculty who wish to embark on a similar journey. However, across the individual contributions one also finds many interesting discussions concerning why people feel that incorporating cultural awareness and diversity into college courses is important. We believe that our book stands as a solid example of an issue that college and university staff and instructors need to address today as a matter of importance.

References

Frederick, P. (1995). Walking on eggs. *College Teaching, 43*, 83–93.

2

Barriers to Diversity

Jerome Branche

There is an oft-quoted reference to Fanon's (1967) description of "the fact of blackness" that bears unerringly on the discussion of the barriers to diversity. It concerns the wonderment and alarm registered by a white child upon suddenly encountering Fanon, a Martinican, one winter's day in Paris ("Look! A Negro! . . . Mama, see the Negro! I'm frightened!" p. 112). It also concerns the psychiatrist's own alarm and wonderment at experiencing being through the eyes of a racial "other." It was a highly charged moment that he deemed unlikely to occur in his homogenous community of origin. If, on the one hand, the child's anxiety was occasioned in the starkness of the corporeal difference of the foreigner, along with the "thousand details, anecdotes, stories," by which he or she might at that tender age have already been affected, it was clearly the starkness of the act of association of his bodily exterior with the troubling content of these "anecdotes" and "stories" that bothered the visitor from overseas. Indeed, the scene might well be described as primordial to the racialized modern West, where similar scenarios of racial difference and racial interaction often are associated with tension and overlaid with connotations of inequality and hierarchy, and where an ever-present history of legal and quasilegal strictures segregates the landscape.

This segregation of the landscape, both interior and exterior, is what imposed itself recently, in the brief space of a semester, when I was repeatedly reminded of the scarcity of the black presence in the rarefied spaces of American academia. In the first two incidents, I was part of a search committee for a new assistant professor for our department, the Department of Hispanic Languages and Literatures. We were conducting preliminary interviews at a hotel in a city away from home, and it fell to me to open the door when the candidate knocked. When I opened the door, the candidate raised his eyes to the room number, as if in a moment of self-doubt, and asked whether he got the room right. I assured him that he did. The second of the two candidates "worthy of recall," if you will, gained this distinction when he turned to me in the course of the interview and excused himself for switching from English to Spanish.

Admittedly, both instances of interracial exchange might be seen as ambiguous. That is to say, there might have been no intention on the part of my interlocutors to "discriminate" or misrecognize me as a black professor, or to indirectly question my competence or whether I was bona fide. In fact, it is not unusual, as one of my colleagues on the search committee pointed out later (and quite reasonably so), that foreign language departments like ours have members of other departments sit on their hiring committees, the implication being that I might have been seen as an outsider by our candidate. For my part, however, I could not escape the possibility that said candidate might well have been working on the subconscious premise that black people, even those teaching in Spanish departments, don't speak Spanish and that whatever intellectual capability might be involved in the mastery of the foreign language did not extend to us. Also, I could not help but be curious at the apparent puzzlement of the first of the two interviewees upon encountering me at the door, because I was the one who had answered the phone when he called up from the lobby asking for the room number. As a person whose professional life is in part based on tuning in to foreign registers in language, could he not have observed the Caribbean cadence in my voice and anticipated meeting a person "of difference"?

The third of these events was essentially not unlike the others. Our department had a very distinguished professor as a guest, and we were feting her at a reception that included several of our graduate students. During the course of introductions, her inquiry of me was illustrative. What was the topic of *my* dissertation? Again, ambiguity? Though she might sincerely have wanted to know what it was that I had studied before entering the profession, it struck me as just as logical that she might have assumed that I, the black guy with the noticeably graying beard of my 40-plus years, was a graduate student. After all, college students are often older nowadays, as a senior police official once told me in the course of an investigation after I had lodged a complaint for racial harassment by campus police. Even where one concedes an inherent ambiguity to these instances, there are no two ways about the way one feels when one is subjected to racial slights, whether these are intended or not. Thankfully, the grief experienced in cases of harassment or negative race or gender interaction is recognized as valid by American jurisprudence. In cases of racial misassumption, given their potential for harm, this is particularly important. Indeed, the slippery realities generated by racial misassumption highlight the value, for aggrieved minorities, of surveys and statistics, of lawyers and cross-examination, and of the access to legal recourse that is provided for, in the final analysis, by our democracy. At another level, if the intentions of the perceived offender are ambiguous, it is no less true that everyday existence for the offended individuals has always meant coping with not only the unsubtle forms of their oppression but also the subtle ones. (I am using *oppression* here not in its traditional sense of springing from a centralized, tyrannical force but in its more recent usage in social theory as the exercise of diffuse power in the "everyday practices of a well-intentioned liberal society" [Young, 1990, p. 41].)

Putting aside my own projections, what was most clear about these events was that this was a case of racial underrepresentation in academia, of underrepresentation both as cause and as effect. Underrepresentation as cause would be a primary derivative of a system of cultural and racial hegemony still resistant to change after half a century of civil rights legislation. It constitutes the major barrier to diversity in higher education. Underrepresentation as effect would explain the misrecognition of a black male who might be deemed to be out of place in a traditionally monochrome professorate. Nationwide only 6% of faculty are black. Another 9% make up the other minorities. Indeed, in the past 10 years of my college teaching, the other black male university employees I have encountered have belonged in their overwhelming majority to nonprofessional or ancillary staff (see U.S. Department of Education, 2006). My black male undergraduate students have likewise been notoriously few, and I have taught but one black male graduate student thus far.

If this resistance to diversity is not as evident as it might be, it could only be the result of accepted norms in thinking in which, as I suggested earlier, the racial profile of the college professor is white. Just as important, accompanying Eurocentric biases in the curriculum are not recognized for what they are. These biases and all that they imply provide the impetus behind the efforts of the editors and contributors in this volume at providing curricular alternatives. Of a truth, the presumed neutrality of schools and schooling, as Henry Giroux (1992) has observed, and their association with the "principles of equal opportunity" (p. 203) remain sharply at odds with the massive inequity in the nation's distribution of wealth, health care, housing, and so forth. One need only look at the effect of California's Proposition 209, passed in 1996 to outlaw preferential treatment based on race, to appreciate the intensity of the ongoing resistance to the civil rights initiative of leveling the historically uneven playing field in education. Ten years after Proposition 209, and although more than 1 million African-Americans live in Los Angeles County and some 10,000 graduated from high school in 2006, a mere 96 of them gained admission to the University of California–Los Angeles. They formed part of the 2% of the incoming black freshmen in fall 2006. Significantly, their numbers represent a decline of 57% over the past decade (Korry, 2006).

Pedro Noguera and Jean Yonemura Wing (2006) have similarly described a strategy for preserving the socioracial status quo at Berkeley High by means of keeping the school segregated "from within," and this in spite of Berkeley High's reputation as the "most integrated high school in America" (p. 17). Noguera and Wing cite formal and informal practices involving resource allocation and advanced placement in math, science, and foreign languages, which favor white and economically advantaged students. These practices lead to the overrepresentation of the latter in positive outcomes and to overrepresentation of black and Latino students in negative outcomes. They further report that of the 8,676 students admitted in 2004 to the University of California–Berkeley, only 211 (2.43%) were black (Noguera & Wing, 2006, p. 14). Here in Pittsburgh the current high school dropout rate for black males is 49%. In fact, only three blacks, out of a population of 10,111 high school students enrolled in the Pittsburgh school district, passed the Advanced Placement exams in 2005. Considering some of the consequences in terms of these students' lack of postsecondary preparedness for the workforce and their susceptibility to racialized exploitation, marginalization, and the prison industrial complex, these are particularly telling statistics (see also Smydo & Grant, 2006; Barlow, 2006).

If we see high school as the initial segment of the pipeline that might later produce college graduates and eventually professors, and possibly rectify the present state of underrepresentation of blacks and other minorities in higher education, it becomes clear that whatever correctives are eventually produced would need to be systemwide. Evident also is the imperative of addressing the matter of racial inequity in education as the first stage of a long-term process that has social justice as its goal. The ideological barriers that produced the rollback of this ideal in the case of California, cited earlier, and its sister state of Texas, where a similar rejection of civil rights advances now obtains, are by no means limited to these regions. They are merely the more glaring examples of the deeply embedded nature of racist ideology and of the limitations of affirmative action legislation in effecting long-term change. As President George W. Bush remarked in an address to the NAACP, it's "a lot easier to change a law than to change a human heart" (Silva, 2006; see also Shelby, 2002). And this in spite of the broad appeal of the American Association of University Professors, which repeated in 1982 its earlier endorsement of the 1965 executive order for affirmative action in recruiting minority persons and women. Although this observation would explain informal policies and practices, which result in limited minority access to higher education, it also accounts for the difficulties experienced by those minority individuals who have been successful in joining the ranks of the professorate.

Anecdotal and documentary sources are replete with references to the feelings of alienation, isolation, and exclusion experienced by minority faculty in predominantly white college environments. These feelings speak to what has come to be known as the "chilly atmosphere" of unwelcome in which minority faculty, sometimes even after years of service, are still made to feel as if they were "in someone else's house" (Turner & Myers, 2000, p. 17). In this atmosphere of unwelcome the racial hostility may be veiled or it may be overt. It may translate in a devaluation of the race-related research undertaken by minority faculty, as if the research pursuits of the majority community were the only ones entitled to legitimacy. Racial hostility is also expressed through the overloading of minority faculty with committee tasks, with the ensuing negative effect on their research, or in suspicion of their qualifications and the feeling that their hiring might have been linked to quotas and tokenism.

In a profession that is by nature competitive and stress ridden and in which networks of information are key to success, the presence or absence of an effective and interested mentor can also make a world of difference for college faculty. Being left out of the loop, a phenomenon disproportionately suffered by minorities, therefore makes a persuasive argument for the premise that what you don't know can hurt you. To the degree that the majority community leaves minority faculty to stumble around the academy in benign neglect, those in the majority make it more difficult for those in the minority to channel their energies into tenurable activities. These and other objective and subjective barriers leave them poorly equipped for the processes of review and promotion.

Repairing the pipeline, increasing the numbers of minority faculty, and improving the quality of the environment in which they work are eminently worthwhile and necessary goals for higher education. Those goals do not constitute, however, the fullest answer to the challenge of diversity. If the traditionalist content of the knowledge that it is the professorate's job to produce and reproduce remains undisturbed, then greater numerical representation of minorities and women is only of limited value. In the final analysis it is a broader politics of course change and curricular change, buttressed by the requisite administrative support, that holds the greatest hope for a new critical pedagogy. It is our hope, as editors and contributors to this volume, that we will have contributed in some modest measure to the advancement of this necessary task. It is all too easy, in other words, for a policy of diversification to produce mere ethnic and gender enclaves within academia and a resultant neglect and ghettoization. On the other hand, as the core of the educational institution, it is of unsurpassable usefulness that there be an ongoing and constructive dialogue among ourselves as faculty to continue the work of transforming and refining the curriculum. This will in the long run better serve all our students as they face an increasingly diverse and globalized world.

References

Barlow, K. (2006, September 28). Racial disparity in performance must be focus, superintendent says. *University Times, 39*(3).

Fanon, F. (1967). *Black skin, white masks.* New York, NY: Grove Press.

Giroux, H. A. (1992). Resisting difference: Cultural studies and the discourse of critical pedagogy. In L. Grossberg, C. Nelson, & P. Treichler (Eds.), *Cultural studies* (pp. 199–212). New York, NY: Routledge.

Korry, E. (2006). *Black student enrollment at UCLA plunges.* Retrieved February 20, 2007, from www.npr.org/templates/story/story.php?storyId=5563891

Noguera, P., & Wing, J. Y. (2006). *Unfinished business: Closing the racial achievement gap in our schools.* San Francisco, CA: Jossey-Bass.

Shelby, T. (2002). Is racism "in the heart"? *Journal of Social Philosophy, 33,* 411–420.

Silva, M. (2006, July 21). "Good rhetoric" falls short. *Pittsburgh Post-Gazette,* p. A6.

Smydo, J., & Grant, T. (2006, July 13). Angry board spurns dropout study. *Pittsburgh Post-Gazette,* pp. A1, A7.

Turner, C. S. V., & Myers, S. L., Jr. (2000). *Faculty of color in academe: Bittersweet success.* Needham Heights, MA: Allyn & Bacon.

U.S. Department of Education, National Center for Education Statistics. (2006). *Digest of Education Statistics, 2005.* Retrieved February 20, 2007, from http://nces.ed.gov/pubsearch/pubsinfo.asp?pubid=2006030

Young, I. M. (1990). *Justice and the politics of difference.* Princeton, NJ: Princeton University Press.

3

Diversity as an Integral Component of College Curricula

Ellen R. Cohn, John W. Mullennix

Institutions of higher education are increasingly focusing attention on academic initiatives that cut across disciplines, majors, and courses. Cross-curricular initiatives may be motivated by one or more of the following reasons:

- *To ensure that graduates will acquire vital competencies and skills* that transcend an individual course, that must be acquired incrementally and practiced frequently, and that are best refined across multiple contexts (e.g., students will acquire oral communication competencies)

- *To remediate weaknesses* in a current generation or group of students (e.g., graduating students will possess knowledge of literary classics)

- *To incorporate new institutional imperatives* into existing academic courses (e.g., upper level courses will incorporate a service-learning component)

- *To address new societal circumstances* (e.g., students will develop a global perspective)

- *To apprise potential employers* of the value that an institution's graduates might bring to their workplace (e.g., students will be able to engage in project management and work effectively in teams)

- *To simultaneously "brand" the institution* (e.g., the university promotes character development) by highlighting areas of professed institutional excellence and *to instill institutional values*

Curricular standards are typically student-centered in that students (as opposed to faculty or members of the academic community) are required to

11

develop and demonstrate standard specific outcomes. However, it is important to recognize that the achievement of standards often requires a high level of commitment and competency within the larger institution, especially among the teaching faculty. Participating faculty must be willing to reach beyond the silos of their courses. Moreover, the institution must invest resources toward both curricular planning and implementation via faculty development.

A Plethora of Cross-Curricular Initiatives

There are numerous potential cross-curricular initiatives. As an example, the University of Maryland University College's School of Undergraduate Studies (2003) stimulates student achievement via six cross-curricular initiatives: civic responsibility perspective, historical perspective, information literacy, international perspective, fluency in information technology, and effective writing. These initiatives are presented in an integrated manner:

> [University of Maryland University College] graduates develop and demonstrate the hallmarks of an educated person: intellectual ability, curiosity, and flexibility; fundamental skills in reasoning, analysis, and expression; understanding of the principles of scientific and intellectual inquiry; awareness of global and historic context; and civic and ethical responsibility. (p. 3)

For each of the six initiatives, cross-curricular faculty "champions" constructed operational definitions, desired student competencies, and model class activities. The initiatives are addressed at "the basic level through a general education requirement" (p. 3) and "at higher levels" via "learning objectives and courses in the academic major and minor" (p. 3).

Other cross-curricular initiatives currently found across colleges and universities are wide ranging and include such areas as mathematics, reading, writing, languages, ethics, critical thinking, arts, music, religion, and even blogging and spreadsheets. Thus, cross-cutting curricular initiatives can focus attention on novel or ongoing programmatic missions or on areas that require remediation. Whatever the motivation, the programming can overwhelm the traditional curriculum, creating courses with unrealistic expectations and requirements both for student and faculty. It is important not to imperil basic course objectives by imposing too many time-consuming or distracting external objectives. Moreover, when an institution's curricular standards are not in concert with a faculty member's skills or ethos, they may collide with individual notions of academic freedom.

Diversity as a Cross-Curricular Initiative_____

Given the existence of many cross-curricular initiatives, we consider one initiative to be of increasing importance in higher education in today's world: diversity and multiculturalism. Why should diversity prevail as a key initiative? Basically, there are four reasons:

- *Diversity-related outcomes cut across multiple curricular competencies.* These include civic responsibility, communication, writing, art, international studies, languages, music, and religion. It is interesting to note that diversity, to some degree, "rides on top of" some other competencies that by their very nature address diversity, such as language and religion. Thus, diversity is already embedded in many curricula as a tacit "supracurricular" initiative. In terms of other basic competencies, such as writing and communication, diversity can be folded into coursework and curricular plans that address these competencies without causing an inordinate increase in faculty workload or course offerings.

- *Globalization and population trends demand that educated individuals are cognizant of diversity and can function in a culturally competent manner, both in the workplace and in the larger community.* There is no question that the world is shrinking and old boundaries between countries, cultures, and peoples are fast disappearing. The internationalization of business and trade has greatly increased since World War II, the number of multinational corporations has grown, there is a continued increase in international travel and tourism, and the growth of transborder media and the Internet has allowed greater communication between different cultures. In the United States, population trends are undergoing drastic change, with greater numbers of Hispanic-American and Asian-American people composing the overall population. What this means to students emerging from institutions of higher learning is that they must be prepared to venture forth into a world where diversity and different cultures are the norm. If a student is not exposed to different cultures or does not develop a sense of cultural awareness and knowledge of cultural differences, he or she will be ill prepared to succeed in a rapidly changing world where different cultures coexist.

- *Diversity-related competencies possess relevance across the life span.* Not only does a student need to possess cultural awareness to succeed in a career, but diversity-related knowledge and skills potentially traverse multiple life areas. If one considers the changing face of the world, one realizes that interpersonal relationships, work, health and wellness, politics, religion, and leisure and entertainment are all affected by changes in cross-cultural exposure. These changes are evidenced in the growing popularity of everything from Japanese anime and graphic novels to Bollywood films and Chinese acupuncture techniques. In terms of politics, people are beginning to realize that they cannot fully understand regional conflicts in the world without understanding more about the cultural norms underlying the countries involved. In academia, recent discussions of university reform have begun to indicate that, in addition to college students' cognitive (intellectual) development, their social and emotional development should also be addressed (Ayers et al., 1999). As Ayers et al. comment, "Promoting diversity across the curriculum subtly alters the university, enhancing the development of empathy, caring, and social skills among its students by inviting them to acknowledge, embrace, and work with differences among people" (p. 163). Thus, knowledge of cultural awareness may directly affect the quality of life experienced by students. Overall, as university reforms advance, we suspect that cultural awareness, as elicited through the acquisition of diversity-related competencies, will become more and more important to various aspects of people's lives.

- *Ethics, diversity, and equity matter.* Many believe that students in higher education, as part of their learning, should develop and maintain a slate of personal and societal standards for ethical behavior. One issue related to ethics is social justice, which is concerned with injustices committed against people due to such factors as racial/ethnic identity, gender, and disability. An important element of teaching ethical standards to students is a comprehensive understanding of different cultures and peoples. Without this understanding, it is difficult to see how an appropriate sense of social justice could be developed.

Characteristics of Diversity-Rich Courses

There are a variety of avenues that one can follow to create a course that promotes diversity. Here are a few examples of some key attributes that one may find in diversity-rich courses, keeping in mind that each course does not necessarily possess all these attributes and that there are other attributes besides the ones we selected. We illustrate selected points with examples from authors of this book.

Includes Other Voices

The focus here is on the inclusion of writings, speeches, dialogues, films, and so forth, that originate from people of different social identities, cultural backgrounds, gender, and disabilities. As Dennis Looney writes in Chapter 13, it is important to have "other voices that might provide alternate perspectives." He aptly follows this advice by including Catherine of Siena in his course on Italian cultural heritage. John Mullennix, in his chapter (41) about teaching the history of psychology, discusses scientific writing that had been ignored for many years from a number of women and ethnic minorities who contributed to the history of psychology. Certainly, the opportunity for students to appraise original work from a diverse set of authors that they may have had little exposure to is extremely useful.

Communicates Interconnectedness

As we mentioned earlier, the world is shrinking. We are able to interact much more easily than ever before with people different from ourselves. Another element of a diversity-rich course is the development of a sense that we are connected to others beyond our immediate experience and geographic area. As María Saavedra puts it in Chapter 19, "Communicating a sense of the interconnectedness of the United States with the rest of the world and the importance of social responsibility and justice on a global scale may be the most important pedagogical goal." This point is illustrated by Jack Meacham's timely chapter (36) on teaching Islam and the Qur'an to students who are not familiar with either. In today's current world political environment, it is important for our students to go out into the world with a better understanding of religions and cultures different from their own. When asked why students should be introduced to Islam and the holy book of Muslims, Meacham says, "Islam is . . . the second most popular religion in the world" and "the number of adherents to Islam is increasing more rapidly than for other world religions." With the current political strife centered on the Middle East, a proper understanding of Islam would seem to go quite a ways in terms of fostering a sense of understanding between disparate cultures in the West and Middle East.

Values Diversity and Equity

A course that embeds information and techniques designed to impart a sense of why diversity and equity are important is valuable. It is hoped that students are eventually able to understand and tolerate those different from themselves, and beyond this, it is hoped that tolerance will give way to acceptance. In Dereece Smither's chapter (40) on cross-cultural psychology, she cites "encouraging understanding of the value of diversity and equity" as a major goal. In her view, three specific learning objectives follow:

- "To examine the social construction of identities and world knowledge by race, gender, ethnicity, class, sexual orientation, physical ability, nation of origin, and so forth"

- "To demonstrate sensitivity to cultural differences by recognizing the students' own and others' biases and to understand how such biases impact social interactions"

- "To differentiate between personal discomfort and intellectual disagreement in social and cultural conflict situations"

Promotes Transformative Thinking

As Kitano (1997) discusses, there is a pedagogical hierarchy by which one can approach the modification of a course to reflect diversity and multiculturalism. Kitano suggests that our goal is to move up the hierarchy of course evolution from exclusion to inclusion and then to transformation. The following excerpts from John Mullennix's chapter (41), based on Kitano's scheme, define the three types of courses along the hierarchy, going from lowest to highest:

An *exclusive course,* as defined by Kitano [1997]:

> presents and maintains traditional, mainstream experiences and perspectives on the discipline. . . . The instructor conveys information in a didactic manner, and students demonstrate their acquisition of knowledge through objective or subjective written examinations. . . . In the exclusive classroom, class time is not given to discussion of social issues not directly related to the discipline. (p. 23)

On the other hand:

> an *inclusive course* presents traditional views but adds alternative perspectives. Content integration in an inclusive course can range from simple addition of new viewpoints without elaboration to efforts at analyzing and understanding reasons for historical exclusion. The instructor uses a wide array of teaching methods to support students' active learning of course content. . . . The instructor monitors student participation and employs learning activities that support participation by all students. (p. 23)

And, finally:

> a *transformed course* challenges traditional views and assumptions; encourages new ways of thinking; and re-conceptualizes the field in light of new knowledge, scholarship, and new ways of knowing. . . . Methods capitalize on the experience and knowledge that students bring and encourage personal as well as academic growth. (p. 23)

Kathryn Russell, in her chapter (38) discussing diversity within the context of a course on prejudice and discrimination, states, "Diversity classes require a transformative pedagogy like that recommended by Paolo Freire in *Pedagogy of the Oppressed* (2000), a process he labeled, 'education for critical consciousness.'" Thus, we would ultimately like courses that incorporate diversity to be of the "transformed" variety. But, when beginning the process of thinking about modifying a course to reflect diversity in some way, sometimes it is useful to begin by analyzing the structure and content of the course as it currently stands within Kitano's hierarchy. Then one can plan on how to move the course upward to either an inclusive course or a transformed course. Many instructors plan these moves in stages over time to see how certain aspects of change play out before making wholesale changes.

Conclusion

Diversity is inescapable in our world and is an intrinsic part of the human experience. It seems obvious to us that embracing diversity prepares citizens to work in a diverse and global society and that knowledge of diverse peoples and cultures fosters transformative thinking. Not only does this knowledge help people in attaining career goals, but perhaps more important, it can have profound individual and societal benefits. If one of the goals of college and university teachers is to teach students how to function in a global environment, then students must develop a sophisticated sense of cultural awareness.

The approach we have taken here is to view diversity within a framework of general curricular initiatives. As a supracurricular initiative, diversity can cut across multiple curricular competencies or can be treated as a separate entity. We provided a few examples of the types of attributes one may find in courses that promote diversity and multiculturalism. But perhaps more important, diversity as a component of a college curriculum has "whole life" relevance. If we are also to assist students in personal growth and an enrichment of the lives ahead of them, then promoting diversity is a critical element of this diversity.

References

Ayers, J. F., Wheeler, E. A., Fracasso, M. P., Galupo, M. P., Rabin, J. S., & Slater, B. R. (1999). Reinventing the university through the teaching of diversity. *Journal of Adult Development, 6,* 163–173.

Freire, P. (2000). *Pedagogy of the oppressed.* New York, NY: Continuum.

Kitano, M. K. (1997). What a course will look like after multicultural change. In A. I. Morey & M. K. Kitano (Eds.), *Multicultural course transformation in higher education: A broader truth* (pp. 18–34). Needham Heights, MA: Allyn & Bacon.

University of Maryland University College, School of Undergraduate Studies. (2003). *Cross-curricular initiatives: Definitions, standards, and suggested activities.* Retrieved February 21, 2007, from www.umuc.edu/prog/ugp/tech_resource/cci.pdf

4

Faculty Members as Architects: Structuring Diversity-Accessible Courses

Ellen R. Cohn, John W. Gareis

Proactive Design for Diversity

Residential homes in the United States are largely inaccessible to persons with physical disabilities. This creates barriers to visitors and even to some of the residents themselves. It is difficult, if not impossible, for wheelchair users to climb stairs, to travel through narrow door frames and halls, to use toilets too low to accommodate transfer, and to store food in kitchen cabinets above their reach. As the U.S. population ages, older adults are increasingly faced with a difficult and expensive choice: move to accessible abodes or retrofit their homes for accessibility. Many are learning the hard lesson that it is less expensive and more effective to build accessible environments to begin with than it is to retrofit inaccessible building structures.

The same concept applies to the architecture of inaccessible web sites. It is easier to create accessible web sites that permit assistive technologies to audibilize text than it is to improve on an inaccessible web site. The same architectural principle translates well to creating diversity-accessible courses by incorporating diverse voices, texts, and graphics. It is easier, in other words, to do it right the first time.

This chapter will present some of the key structural elements to consider when designing a diversity-friendly course: the syllabus, the textbook and readings, the assignments, and the participation norms.

Structural Elements

The course syllabus typically outlines much of the course structure, including statements of values, course objectives, lectures schedule, textbooks and readings, assignment due dates, expectations for attendance and participation, and grading policies. This document is thus well suited to serve as a blueprint for diversity for both the instructor and the students to follow over the course of a semester. There are several key points to keep in mind when constructing a syllabus for a diversity-friendly course.

Statements of Values and Policy

Without question, the primary place to signal the importance of, and attention that will be given to, diversity in the course is the statement of values. Here the instructor can set the tone for a class experience that is supportive of diversity by articulating (and abiding by) statements of values and policies. Four types of statements are included as examples.

Institution's values. It is important for students to recognize that diversity-supportive classes reflect the ethos of the institution, as the following statement of policy shows:

> The University of Pittsburgh, as an educational institution and as an employer, values equality of opportunity, human dignity, and racial/ethnic and cultural diversity. Accordingly, the University prohibits and will not engage in discrimination or harassment on the basis of race, color, religion, national origin, ancestry, sex, age, marital status, familial status, sexual orientation, disability, or status as a disabled veteran or a veteran of the Vietnam era. Further, the University will continue to take affirmative steps to support and advance these values consistent with the University's mission. (University of Pittsburgh, 1992)

Instructor's values. Placing a statement of the instructor's values in the syllabus sends a clear message concerning the classroom climate. An example follows:

> I am committed to providing you with an excellent course experience within an atmosphere of mutual respect and trust. In creating such an environment I want you to know that I value academic excellence, academic integrity and respect for one another. As such, I expect all those participating in the course to abide by the University of Pittsburgh policies concerning academic integrity, anti-harassment and anti-discrimination. I welcome your comments and suggestions.

Students with disabilities. It is standard now in many institutions of higher education to include a statement in the syllabus that articulates a commitment to offering course-related accommodations to persons with disabilities. As an example, here is the statement from the University of Pittsburgh:

If you have a disability for which you are or may be requesting an accommodation, you are encouraged to contact your instructor and Disability Resources and Services, 216 William Pitt Union, 412-648-7890 or 412-383-7355 (TTY) as early as possible in the term. Disability Resources and Services reviews documentation related to a student's disability, provides verification of the disability, and recommends reasonable accommodations for specific courses. (University of Pittsburgh, Office of Disability Services, 2006)

Expectations for communication. Ground rules for class participation posted in the syllabus can promote comfortable learning environments that encourage and support diversity. Examples include the following:

- Discussion in this class will be conducted in adherence to the University of Pittsburgh's nondiscrimination policy.

- We should respect diverse points of view. We do not need to come to an agreement on any particular issues; we can agree to disagree.

- Our use of language should be respectful of other persons or groups. (As your instructor, I will not let injurious statements pass without comment.)

- You need not represent any group, only yourself, though you may choose to represent a group if you wish.

- If you feel uncomfortable about any aspect of the class environment, it is your responsibility to discuss it with the instructor.

Many instructors not only publish and discuss ground rules, but they ask their classes to provide feedback concerning the rules and to offer suggestions for changes or additions. It is also important that faculty do not ignore or single-out students and that they get to know students as individuals.

Course Objectives and Learning Outcomes

Again drawing on an architectural analogy, the course objectives and associated learning outcomes set the plan for the course. We encourage instructors to make a commitment to integrate diverse voices throughout the course in a manner that fosters integration but not tokenism. An excellent guide on inclusive teaching authored by a center at the University of North Carolina–Chapel Hill (1997) recommends that instructors:

- "Integrate the diverse perspectives into other concepts [they] teach" (p. 30)

- Show that an author "is worth studying on his own merits, and not simply because of his ethnic identity" (p. 30)

- "Avoid placing topics related to diversity last on [the] syllabus or last within a unit" (p. 30)

Textbook Selection/Readings

The course textbooks and/or readings selected by instructors to present their disciplines send powerful messages concerning the value they place on diversity. It is important to consider nonverbal as well as verbal inclusiveness and to be alert to silences and omissions, as well as to distortions. A study by Gullicks, Pearson, Child, and Schwab (2005) found that photos in the top 10 textbooks on public speaking more often pictured men in positions of power than women and aptly notes, "Textbooks must provide students with images of possibility that empower and encourage all voices" (p. 2).

Questions to consider when selecting a textbook include the following:

- Does the textbook include minorities, women, and persons with disabilities as content experts or authorities?

- Do the examples and applications of textual material extend to minorities, women, and persons with disabilities?

- In photographs and graphics, are minorities, women, and persons with disabilities depicted in positions of power with the same frequency as those in the majority?

Remember that textbooks, like other products, are formulaic and market driven. Publishers will only supply a proven product that the market will buy. If academics are to see more than a smattering of inclusive textbooks from more than a few independent presses, then the primary users of textbooks must demand such products.

Assignments

Assignments can represent a vehicle for students to personalize a course and give it individual meaning. Consider another architectural analogy: "Hard architecture" does not respond to the needs of the user, but "soft architecture" takes the needs of the user into account (Sommer, 1974). Soft versus hard assignments allow students to select their own topics—ones they are comfortable with exploring. The University of North Carolina–Chapel Hill (1997) recommends that faculty "depersonalize controversial topics and structure assignments to let students choose topics with which they are comfortable" (p. 36) as well as to accommodate different learning styles. It is incumbent on faculty to model this approach throughout their courses.

Course Evaluation

In addition to formalizing a commitment to diversity in the syllabus, faculty members should discuss their intent when reviewing the syllabus and operationalize the commitment throughout the semester. The end-of-semester course evaluation can be used to determine whether students perceived that these goals were met. Sample evaluation items are as follows:

- To what extent did the instructor foster a class environment in which diverse points of view were respected?

- To that extent did the course content incorporate diverse voices and populations?

- To what extent did the assignments allow students to incorporate content related to diverse and/or underserved populations?

Conclusions

This brief chapter has reviewed some of the key structural elements to consider when designing a diversity-friendly course: the syllabus, the textbook and readings, the assignments, and the participation norms. The chapter in this volume by Barbara Frey converges on this theme with a view toward assessment practices that are supportive of diversity.

References

Gullicks, K. A., Pearson, J. C., Child, J. T., & Schwab, C. R. (2005). Diversity and power in public speaking textbooks. *Communication Quarterly, 53*(2), 247–258.

Sommer, R. (1974). *Tight spaces: Hard architecture and how to humanize it.* Englewood Cliffs, NJ: Prentice Hall.

University of North Carolina–Chapel Hill, Center for Teaching and Learning. (1997). *Teaching for inclusion: Diversity in the college classroom.* Chapel Hill, NC: Author.

University of Pittsburgh. (1992). *Nondiscrimination policy statement.* Retrieved February 20, 2007, from www.hr.pitt.edu/empreledu/affirm.htm

University of Pittsburgh, Office of Disability Services. (2006). *Recommended syllabus statement.* Retrieved February 20, 2007, from www.drs.pitt.edu/facstaff.html

5

Practices That Facilitate Diversity Across the Curriculum: Inclusive Classroom Assessment

Barbara A. Frey

Never before has higher education faculty faced such diversity in student populations. Inevitably, instructors find themselves teaching learners with backgrounds very different from their own. In American colleges and universities, "slightly over half of the students on most campuses are women, and nearly 25 percent of all undergraduates are nonwhite" (Light, 2001, p. 129). Students come to campus with different racial, ethnic, sexual, political, geographic, religious, and economic backgrounds. Teaching these diverse populations requires coordinating course content, learning activities, and assessment strategies that meet the needs of all students. This chapter examines effective strategies for the planning and implementation of inclusive classroom assessment. In particular, portfolios are discussed as a flexible, comprehensive assessment strategy, and rubrics are presented as a strategy for delivering culturally responsive, objective feedback to learners.

Assessment is a process of gathering information from multiple sources and indicators to make judgments about student learning, achievement, progress, and performance. In many higher education settings, assessment entails several multiple choice exams administered at the end of textbook chapters or units. Such exams often consist of low-level, electronically scored questions. Student grades are then based on a cumulative average earned throughout the term. Although this process is not the ideal system, it enables faculty to manage large enrollments and heavy workloads. Many instructors, however, value the diversity of their students and seek a more effective way to evaluate their students' learning.

It follows, then, that in the multicultural classroom, assessment necessitates inclusive approaches that recognize the uniqueness of individual students but does not compromise the standards of achievement. In 2000, the Educational Alliance at Brown University introduced educators to the standards movement to emphasize that "education standards are meant for all students" (Lachat, 1999, p. 1). No matter what a student's educational level is, standards define what every student should know and be able to do. Therefore, assessment should be integrated with instruction and focused on what students understand and can do. However, the Educational Alliance goes on to note current inequities in classrooms: Although "all minority students master basic skills by age 17, disproportionately few master the higher level skills" (Lachat, p. 9). Actually, minority students may enter higher education classrooms underprepared for the problem solving, critical thinking, and higher level skills that are expected of them. As a result, before administering assessments, instructors should consider the knowledge and skills that learners bring to the classroom. Moreover, faculty need to model and provide practice for the higher level thinking skills required for assignments, exams, and evaluations.

Wlodkowski and Ginsberg (2003), who studied cultural diversity, noted that instructor judgments made when assessing learners are subject to subtle forms of bias that impact student motivation. For example, there may be a tendency for faculty to reward white male students who appear attentive and assertive during class. The culture of these white students may have prepared them to fit the "stereotype of learning" (Wlodkowski & Ginsberg, p. 233), which includes behaviors such as making eye contact, sharing information, and asking questions of an authority figure. Interestingly, male undergraduates are more likely to overestimate their abilities, whereas women are more likely to underestimate theirs. Wlodkowski and Ginsberg explained that students of color often distrust the perceptions of their instructors. These learners may have experienced assessment processes "that reward students who best conform to the instructor's norms and values" (p. 238). Obviously, the impersonal, one-dimensional formal testing model with its limited feedback may impair the motivation of some diverse learners.

By the same token, research from the University of Michigan also found student awareness of classroom bias. Its Center for Research on Learning and Teaching conducted 15 focus groups with undergraduate students of color (Chester, Wilson, & Milani, 1993). Several important themes emerged: (1) faculty tended to have low expectations for students of color; (2) the curriculum and classroom interaction often excluded students of color; and (3) classroom structures and pedagogical approaches were limited. This student feedback indicated that the instructors' attitudes and the structure of their courses may contribute to limiting some students' learning experiences.

Where do faculty begin in designing inclusive assessments? The first step in planning fair assessment of all learners is a thoughtful instructional plan of what students must learn and what they should be able to do. The psychology instructor whose goal is for learners "to critically analyze information on mental health disorders presented in the media" has set the foundation of an assessment plan. How will students demonstrate that they can analyze mental health information? It might be demonstrated through a case study essay question, or students might demonstrate their knowledge through a team presentation analyzing information from popular magazines or movies. Or a biology instructor may want students "to apply biology principles to common environmental issues and concerns." These students may be assessed through a term paper on such topics as controlling the deer population or addressing acid rain runoff. They also could be evaluated through a journal relating environmental issues to principles discussed in their textbooks or class sessions. Clearly, well-defined goals of what students should know and be able to do are a major component of any type of learner-centered assessment.

After establishing clear goals, many faculty seeking fair assessment strategies as alternatives to traditional paper-and-pencil exams have adopted assessment portfolios—collections of students' work representing effort, progress, or achievement in one or more areas. Diverse students benefit from this opportunity to customize the evidence of their learning. In fact, Calvin (as cited in Banta, 2003) found that when students were assessed using authentic materials such as portfolios, bias was reduced. And Wiggins (1994) wrote that "the use of a single grade to represent achievement, progress, and growth leads to the difficulty of grading fairly" (p. 33). Boyle (1994) reported that portfolios "captured the interest of many instructors who want a more comprehensive way to assess their students' knowledge and skills" (p. 10). Increasingly, faculty "recognize that no single instrument can measure all that students know about a concept or issue, that not every student will be up to giving their best performance on any specific occasion, and that the important element of growth over time cannot be assessed with a single measurement" (Banta, 2003, p. 1). Ultimately, portfolios may provide the assessment instrument that faculty seek as students use artifacts and media to demonstrate their unique knowledge, skills, and talents.

Portfolios can demonstrate learners' accomplishments in a single course or program or can be a multiyear project demonstrating progress through their college experience. Instructional goals may require students to provide evidence of applying knowledge to practice, reporting an experiment, evaluating others' research, interpreting results or data, or analyzing contemporary issues. Additionally, portfolios can consist of a wide variety of materials, such as instructor notes, self-reflection journals, written assignments, term papers, exams, and multimedia files. Through portfolios, students are actively involved in a structured assessment process by providing evidence that they have mastered goals established by faculty or the institution.

Generally, portfolios have a critical reflection component in which students review, organize, and annotate their progress. This self-reflection is a major component of portfolios and is especially beneficial to minority students as they make connections and derive meaning from their learning experiences. "Self-assessment offers students a way to transcend stereotypes and to make well-reasoned connections between their actions and learning" (Wlodkowski & Ginsberg, 2003, p. 240). Portfolios also empower students and enhance their motivation to learn and achieve—the evaluative feedback that they receive about their learning performance is a powerful tool that can strongly affect effort and attitude (Spicuzza, 2003). Cook-Benjamin (2003) emphasized, however, that portfolios continuously evolve and that there is no one correct way to create or assess a portfolio.

Likewise, rubrics are culturally responsive assessment tools that provide timely, objective, and consistent feedback on complex assignments, such as portfolios. Rubrics are particularly useful for subject areas and topics that require a judgment of quality, rather than a simple correct answer. There are two main types of rubrics—the holistic and the analytical. The *holistic rubric* assesses student work as a whole. It does not assess individual criteria; it looks at levels of performance across all criteria or components of an assignment. The levels of performance may be somewhat descriptive ("excellent," "competent," and "needs work"), numerical (5, 4, 3, 2, and 1), or letter based (A, B, C, D, and F). The following is the holistic description for a writing assignment that received an A: "Excellent. Thesis is well defined and clear; topic complexities are explored; logic is presented in organized manner; references are used properly and effectively; grammar and mechanics are correct; writing style is appropriate; APA format is correct."

The *analytical rubric* is a grid that considers levels of performance for each component or criterion of an assignment (e.g., content, self-reflection, organization, grammar, and progress). For example, a rubric to assess student performance in a science lab may consider the criteria of preparation, procedures, safety, and clean-up. Figure 5.1 shows a rubric for assessing student participation in an online discussion. Here the criteria include frequency, initial assignment posting, follow-up postings, content contribution, references, and mechanics.

One major advantage of an analytical grading rubric is that the instructor clearly defines what constitutes success and the measurable criteria required to reach it. This approach naturally increases the objectivity of precise assessment and saves instructors time because they use a consistent structure for evaluating the same assignments. Rubrics also increase interrater reliability for large enrollment courses with several graders. Students obviously appreciate the meaningful feedback provided by rubrics because levels of performance are clearly described and differentiated. Some faculty members even involve students in designing the rubric, thus giving them a sense of ownership in the assessment process and the ability to assess themselves. This rubric is used for students to assess their own participation in online discussions in a web-based distance education course. The left-hand column states the criteria or category of assessment. The levels of proficiency are described in each row.

Figure 5.1

Rubric for Asynchronous Discussion Participation

Name_____

Asynchronous discussion enhances learning as you share your ideas, perspectives, and experiences with the class. You develop and refine your thoughts through the writing process, plus broaden your classmates' understanding of the course content. Use the following feedback to improve the quality of your discussion contributions.

Criteria	Unacceptable 0 Points	Acceptable 1 Point	Good 2 Points	Excellent 3 Points
Frequency	Participates not at all	Participates 1–2 times on the same day	Participates 3–4 times but postings not distributed throughout week	Participates 4–5 times throughout the week
Initial Assignment Posting	Posts no assignment	Posts adequate assignment with superficial thought and preparation; doesn't address all aspects of the task	Posts well-developed assignment that addresses all aspects of the task; lacks full development of concepts	Posts well-developed assignment that fully addresses and develops all aspects of the task
Follow-Up Postings	Posts no follow-up responses to others	Posts shallow contribution to discussion (e.g., agrees or disagrees); does not enrich discussion	Elaborates on an existing posting with further comment or observation	Demonstrates analysis of others' posts; extends meaningful discussion by building on previous posts
Content Contribution	Posts information that is off-topic, incorrect, or irrelevant to discussion	Repeats but does not add substantive information to the discussion	Posts information that is factually correct; lacks full development of concept or thought	Posts factually correct, reflective, and substantive contribution; advances discussion

Figure 5.1 (continued)

Rubric for Asynchronous Discussion Participation

Criteria	Unacceptable 0 Points	Acceptable 1 Point	Good 2 Points	Excellent 3 Points
References and Support	Includes no references or supporting experience	Uses personal experience, but no references to readings or research	Incorporates some references from literature and personal experience	Uses references to literature, readings, or personal experience to support comments
Clarity and Mechanics	Posts long, unorganized, or rude content that may contain multiple errors or may be inappropriate	Communicates in friendly, courteous, and helpful manner with some errors in clarity or mechanics	Contributes valuable information to discussion with minor clarity or mechanics errors	Contributes to discussion with clear, concise comments formatted in an easy-to-read style that is free of grammatical or spelling errors

Examples of postings that demonstrate higher levels of thinking:

- "Some common themes I see between your experiences and our textbook are . . ." (analysis)
- "These newer trends are significant if we consider the relationship between . . ." (synthesis)
- "The body of literature should be assessed by these standards . . ." (evaluation)

Although the construction of a rubric might be an unfamiliar process and seem to be a daunting task at first glance, there are many resources and tools to draw on. First, to create a rubric, faculty should clearly define the evidence or criteria that are needed to evaluate the knowledge, skills, and attitudes demonstrated in the assignment. It is helpful to examine a few examples of rubrics from similar disciplines. Regardless of the approach, faculty must be sure to differentiate clearly between the levels of performance. A review of student assignments from previous classes can help define these degrees of proficiency.

Remember, a rubric does not have to lead to a grade—many faculty consider it to be a tool to enhance learning and feedback. If using it for grading, however, consider the criteria and how the levels should be weighted because all the criteria categories may not warrant the same value. The criteria can be weighted by percentages, points, or verbal descriptions (i.e., "excellent," "good," "needs improvement"). Like the assessment portfolio, the rubric is a dynamic tool that undergoes numerous modifications through its life cycle.

Ultimately, inclusive assessment involves faculty awareness and sensitivity to student diversity in the classroom. Faculty must be willing to assess their own teaching styles and practices. More research is needed to identify specific ways that faculty demonstrate assessment bias and to determine how to address that problem.

In a multiracial society, higher education faculty must develop instructional approaches and assessments that accommodate the needs of their diverse students. Inclusive classroom assessment should consider the setting and the learners and be based on the goals and objectives of the course. Portfolios, one alternative to traditional paper-and-pencil assessments, require students to demonstrate their learning and progress over time. When providing constructive comments to learners, rubrics are effective tools to provide feedback regarding complex, multifaceted assignments. Rubrics help faculty deliver consistent, objective feedback in a timely manner. Ultimately, inclusive assessment facilitates learning for all students and is one of the most important responsibilities of faculty.

References

Banta, T. W. (2003). Introduction: Why portfolios? In T. W. Banta (Ed.), *Portfolio assessment: Use, cases, scoring, and impact* (pp. 1–5). San Francisco, CA: Jossey-Bass.

Boyle, J. E. (1994). Portfolios: Purposes and possibilities. *Assessment Update, 6*(4), 10–11.

Chester, M. A., Wilson, M., & Milani, A. (1993). Perceptions of faculty behavior by students of color. *The Michigan Journal of Political Science, 16*, 54–79.

Cook-Benjamin, L. (2003). Portfolio assessment: Benefits, issues of implementation, and reflection on its use. In T. W. Banta (Ed.), *Portfolio assessment: Use, cases, scoring, and impact* (pp. 11–15). San Francisco, CA: Jossey-Bass.

Lachat, M. A. (1999). *Standards, equity and cultural diversity.* Providence, RI: LAB at Brown University, Education Alliance.

Light, R. J. (2001). *Making the most of college: Students speak their minds.* Cambridge, MA: Harvard University Press.

Spicuzza, F. J. (2003). An evaluation of portfolio assessment: A student perspective. In T. W. Banta (Ed.), *Portfolio assessment: Use, cases, scoring, and impact* (pp. 63–72). San Francisco, CA: Jossey-Bass.

Wiggins, G. (1994). Toward better report cards. *Educational Leadership, 52*, 28–37.

Wlodkowski, R. J., & Ginsberg, M. B. (2003). *Diversity and motivation: Culturally responsive teaching.* San Francisco, CA: Jossey-Bass.

6

Diversity and Disciplinary Practices

Jean Ferguson Carr

I have worked on diversity issues within English departments (developing courses and assignments on gender; revising existing courses; addressing diversity issues in pedagogy, admissions, career development, and evaluation) and on a national level (revising curricula and developing anthologies, addressing issues of discourse and hate speech, writing about ways to rethink literary culture). From 1995 to 1999, I led sessions in and then codirected the faculty seminar on diversity at the University of Pittsburgh, a seminar in which faculty from the range of disciplines and professional schools meet to discuss and revise course syllabi. The issue that I found most challenging in the faculty seminar and in my own professional work is the question of disciplinary practices, those entrenched and valued procedures that faculty bring with them to diversity discussions.

Disciplinary practices shape our knowledge, methods, and materials; they foreclose certain inquiries and make others seem central or pressing. They inevitably affect discussions among faculty from different parts of a university. What goes without saying in one field, may be the subject of endless debate in another. Disciplinary traditions thus frame discussions about curricular change, even when practitioners focus on other issues, like issues of pedagogy or diversity. In an interdisciplinary faculty seminar on diversity, disciplinary practices are both powerful and difficult to negotiate—partially because they are often unexamined or unacknowledged. One of the key values of such a seminar is pressuring the articulation of—and reflection on—such practices and bringing them into productive exchange.

In their influential diversity schema of "stages of curricular transformation," Schuster and Van Dyne (1985) mark the "challenge to the disciplines" as an advanced stage, a movement beyond the search for new content or expertise.[1] Yet much of the work of revising syllabi or improving teaching in U.S. higher education in the past few decades has focused on their scheme's earlier stages: on revising and adding content, expanding the list of authorities and authors, and devising exercises that pressure students' engagement with the politics of race or gender. Such interventions have often been discipline neutral, offered by experts in educational methods, technology, library research, or the so-called skills (the teaching of writing, communication, small-group dynamics, etc.). Individual faculty often go to a learning center to "repair" individual syllabi, to add proven kinds of assignments, to address questions of classroom climate, or to delete offensive formulations or representations. The disciplines are often, in this model, addressed as distinct teaching traditions, requiring advice tailored to the humanities, social sciences, or sciences, usually about particular pedagogical "problems" (negotiating experimental procedures, writing research papers, handling large or small classes).

One of the effects of treating diversity in this centralized way is that students often experience "the diversity issue" in familiar—and limited—ways, as certain texts, topics, and activities circulate across the curriculum. Such diversity work—however important and influential—does not necessarily affect their understanding of the other issues of the course. It is too easy for students to recognize (and bracket) diversity in their courses and in the curriculum as a whole.

The diversity "agenda" itself has been primarily articulated by experts in humanities and social sciences—women's studies, black and ethnic studies, critical pedagogy, sociology of education, and feminist psychology. Its "advice" favors the solutions apparent to those disciplines. It has focused less attention on issues from the sciences or from empirical fields, which often seem "beyond" the questions of diversity in terms of subject and method, if not in terms of pedagogy.[2] The diversity effort has most successfully addressed issues of diverse subjects and experts and such "diversity" topics as discrimination, identity, access, power, authority, the body, sexuality, and race. Even within the most active parts of the curriculum, diversity has been figured as a contemporary issue, often sharply inflected by its association with U.S. politics and social structures, shaped by the civil rights movement of the 1960s and the feminism movement of the 1970s. It has a less worked-out relationship to international or global formulations and to fields focusing on earlier periods or cultures.

The pressures for diversity change have been strong in general education courses, especially threshold courses like freshman composition that reflect on the identity and socialization issues facing incoming students. Women's studies and black studies are arenas of the academy shaped by (and shaping) diversity discussions by the need to "include" and refashion the curriculum and reading lists and by the need to transform the academy (classroom climate and pedagogy, the makeup of the faculty and student populations, notions of access and advancement). These fields have subsequently influenced content-related areas like history, political science, and sociology. Diversity reform has taken hold in the past decade in professional fields like nursing and social work, under pressure from the professional organizations and the governmental and granting agencies to become more diverse in materials, practices, and outlook.

Fields like the so-called hard sciences, philosophy, theoretical political science, and those parts of disciplines focusing on older periods or on less "diverse" populations have seemed less immediately available to diversity work.[3] "What does it have to do with my field?" asks a professor of ecology and natural sciences. "Where do I find examples of high-achieving women or persons of color?" asked the professor of 18th-century music. Students thus face a gap in the curriculum that may reinforce the problems diversity attempts to address; they are hard pressed to understand how the issues that seem so crucial in part of the academy have no place in other arenas. They may read diversity as an issue of the contemporary scene, not something that depends on or touches older periods or that operates within more "abstract" subjects.

More significant and lasting challenges to the curriculum need to engage the wider array of disciplines and concerns, and to develop a more challenging repertoire of diversity reforms. Instead of pressuring each discipline to pay lip service to a uniform program of race/gender awareness, such an engagement asks what each discipline contributes to the diversity agenda—in terms of its research methodologies, its history and traditions of instruction, its favored educational materials, its culture of learning and expertise. What are the aspects of a modern debate about diversity that are shaped by (or rendered invisible by) particular disciplinary traditions? How would attention to diversity enhance disciplinary work? A broader transformation would help students negotiate diversity issues across the curriculum.

Suggestions for Disciplinary Change

1. *Investigate what a particular discipline contributes to the academic discussions about diversity and what might be particular diversity concerns.*

This inquiry is best done by experts in each field in dialogue with diversity experts and other interested faculty who can speak to what promotes or hampers curricular change. Faculty can investigate contemporary diversity initiatives to consider what issues or assumptions emerge, in a sense, from their arena of expertise. Philosophers, for example, may work on how their educational traditions promote notions of dispassionate and generalized standards—notions of "beauty" or "the good"—that then box in contemporary debates about cultural difference or change. Their diversity agenda might be to explore how such standards emerge from particular historical circumstances or how the translation of such categories occurs across time or situation. Literature professors might investigate how values of "classic" or "popular" serve to divide kinds of literary texts and ways of reading, marking some as privileged and others as superficial. Music faculty might investigate how issues of performance shape value and taste; mathematics faculty might develop discussions about issues of proof and evidence; empirical scientists might focus on how experiments are established and authorized. These issues are core concerns of disciplinary curriculum; they can also serve the broader curriculum by suggesting their ongoing influence on contemporary debates.

2. *Investigate how disciplinary concerns operate to shape, authorize, and articulate knowledge across the curriculum.*

As Adrienne Rich (1979) writes, it is crucial to "understand the assumptions in which we are drenched" (p. 35). Among the powerful assumptions that need to be understood are the ways various disciplines are implicated in issues of diversity and privilege and how this has shaped the curriculum. Some fields may be the visible arenas in which diversity issues are most readily displayed. Political science, education, literature, history, psychology—these are all disciplines that address how people are valued, ranked, represented, accounted for, moved, or affected. But other fields contribute less direct frameworks to the diversity debate. Art history's tradition of valuing originality, for example, shapes modern discussions of folk art. Even when (especially when?) such issues are treated as general categories (e.g., "the role of the artist"), they have implications for diversity discussions. They are, in a sense, the basis for many concrete claims about value and difference. Older fields often shape the dichotomies that underwrite contemporary debates: consider, for example, the long-lasting influence of such early notions as the Greek concept of the barbarian or medieval debates about the body and soul. The contemporary diversity debate often has "forgotten" such powerful designations and so struggles with the effects rather than the conditions of knowledge.

3. *Given each discipline's traditional and professional concerns, consider where the curriculum can be most readily changed.*

Academic disciplines have different control over curriculum: some are strongly shaped by professional organizations, work conditions, or entrance requirements. It is important for faculty to recognize which parts of the curriculum require collective agreement, are authorized by professional or national debates, or carry out ensconced traditions (e.g., core knowledge, revered texts, or established sequences). Some parts of the curriculum may call for variation, and these may be the best places to try out curricular change. Diversity reform can be a way to enliven a stale course, to refashion sequences that seem old fashioned or irrelevant to students. Diversity issues can draw students to parts of the curriculum they would not normally enter. Diversity change, like other forms of curricular revision, is linked to teacher training (particularly in large courses with teaching assistants, lab assistants, or graders), as well as to assessment and evaluation (how is learning to be measured or evaluated, or how is good teaching to be measured?). Changing an assignment can change a course, which can pressure changes across a curriculum and a department.

   4. *Pressure the curriculum to articulate the relationships between and across disciplines.*

One of the difficulties in making curricular change effective is that change often occurs in pockets in the curriculum, within departments or levels of study. Students need to translate from one arena to another and need to negotiate different academic methodologies and authority. Students may well learn something important about diversity in a particular course, but that learning is not necessarily reinforced, complicated, or extended in the next class. Indeed, subsequent courses may call into question earlier study, marking it as elementary or preprofessional, the interest of particular social groups but not something to generalize.

   Faculty members committed to profound diversity change need to move beyond revising individual syllabi to articulating the shape of the larger curriculum. A philosophy course in aesthetics, an art history course, and a course in women's history, for example, might articulate the relationship among abstract claims about aesthetic value, the emergence and valuing of particular media, and the particular situation of women artists or audiences. A course in literary theory or empirical science or statistics might invite students to compare notions of evidence and value across these different fields. Such additions to courses need not be large or totalizing; courses need not be recast as multidisciplinary to suggest such connections. Nor do such activities need to be isolated in a marked "diversity" section; in fact, diversity work is probably most effective when it is articulated with a course's ongoing topics and assignments. The work of articulating the curriculum can be as small as a well-placed comment, a brief reading or homework assignment, an exam question or reflective discussion, an invitation to cross boundaries or to look back at earlier levels of schooling. Faculty may do the work of investigating the implications of other fields or courses, but faculty may also invite students to bring such matters forward, to draw on their experience with the curriculum's continuities and differences.

   5. *"Translate" modern and U.S.-based diversity issues to alternative times, places, or academic areas.*

Diversity issues need to expand beyond their immediate relevance to less visibly connected areas. Shifting the focus of Shakespeare studies from the author to the many different audiences and their literacy expectations has been an exciting and productive critical and pedagogical move. Expanding the notion of race from its U.S. contexts to address such categories as the ancient Greek "barbarian" or the 18th-century British treatment of the Irish makes race a critical tool and extends its possible meanings or uses. Questions of value, of hierarchy, and of priority, notions of logic and causality—these are all charged issues that underwrite contemporary debates.

The activity of reflecting on disciplinary practices can ultimately energize more productive change, change that addresses what is important or central to a discipline and that furthers a disciplinary agenda for teaching. Diversity can be an impetus for thinking about the shape and trajectory of the discipline's history, its teaching traditions and commitments, and its central concerns. It can help students to understand what a discipline contributes to the larger field of knowledge and curriculum and to understand why its diversity investment is different from that of another field's.

Endnotes

1. Schuster and Van Dyne (1985) urge both administrators and faculty to be "patient" with the "long-term process" of curriculum transformation, to "counter their impatience for the finished product, their understandably urgent demand for the transformed syllabus, the fully integrated textbook, the inclusive general education requirements, the truly liberal core curriculum" (p. 13). Focusing on questions of gender, the authors' "stages of curriculum transformation" begin with changes in content, followed by epistemological changes.

2. There are many excellent examples of diversity work in the sciences and empirical fields. See, for example, Cerrito, 1994; Fausto-Sterling, 1992; Haraway, 1988; and Hovland, 2006. But many of the curricular projects have been developed by faculty from the social sciences (Hill, 1995) or humanities (Gates, 1986; Lauter, 1994).

3. Ancient Greek rhetoric and Renaissance literary studies are two examples of areas focused on earlier periods in which revisionary scholarship and curricular work has transformed the field. In the past few decades, scholars of ancient Greek rhetoric have published books on "regendering the tradition," "bodily arts," "reclaiming rhetorica," "women's rhetoric(s)," and "rereading the Sophists" (see Glenn, 1997; Hawhee, 2004; Lunsford, 1995; Ritchie & Ronald, 2005; Jarratt, 1998). In Renaissance studies, there have been a surge of books "rewriting the Renaissance" (to quote the title of a 1986 book edited by Ferguson, Quilligan, & Vickers) on such topics as global interests; Renaissance feminism; medical science and the Renaissance notion of woman; literacy, territoriality, and colonization; and convents and the body politic (see Jardine & Brotton, 2005; Jordan, 1990; Maclean, 1983; Mignolo, 2003; Sperling, 2000).

References

Cerrito, P. (1994). Demonstrating the need for diversity in teaching statistics. *Transformations, 5*(2), 100–109.

Fausto-Sterling, A. (1992). Race, gender, and science. *Transformations, 2*(2), 4–12.

Ferguson, M. W., Quilligan, M., & Vickers, N. (Eds.). (1986). *Rewriting the Renaissance: The discourse of sexual difference in early modern Europe.* Chicago, IL: University of Chicago Press.

Gates, H. L., Jr. (1986). Writing "race" and the difference it makes. In H. L. Gates (Ed.), *"Race," writing, and difference* (pp. 1–20). Chicago, IL: University of Chicago Press.

Glenn, C. (1997). *Rhetoric retold: Regendering the tradition from antiquity through the Renaissance.* Carbondale, IL: Southern Illinois University Press.

Haraway, D. J. (1988). Situated knowledges: The science question in feminism. *Feminist Studies, 14*(3), 575–599.

Hawhee, D. (2004). *Bodily arts: Rhetoric and athletics in ancient Greece.* Austin, TX: University of Texas Press.

Hill, L. I. (1995). Rethinking the social sciences: A multi-lensed perspective for curriculum transformation. *Transformations, 6*(1), 1–15.

Hovland, K. (2006). Science diversity, and global learning: Untangling complex problems. *Diversity Digest, 9*(3), 1.

Jardine, L., & Brotton, J. (2005). *Global interests: Renaissance art between East and West.* London, UK: Reaktion Books.

Jarratt, S. C. (1998). *Rereading the Sophists: Classical rhetoric refigured.* Carbondale, IL: Southern Illinois University Press.

Jordan, C. (1990). *Renaissance feminism: Literary texts and political models.* Ithaca, NY: Cornell University Press.

Lauter, P. (1994). Feminism, multiculturalism, and the canonical tradition. *Transformations, 5*(2), 1–17.

Lunsford, A. A. (1995). *Reclaiming rhetorica: Women in the rhetorical tradition.* Pittsburgh, PA: University of Pittsburgh Press.

Maclean, I. (1983). *The Renaissance notion of woman: A study in the fortunes of Scholasticism and medical science in European intellectual life.* Cambridge, UK: Cambridge University Press.

Mignolo, W. (2003). *The darker side of the Renaissance: Literacy, territoriality, and colonization.* Ann Arbor, MI: University of Michigan Press.

Rich, A. (1979). When we dead awaken: Writing as revision. *On lies, secrets, and silence: Selected prose, 1966–1978* (pp. 33–49). New York, NY: Norton.

Ritchie, J. S., & Ronald, K. (Eds.). (2005). *Available means: An anthology of women's rhetoric(s).* Pittsburgh, PA: University of Pittsburgh Press.

Schuster, M., & Van Dyne, S. (1985). Stages of curriculum transformation. In M. Schuster & S. Van Dyne (Eds.), *Women's place in the academy* (pp. 13–29). Totowa, NJ: Roan and Allanheld.

Sperling, J. G. (2000). *Convents and the body politic in late Renaissance Venice.* Chicago, IL: University of Chicago Press.

Part II

Diversity Initiatives at Six Institutions

7

Multiculturalism and Diversity: One Institution's Cultural Journey

Jaime P. Muñoz, Laurel Willingham-McLain

Universities face many challenges in implementing organizational changes to promote campus diversity and multicultural infusion across the curriculum (Smith & Wolf-Wendel, 2005). Research demonstrates the educational benefits students derive when they interact with diverse peers (Antonio, 2004; Hurtado, 2003), and blueprints exist for building an inclusive campus climate (Brown, 2004; Smith, 1997; Smith & Wolf-Wendel, 2005). Contextual factors unique to each institution support or create barriers to effective multicultural policies and procedures (Lopez-Mulnix & Mulnix, 2006; Morey 1997). Developing a diverse campus is a dynamic, ongoing process for which each institution sets its own pace. Each stage of the journey reflects a different level of multicultural understanding and readiness for change, and each milestone provides a new departure point for continuing the journey (Siegel, 2003). This paper describes some points along the multicultural journey of a midsized Catholic university and discusses landmarks we envision for the road ahead.

Institutional Context

Duquesne University is located in Pittsburgh, Pennsylvania. Founded in 1878 by members of the Congregation of the Holy Spirit, Duquesne's mission is

> to serve God by serving students—through commitment to excellence in liberal and professional education, through profound concern for moral and spiritual values, through the maintenance of an ecumenical atmosphere open to diversity,

and through service to the Church, the community, the nation, and the world. (Duquesne University, n.d.)

Duquesne currently enrolls about 10,000 students in its 10 schools, which offer baccalaureate, professional, master's, and doctoral degrees. The student body and faculty consist largely of European Americans; about 3.5% of the student body is African-American, 2.5% is other ethnic minorities, and 3.5% is international students (Duquesne University, 2006a).

In this chapter we discuss the creation, efforts, and life cycle of the Diversity Network, an organic, informal group that initially provided a vehicle for discussion of multicultural education, but which also served to concentrate a collective desire for action and capacity building and laid the groundwork for university-wide actions to target diversity goals in organizational decision-making. Our story also highlights the leadership provided by two of Duquesne's central offices—the Learning Skills Center (primarily serving students) and the Center for Teaching Excellence (primarily serving faculty)—which worked hand in hand to support the Diversity Network. Although valuing diversity has always been a foundational component of the mission of Duquesne University, in this chapter we describe how current steps in our multicultural journey include a more intentional focus on these aspects of the university's mission.

The Diversity Network: A Faculty- and Staff-Initiated Collaborative

In the fall of 1999, Duquesne University did not require students to take a course in cultural diversity as part of their core liberal arts and sciences curriculum. At that time, electives focusing on diversity, social justice, or global perspectives did exist, and several professional schools had implemented requirements ranging from one course to a series of transcultural courses and clinical experiences.

The Duquesne Center for Teaching Excellence (CTE) routinely sponsored diversity-related workshops and, in the fall of 1999, collaborated with the Learning Skills Center to offer a workshop titled "Teaching Across Racial Lines." The workshop leaders used the film *Skin Deep* (Reid, 1995), and it sparked a lively discussion that focused on faculty and staff members' own perceptions of their cultural identities; on the sense of isolation experienced by those who addressed issues of diversity, multiculturalism, and inclusion; on successes and frustrations in educational strategies; and on the prevailing campus climate. At the end of the workshop, the 20 participants requested continued dialogue on these topics, and from these beginnings a faculty- and staff-initiated group called the Diversity Network emerged.

Members of the network established the primary purpose of the group as follows: to celebrate the diversity that already exists at Duquesne and to work toward fostering a climate of inclusion by infusing teaching, learning, and the Duquesne community culture with an understanding of, and respect for, people of diverse cultures. In retrospect, collaboration between CTE and the Learning Skills Center was critical for maintaining the momentum of this fledgling group. The staff at CTE brought expertise and a campus-wide reputation needed to coordinate, document, and advertise events, and to develop a resource collection of multicultural teaching and learning materials both in print and online, something no single faculty member or department could accomplish alone. The Learning Skills Center had a strong reputation on campus for promoting diversity and for helping students and staff alike in understanding and thriving in an academic community. CTE and Learning Skills Center leaders leveraged administrative support for regular Diversity Network meetings, including guest speakers, workshops, book studies, and informal discussions of multicultural issues over dinner. Sample workshop topics included developing intercultural competency through community service and multicultural course transformation (Morey & Kitano, 1997).

Beginning in the fall of 1999 and continuing through 2003, the Diversity Network met several times, with a core group of faculty and staff planning the meetings. Members discussed such topics as race relations and the campus diversity climate, the status of women and minorities in the faculty and administrative hierarchy, and the experience of gay and lesbian faculty and students at Duquesne. At each meeting we identified strategies for supporting a more inclusive campus climate that promoted dignity and equity for all, and we generated ideas for future multicultural learning events. During this time the network grew to include over 70 members from both student life and academic affairs.

Building capacity in faculty and staff was a key focus of the Diversity Network, and the organizers of the group experimented with various strategies to accomplish this task, most of which were recommended by members themselves. Primary strategies included maintaining connections between faculty and staff through an email list, creating a repository of multimedia resources in the university library, announcing educational and cultural events, and sharing resources and ideas for multicultural training in regular Diversity Network meetings. For example, using a brief email survey and following it with a lengthier one, the network collected faculty members' descriptions of strategies they were using to integrate multicultural education into their teaching and interaction with students; and it queried members about diversity-related programs or organizations they were involved in, their goals for the Diversity Network, and the level of participation they wanted to have in it. Members were also asked to share their syllabi and learning activities and to alert other members to relevant events.

When the Association of American Colleges and Universities (AAC&U) held its diversity and learning conference in Pittsburgh in 2000, many faculty, teaching assistants, and administrators from Duquesne attended. The entire Duquesne community was invited to attend the opening event, "I am that I am: Woman, Black" by Adilah Barnes, because Duquesne University cosponsored the reception. Informal sessions that followed the AAC&U conference focused on sharing what we had learned and brainstorming ideas to implement key strategies within the Duquesne community.

Sharing between network members was a critical strategy for capacity building. Organizers found that scheduling meetings over meals helped increase attendance and allowed members to fit meetings into their perpetually full schedules. Some of the most successful sharing occurred in meetings where participants were asked to briefly describe a *lesson* they had learned related to teaching cultural diversity as well as a *challenge* they continued to face. Discussions of such practical topics led to a renewed commitment and energy for continuing to meet in order to understand how different faculty and support staff at Duquesne were approaching multicultural education, to share resources, and to promote systemic action in the university community. In one such meeting faculty from occupational therapy and education shared how they approached issues of institutional, personally mediated, and internalized racism using popular films such as *A Time to Kill* (Hunt, Grisham, & Schumacher, 1996). In others we invited nationally and regionally known guest speakers to address the topics of multicultural teaching and the importance of multicultural understanding in the global marketplace.

The life cycle of the Diversity Network was fairly short, lasting about three years. Network members, however, have moved from informal discussion to participation in organizational changes brought about by the university leadership. A key sign of Duquesne's intention to take diversity seriously came when the then director of mission and identity invited network members to provide feedback on a white paper he had written outlining foundations for diversity at Duquesne, Duquesne's policy on nondiscrimination and nonharassment, the hallmarks of Duquesne's vision for diversity, and specific areas in need of attention.

Making Diversity Tangible at Duquesne

The grassroots efforts of the informal Diversity Network clearly prepared the way for Duquesne University to take action toward creating a more diverse campus and systematically integrating multiculturalism into the curriculum. The network facilitated important consciousness-raising and capacity-building activities, and it provided momentum for continued progress on the institution's cultural journey that would include actions in curriculum, personnel, student recruitment, organizational structure, budgeting, and policy. We will list here selected ways in which the network's commitment to diversity—both for social justice and educational quality—has become tangible throughout various levels and areas of Duquesne.

The Diversity Network met with the then new provost in November 2001 and learned of his commitment to providing multicultural education, to exploring the possibility of a core curriculum requirement, and to including diversity in the strategic planning process. The strategic plan for 2003–2008 did indeed include targets for integrating a global perspective into the general education requirement; creating a center for Catholic social thought with a focus on interreligious dialogue, racism, and poverty; and designating that "the university will increase its diversity. Numbers from underrepresented groups will increase. More women and minorities will have leadership roles" (Duquesne University, 2002). The provost and human resources staff partnered to create a hiring policy requiring search committees to recruit a diverse pool of candidates and to provide incentives to departments to hire faculty of color. The university has recently hired several women of color for leadership positions (e.g., a dean, an associate dean, a school registrar, an assistant director of human resources, and a campus minister), and women were also hired for other key positions in which men had previously served (e.g., a university librarian, two deans, an executive director of international programs, and a vice president for advancement). Many departments have hired faculty of color, and in particular, Duquesne has successfully recruited black male Catholic theologians.

The Office of International Programs at Duquesne has a long and successful history of supporting international students coming to Duquesne but has recently reorganized to include a centralized office for expanding the study abroad program. In conjunction with this, the college of liberal arts developed an intercultural study certificate that includes core courses in sociology and communication, study abroad, and an intercultural interpretation seminar upon students' return to the United States. In student life, the Office of Multicultural Affairs was founded to support individual minority students, often first-generation, in learning how to succeed in college. It also offers programming that celebrates diversity, provides opportunities for multicultural exchange between students and faculty, and creates forums for cross-cultural dialogue.

Although diversity, globalism, and ecumenism have figured in the mission statement for over a decade, recently the executive director of mission and identity foregrounded their importance and has been appointed the chair of a presidential task force on diversity. He also led the process of creating a gay-straight alliance to ensure dignity and justice toward gay members of the Duquesne community and to offer relevant educational opportunities. The provost also chairs a social justice committee, which seeks to ensure that social justice issues of national or international importance that are pertinent to university life—such as sweatshops and university apparel, living wage, and health—enter into the broader university discourse on justice, equity, and action.

A series on the foundations of successful management, required of all leaders on campus, begins each year with a joint session on the mission of Duquesne and "managing with diversity," co-facilitated by the executive director of mission and identity and a regionally known diversity trainer. The same kind of session also serves to introduce the new seminar series for academic chairpersons. The five pillars of the mission are presented to all new employees, and an ongoing discussion of these is promoted among current employees. Newly established faculty and staff expectations include fostering an atmosphere of openness and appreciating and working to enhance diversity to complement the longstanding student expectation of appreciating diversity and being open minded.

For nearly 20 years, the Spiritan campus ministry has sponsored cross-cultural trips that focus on helping students understand the cultural realities of others through firsthand experience. Duquesne was one of the first universities to take students to live with, work with, and learn from migrant farm workers in southwest Florida. Leaders use guided reflection before, during, and after these trips to help students build a deeper understanding of self and others. This theme of understanding others through cross-cultural encounter is now interwoven into the Duquesne educational experience for all students. Two components of the recently approved core curriculum, a global diversity course and a service-learning requirement for all undergraduates, are intended to help students "develop a global perspective through investigating diversity within global, national, and local contexts" (Duquesne University, 2006c). The service-learning initiative, as well as the broader community outreach, focuses on building a mutually beneficial relationship with surrounding communities. These represent populations distinct from that of the majority of Duquesne students in social class, ethnicity, and religion. Finally, the revised university-wide assessment initiative requires that each academic program report on student learning outcomes relevant to the five dimensions of a Duquesne education, including diversity and global mindedness (Duquesne University, 2006b).

The Duquesne leadership has stated the importance of the Diversity Network's early work in laying the foundation for the systemic commitments Duquesne has recently made. But we clearly haven't arrived. In fact, it's not so much about arriving as about keeping at the forefront of all we do the question of how we can best educate our students and model for them a community where we seek justice and dignity for all persons.

Continuing the Journey

As with any journey, the pictures we share in this short chapter do not reflect all the efforts to infuse multiculturalism into the institutional context of Duquesne University. Challenges persist in the road ahead. We have not yet met our goal of recruiting and supporting a significantly diverse student body and employee community. In fact, our students reported in the 2003 and 2004 National Survey of Student Engagement that they had significantly fewer serious conversations than their peers at other doctoral-intensive schools with students of a different ethnicity and that Duquesne contributed significantly less to their understanding of people of other racial and ethnic backgrounds. We are concerned about this finding and realize our need to provide support to talented minority students who are unable to pay the high costs of college. In so doing, we would honor the Spiritan priests who founded Duquesne in 1878 specifically to provide an education and safe, professional employment to immigrant children—the educationally underserved population of that day in Pittsburgh.

References

Antonio, A. L. (2004). When does race matter in college friendships? Exploring men's diverse and homogeneous friendship groups. *Review of Higher Education, 27*, 553–575.

Brown, L. I. (2004). Diversity: The challenge for higher education. *Race, Ethnicity and Education, 7*, 21–34.

Duquesne University. (2002). *Duquesne University strategic plan, 2003–2008*. Retrieved February 21, 2007, from www.duq.edu/frontpages/aboutdu/stratplan.html

Duquesne University. (2006a). *Duquesne University fact book*. Retrieved February 21, 2007, from www.irp.duq.edu/pdf/2006_Fact_Book.pdf

Duquesne University. (2006b). *Dimensions of a Duquesne education*. Retrieved February 21, 2007, from www.aloa.duq.edu/dimensions.html

Duquesne University. (2006c). *University core curriculum*. Pittsburgh, PA: Author.

Duquesne University. (n.d.). *Duquesne University mission statement*. Retrieved February 21, 2007, from www.mission.duq.edu/index.html

Hunt, L. (Producer), Grisham, J. (Producer), & Schumacher, J. (Director). (1996). *A time to kill* [Motion picture]. United States: Warner Home Video.

Hurtado, S. (2003). *Preparing college students for a diverse democracy: Final report to the U.S. Department of Education, OERI Field-Initiated Studies Program*. Ann Arbor, MI: Center for the Study of Higher and Postsecondary Education.

Lopez-Mulnix, E. E., & Mulnix, M. W. (2006). Models of excellence in multicultural colleges and universities. *Journal of Hispanic Higher Education, 5*(1), 4–21.

Morey, A. I. (1997). Organizational change and implementation strategies for multicultural infusion. In A. I. Morey & M. K. Kitano (Eds.), *Multicultural course transformation in higher education: A broader truth* (pp. 258–277). Needham Heights, MA: Allyn & Bacon.

Morey, A. I., & Kitano, M. K. (1997). *Multicultural course transformation in higher education: A broader truth*. Needham Heights, MA: Allyn & Bacon.

Reid, F. (Producer). (1995). *Skin deep* [Video]. (Available from Iris Films, 2600 10th Street, Suite 413, Berkeley, CA 95710)

Siegel, D. J. (2003). *The call for diversity: Pressure, expectation, and organizational response in the postsecondary setting.* New York, NY: Routledge.

Smith, D. G. (1997). *Diversity works: The emerging picture of how students benefit.* Washington, DC: Association of American Colleges and Universities.

Smith, D. G., & Wolf-Wendel, L. E. (2005). *The challenge of diversity: Involvement or alienation in the academy?* San Francisco, CA: Jossey-Bass.

8

Diversity Initiatives in an Online University

Helen Bond

University of Maryland University College _____

Mission and Vision

University of Maryland University College (UMUC) is one of the 11 public degree-granting institutions in the University System of Maryland (USM). Founded in 1947 as the College of Special and Continuation Studies at the University of Maryland–College Park, UMUC became a separate degree-granting institution in 1970. UMUC offers degree programs from the associate of arts through the doctor of management and several certificate programs. UMUC is now a global university with worldwide headquarters in Adelphi, Maryland, and regional headquarters in Europe and Asia. These overseas operations enable UMUC to offer educational opportunities to geographically dispersed individuals, such as military service members and their families.

The principal mission of UMUC is to serve the needs of nontraditional students. UMUC accomplishes this by offering high-quality distance education as a means of engaging faculty, students, and others in the world community. UMUC was awarded the International Council for Open and Distance Education 2004 Prize of Excellence in the fields of open, distance, virtual, and flexible learning. The vision of UMUC is to become the premier global university serving nontraditional students, recognized by the accessibility and affordability of its programs; the quality of its teaching, learning, and student services; and its commitment to the success of its students (UMUC, 2004a).

Student Demographics

UMUC is the most racially diverse institution within the USM. With an online enrollment of over 126,000 in 2004, UMUC enrolls more African-American students than any other public four-year institution in Maryland, including Historically Black Colleges and Universities (UMUC, 2005). *Black Issues in Higher Education* (Borden & Brown, 2003) reported that UMUC ranked 27th in the number of master's degrees awarded to minority students in 2002. Approximately 58% of stateside undergraduate students are female and 32% of stateside undergraduate students are African-Americans. Women made up 52% of the graduate students in fall 2004, and minority students represented 55% of the graduate students in fall 2004 (UMUC, 2005).

Diversity Programs

The Office of Diversity Initiatives

With UMUC's global footprint and diverse student body, it is critical that the university fosters a climate of respect. Progress is made toward this goal in several ways. The Office of Diversity Initiatives located in Adelphi, Maryland, is responsible for promoting diversity and human relations through the efforts of a diversity council. Council members are staff and faculty from UMUC Adelphi, Asia, and Europe. Members serve as liaisons to their institutions by collaborating and sharing resources. This cooperation enables the Office of Diversity Initiatives to feature speakers, presentations, films, and other programs to promote a greater awareness and appreciation for diversity.

The "Meet the Ambassador" series, cosponsored by the Office of Diversity Initiatives and the Alumni Association, is one example of the programs offered. It enabled students, staff, faculty, and community to meet ambassadors from Argentina, Afghanistan, and Switzerland and hear them speak about important issues in their countries. Because UMUC is a virtual university with students and faculty located worldwide, many presentations and events are captured as web casts for viewing on the university's web site.

The Office of Diversity Initiatives also ensures compliance with affirmative action policies, assists in conflict resolution, and helps the university maintain a diverse workforce. The Office of Human Resources supports these efforts by offering workshops that address effective management practices for a diverse and equitable workplace.

Diversity Network Faculty Initiatives Committee

A second way in which UMUC seeks to provide a climate of respect is through membership in the USM Diversity Network. Established in 1995, the Diversity

Network cooperates with the administration of the 13 USM institutions in making diversity an institutional priority. The Diversity Network is composed of the Faculty Initiatives Committee; Lesbian, Gay, Bisexual, and Transgender (LGBT) Committee; and Student Initiatives Committee. These committees collaborate in ways that expand diversity awareness by transforming the curriculum, conducting and disseminating research, and sponsoring an annual conference.

For example, the Faculty Initiatives Committee focuses on concerns of faculty members within the 13 member institutions and beyond. The committee sponsors an annual conference that provides a forum for exchanging ideas, sharing best practices, and engaging in thought-provoking conversations about diversity. The LGBT and Student Initiatives Committees participate in the planning of the conference so that a wide range of perspectives are included. The conference has grown to include student research, the K–12 school community, and participants outside the USM community.

Curriculum Transformation

International Perspectives

To remain viable UMUC must prepare students with 21st-century skills. The curriculum must be revised and updated to meet the needs of a highly diverse, global, and technological world. To help accomplish this, UMUC draws on its virtual capacity in connecting with institutions in Latin America, Europe, and Asia and developing partnerships to jointly deliver courses. To sustain and grow the partnerships, the curriculum must reflect a more international perspective. UMUC is often challenged by its mandate to meet the needs of a growing workforce within Maryland and the need for a more interdisciplinary focus from the regional headquarters in Europe and Asia (UMUC, 2005). General education courses with an interdisciplinary cross-curricular focus have been included in the School of Undergraduate Studies so that students' learning experiences would be "engaging and negotiating different perspectives and exercising ethical judgment in their personal and professional lives" (UMUC, 2004c, p. 21).

Core Learning Areas

Finally, demonstrating the knowledge, skills, and dispositions necessary to function effectively as a global citizen is a core learning area for both the School of Undergraduate Studies and the Graduate School of Management and Technology at UMUC. Core learning areas were adopted in 2003 as clearly defined expectations of what students should know and be able to do upon completing their programs at UMUC. Core learning areas were determined by Middle States Association Commission on Higher Education accreditation guidelines,

Maryland Higher Education Commission guidelines on student learning outcomes, and the mission and vision of UMUC (UMUC, 2004b). Making globalization and diversity a core learning area for the university will help the university stay focused on achieving the skills, knowledge, and ethics that promote and respect diversity.

References

Borden, V. M. H., & Brown, P. C. (2003). The top 100: Interpreting the data. *Black Issues in Higher Education, 20*(10), 40–62.

University of Maryland University College. (2004a). *Five-year strategic plan, FY 2005–2009: "Transforming the university."* Adelphi, MD: Office of the President.

University of Maryland University College. (2004b). *Institutional plan for the assessment of student learning outcomes.* Adelphi, MD: Office of Outcomes Assessment.

University of Maryland University College. (2004c). *Undergraduate catalog, 2004–2005.* Retrieved February 21, 2007, from www.umuc.edu/prog/ugp/catalog04_05/catalog04_05.pdf

University of Maryland University College. (2005). *Middle States self-study.* Retrieved February 21, 2007, from www.umuc.edu/middlestates/index.shtml

9

"The City in Transition": A Multiyear Thematic Initiative at an Urban Institution

David Bogen

This chapter reports on a thematic initiative that was begun at Emerson College in fall 2002 and concluded in spring 2005. The purpose of this initiative was to provide focus, resources, administrative support, and visibility for curricular projects and cultural events that explored the interface between the college and its surrounding communities. The chosen theme for this initiative—"The City in Transition"—reflects the complex relationship between urban institutions, local communities, government agencies, businesses, and the many other constituencies and interests that shape the development of urban centers. Institutions of higher education have the potential for broad impact, both positive and negative, on their surrounding communities. Similarly, the city provides the physical, cultural, and economic context within which urban institutions exist, and their development can either be enabled or hindered by that relationship. At its core, the "City in Transition" initiative was conceived as a practical way of building awareness around issues of diversity and creating positive patterns of interaction between the college and the people and organizations that compose its local environment. Although it is only one element in a larger institutional strategy for addressing matters of race, class, gender, and ethnicity, it provides a model approach for bringing questions of diversity directly into the experience of faculty, students, and the curriculum.

Emerson College is a privately controlled institution located in the center of Boston, with approximately 3,000 undergraduate and 800 graduate students. Its mission focuses on programs in the arts and communication disciplines, and its seven departments include performing arts; visual and media arts; writing, literature, and publishing; organizational and political communication; marketing communication; journalism; and communication sciences and disorders. Emerson is also the home of the Institute for Liberal Arts and Interdisciplinary Studies, which was created in 1997 as a center of innovation in scholarship and teaching of interdisciplinary studies and integrated curriculum in the liberal arts.

Since the early 1990s, the college has undergone a series of transformations in its physical plant, technological infrastructure, and academic and curricular organization. Perhaps the most critical change has been the movement of the Emerson campus from a collection of brownstones in Boston's Back Bay area to a group of renovated and newly built highrises in the midtown cultural district. From an internal perspective, this move has meant a thorough rethinking of the college's sense of place and identity as an academic community. Externally, the relocation to the city center has been part of a larger movement to develop properties in and around the Boston Common and to revitalize the cultural and civic life of this area. These patterns of development also place new pressures on many of the residents and communities in the area, including rising real estate costs and a depletion of low- and moderate-income housing. In Emerson's view, the core questions of diversity curricula—issues of race, class, gender, and ethnicity—are manifest in this new set of relationships and everyday behaviors that have arisen as part of Emerson's relocation and the implications of gentrification in the surrounding neighborhoods.

During the 2000–2001 academic year, a group of faculty and administrators met in the context of college-wide strategic planning to create a new academic vision for Emerson College. Their work was informed by Emerson's emerging identity as an agent of change in the midtown cultural district and the opportunities and responsibilities this implies. In their final report, this group articulated a vision in which teaching and learning would be "extended beyond the classroom," the college would become more "permeable," and students would be provided with opportunities to "participate in the democratic process" and "to use their skills to improve the quality of life in local communities" (Emerson College, 2005, p. 2). During the summer and fall of 2001, a planning group in the Office of Academic Affairs developed the concept of the "City in Transition" initiative as one strategy for implementing this new academic vision. The stated goals of this initiative were:

- To enhance interdisciplinary connections between different academic disciplines

- To increase the exchange and "permeability" between the college and its surrounding communities

- To provide an organizing principle for college-wide events, student work, and discussion that is penetrating, coherent, and enduring

With funding from the Office of Academic Affairs, a coordinating group was formed within the Institute for Liberal Arts and Interdisciplinary Studies. Over the next three years, this group worked with other schools and departments, student groups, Emerson faculty, and a variety of on-campus and community partners to produce a wide array of courses, events, and projects associated with this initiative. These included the creation of over 12 new courses focused on issues of diversity and urban life; sponsorship for more than 30 residencies, exhibitions, and public lectures on themes related to the culture and politics of the city; the formation of new partnerships with a wide variety of community organizations and artistic and cultural groups, including the Chinatown Coalition, the Center for Latino Arts, and the Boston YMCA; and the development of the Office of Service Learning and Community Action as a central resource for the creation of engaged curricula.

The "City in Transition" initiative is testimony to the impact that strong academic leadership accompanied by modest amounts of funding can have at critical junctures in an institution's history. For three years it provided a focus and an impetus for faculty and students to participate in the creative exploration of Emerson's new academic vision, and it has led to sustainable curriculum, partnerships, and institutional infrastructure in support of that vision. Much of this work has been archived online, and readers are encouraged to visit the web sites listed here to learn more about these projects.

References

Emerson College. (2005). *Building on a solid foundation: A strategic plan for 2001–2005.* Boston, MA: Author.

Resources

The "City in Transition" main web site: www.emerson.edu/city

"Moving Out/Moving In" course site: http://institute.emerson.edu/movingoutmovingin/

"Boston: City in Transition" graduate journalism course site: http://journalism.emerson.edu/changingboston

"Invisible Cities" course site: http://institute.emerson.edu/spring04/IN308/flash/index.php

Charles Beard Arts and Communication Exploration Program: http://institute.emerson.edu/youngachievers/2004/

10

Diversity Initiatives at the University of North Carolina–Chapel Hill

Lynne Degitz

The University of North Carolina–Chapel Hill (UNC–Chapel Hill) was the nation's first state university and the only public university to award degrees in the 18th century. Now in its third century, the university offers bachelor's, master's, doctoral, and professional degrees in academic areas critical to North Carolina's future: business, dentistry, education, law, medicine, nursing, public health, and social work, among others. In fall 2005, UNC–Chapel Hill enrolled more than 27,000 students from all 100 North Carolina counties, the other 49 states, and more than 100 other countries. Eighty-two percent of its undergraduates come from North Carolina. Those students learn from a 3,100-member faculty. Offerings include 71 bachelor's, 110 master's, and 77 doctorate degree programs. The health sciences are well integrated with liberal arts, basic sciences, and high-tech programs. Patient outreach programs affiliated with UNC–Chapel Hill and the UNC Health Care System serve citizens in all 100 North Carolina counties. The mission of the university is to serve all the people of the state, and indeed the nation, as a center for scholarship and creative endeavor. The university exists to teach students at all levels in an environment of research, free inquiry, and personal responsibility; to expand knowledge; to improve the condition of human life through service and publication; and to enrich our culture.

Several national publications regularly publish rankings that have listed UNC–Chapel Hill prominently in categories ranging from academic quality to affordability, to diversity, to public service, to international presence. Several national publications regularly publish rankings that have listed UNC–Chapel Hill prominently in categories ranging from academic quality to affordability, to diversity, to public service, to international presence, including *U.S. News & World Report*, *Kiplinger's Personal Finance*, *The Princeton Review*, and the *Fiske Guide to Colleges*.

Program Descriptions_____

UNC–Chapel Hill has committed to a variety of steps to embrace diversity and ensure that diversity is incorporated into curricula, including the following.

Diversity Values

The university upholds the following diversity values as part of an institutional commitment to building an inclusive climate for all members of the campus community:

- The university supports intellectual freedom, promotes personal integrity and justice, and pursues values that foster enlightened leadership devoted to improving the conditions of human life in the state, the nation, and the world.

- The university believes that it can achieve its educational, research, and service mission only by creating and sustaining an environment in which students, faculty, and staff represent diversity, for example, of social backgrounds, economic circumstances, personal characteristics, philosophical outlooks, life experiences, perspectives, beliefs, expectations, and aspirations, to mention some salient factors.

- The university will achieve and maintain diversity on the campus through the admission of students and the employment of faculty and staff who broadly reflect the ways in which people differ.

- The university promotes intellectual growth and derives the educational benefits of diversity by creating opportunities for intense dialogue and rigorous analysis and by fostering mutually beneficial interactions among members of the community.

- The university provides an environment that values and respects civility and cordiality of discourse so that all members of a diverse community feel welcomed and feel free to express their ideas without fear of reprisal. (University of North Carolina–Chapel Hill, 2005, pp. 7–8)

Academic Plan

The university's academic plan articulates diversity as one of six key priorities for the institution's overarching educational goals. Specifically, the plan outlines the importance of efforts that ensure that the diverse members of UNC–Chapel Hill's community feel welcome as students or as members of the faculty and staff. Continued support and strengthening of key units—such as African-American Studies, the Sonja Haynes Stone Black Cultural Center, and Diversity and Multicultural Affairs—are critical components of building an inclusive learning environment. In addition, the plan recommends implementing a U.S. diversity requirement for undergraduates because diversity is critical to the university's effectiveness as an educational institution. The establishment and deepening of educational collaborations with historically minority colleges and universities in North Carolina is an additional key component of the academic plan (University of North Carolina–Chapel Hill, 2003).

Diversity and Multicultural Affairs

Diversity and Multicultural Affairs' mission is to provide university-wide leadership, consultation, and project management for policies, programs, and services that promote diversity as a means of achieving educational excellence and enhancing the quality of life for all members of the university community. Diversity and Multicultural Affairs provides substantial leadership and guidance to university-wide diversity assessments and to the development and implementation of an institutional diversity plan. Diversity and Multicultural Affairs is situated under the Office of the Provost and the executive vice chancellor.

References

University of North Carolina–Chapel Hill. (2003). *Academic plan.* Retrieved February 21, 2007, from http://provost.unc.edu/academicplan

University of North Carolina–Chapel Hill. (2005). *Report of the chancellor's task force on diversity.* Retrieved February 21, 2007, from www.unc.edu/minorityaffairs/assessment/diversityreport.pdf

11

Diversity Initiatives at St. Louis Community College

Diane Pisacreta

St. Louis Community College (STLCC) is the largest community college in Missouri and one of the largest in the United States. Enrollment at the college averages around 32,000 students per semester; by that head count STLCC is the second largest institution of higher education in Missouri. STLCC is composed of three campuses: Florissant Valley, Forest Park, and Meramec. These campuses provide services to both the city of St. Louis and to St. Louis County. The focus of STLCC, like other community colleges, is to offer freshman- and sophomore-level college transfer courses and a variety of career programs. In addition, STLCC also offers many noncredit continuing education courses to the community.

The college's mission statement plays a strong role in shaping the services the school provides. The following items represent some of the goals that are set forth in STLCC's mission statement:

- To prepare students for a college or university transfer, up through the associate degree

- To prepare students for occupational entry at both the vocational and the paraprofessional or technical level, up through the associate degree

- To provide occupational upgrading and retraining in credit and noncredit courses and certificate programs

- To provide counseling and other student support services, particularly personal, academic, and career advisement, as well as job placement

58

- To provide programs for special student groups, such as disabled, limited-English-speaking, talented and gifted persons

- To provide continuing education courses for academic, social, cultural, recreational, and personal enrichment

- To engage in educational and collaborative partnerships with business, industry, labor, government, and other institutions, including secondary schools and other colleges and universities

As indicated by those goals, STLCC differs in significant ways from universities. An important part of its vision is focusing on career programs and establishing collaborative relationships with businesses and industries. In addition, STLCC's relationship to the community is different: rather than enriching the community through conducting research, it enriches the community through programming and continuing education. Because the college is working to prepare the future workforce and looking to connect to the community around it, it has a particular responsibility to respond to the issue of diversity.

The face of the U.S. population is changing; it is becoming more diverse. According to the U.S. Census Bureau (2001, p. 17, Table 15), minority populations grew between 1980 and 2000: the African-American population grew by 28%, the Native American population grew by 55%, the Hispanic population grew by 122%, and the Asian population grew by 190%. Johnson and Packer (1987) predict that by 2030 the United States will be a global society, a society in which racial minorities will come to represent nearly half of all Americans.

Preparing students for the workforce and making connections to the community entails that the college work toward its own cultural competency and the cultural competency of its students. Being culturally competent is not limited to issues of race but rather includes all forms of diversity—gender, ethnicity, age, and ability. STLCC has developed various programs and resources to develop a sense of cultural competency at the institutional level that can then be brought into the classroom and into the community.

Some initiatives include a district-wide diversity committee, the Global Studies Program, and activities during African-American History Month and Women's History Month. The district-wide diversity committee addresses issues of diversity on a cross-campus level. Initiatives include working on a policy for domestic partners and working to make the college more attractive to minority applicants. Though these initiatives do not deal with curriculum directly, their impact on students is felt. Knowing that work is being done on these issues sets the tone for the institution as a whole.

The Global Studies Program has a more direct impact on curriculum development. Its mission statement "encourages development of global content in courses across the curriculum by providing educational opportunities for faculty to expand their knowledge of various regions of the world." The program works to provide resources for faculty that will facilitate the inclusion of global issues into their teaching; this includes the development of curriculum modules that faculty can modify for their own use. The Global Studies Program focuses on the following goals: curriculum development, staff development, international student support, and travel opportunities for faculty and students. In addition, Global Studies contributes to the campus culture by bringing in speakers and events, including activities for African-American History Month and Women's History Month. The presence of this type of programming creates an easy way for faculty to introduce students to diversity and links the campus to the surrounding community.

Example of a Diversity Initiative: Women's Studies _____

In general, addressing issues of diversity plays a central role in the ways the STLCC curriculum is organized. I teach Introduction to Women's Studies; this course works as an example for how instructors can address the issue of diversity within a classroom setting. When I arrived at STLCC, the course had never been taught at this community college. In fact, it is a rarity to see women's studies curriculum at the community college level. Though the course met some resistance, it gained district-wide acceptance. The course explores women's issues from a variety of disciplines. An emphasis is placed on the diversity of women's personal experience and its relationship to larger social structures. The focus of this course is to develop a sense of empowerment and critical thinking. Students are presented the following learning objectives:

- The issue of diversity

- Gender as a social and personal construct

- The women's movement

- The varieties of feminism

- The intersectional model of identity

- Gender in relation to class, race, and sexual orientation

- Women's roles in the family

- Women's role in the economy

- Women's relationship to the media

- The continuum of violence against women

- The ideas of coalition building and forming alliances and social movements

- Relationships and applications of concepts to personal experience

The focus of these objectives is for students to engage in the material on a personal level. Connecting theory to personal experience brings the material to life in a meaningful way for them.

I take two approaches to addressing issues of diversity within the classroom: 1) I make it a point to link the theory that the class is discussing to students' personal lives; and 2) if they are members of the dominant group, I encourage students to think through the issue of privilege and how they have personally benefited from systems of oppression. Often, at the beginning of the semester, students gloss over issues of difference; they are unable to see the ways power differences can organize their lives. Students can be very resistant to the idea that sexism exists. Along with theory I include personal narratives, a module on violence against women, and writing exercises that have students contemplate the ways their lives are organized by sexism. Once they start to make those connections to their own experience, it becomes very easy to educate them on other forms of oppression.

A challenge in educating students on issues of diversity is getting students from the dominant class to engage in the material in a straightforward manner. For example, having white students read McIntosh's (2003) "White Privilege: Unpacking the Invisible Knapsack" or having heterosexual students read Pharr's (1988) *Homophobia: A Weapon of Sexism* can be very emotionally and intellectually challenging for students. Students are often trained to think about racism, sexism, and homophobia as individual acts. They do not see these as systems of oppression. They fundamentally believe that if they personally do not behave in a racist or sexist manner, they are exempt from participating in these systems. As members of the dominant class, they often fail to see the ways that they benefit from these systems of oppression; they have a difficult time admitting to and owning their own privilege. This is the main challenge in teaching students regarding issues of diversity. They can easily recognize racism or sexism, but they are often blind to the privilege that results from the existence of these systems. Students often clam up at this point in the semester—guilt, a resistance to letting go of their privilege, and an inability to engage can all prevent students from opening up. I encourage students to list the ways that they may personally benefit from being white, male, or heterosexual. I then ask them to think of creative ways they can extend these benefits to others—often students come to the realization that this extension of benefits does not diminish their own possibilities.

Though it is challenging to have students deal with such heated topics, it is both professionally and personally rewarding to see the ways students can grow and stretch. I warn students at the beginning that this class will change the way they view the world. I tell them that by the end of the semester, they will have their women's studies glasses, a new set of lenses through which they will view the world—and it won't look the same. Some of them might not like what they see, some might not like wearing new glasses, and some will feel as if they are seeing everything clearly for the first time. The response from students can be overwhelming. Teaching a course that focuses exclusively on issues of diversity gives students not only a language but also a safe space to discuss the very issues that impact their lives. Colleges and universities should be committed to encouraging faculty to integrate issues of diversity into the curriculum; they should also consider requiring students to take courses whose sole purpose is educating students regarding diversity.

References

Johnson, W. B., & Packer, A. H. (1987). *Workforce 2000: Work and workers for the 21st century.* Indianapolis, IN: Hudson Institute.

McIntosh, P. (2003). White privilege: Unpacking the invisible knapsack. In A. Kesselman, N. Schniedewind, & L. McNair (Eds.), *Women: Images and realities, a multicultural anthology* (3rd ed., pp. 424–426). New York, NY: McGraw-Hill.

Pharr, S. (1988). *Homophobia: A weapon of sexism.* Little Rock, AR: Chardon Press.

U.S. Census Bureau. (2001). *Statistical abstract of the United States: 2001.* Washington, DC: Author.

12

Institutional Diversity Initiatives: Theory and Practice

Xaé Alicia Reyes

In this essay I posit there are strategies employed by institutions of higher learning that are aimed at appearing "diversity compliant" but that undercut the supposed objectives of diversity. These strategies include the hiring of candidates who have the appropriate minority surname or skin color but who espouse assimilationist and dominant ideologies, pedagogies, or goals. Indeed, it often turns out that when an ethnically, culturally, or linguistically diverse candidate is hired, the differences celebrated during the hiring process are the very things that eventually marginalize him or her (Reyes, 2004, 2005; Reyes & Rios, 2005). Such practices are in conflict with the lofty missions and visions outlined for institutions of higher education. Unfortunately, it is not surprising to find skepticism and disdain instead of a willingness to entertain self-critique or to recognize individual notions of superiority among academics of the majority group. Without true acceptance of "others" as equals and contributors, diversity plans, curricula, and infusing other perspectives into courses and dynamics of our institutions turn out to be simply linguistic exercises—wordsmithing that is meant to look good on paper only. The undermining of diversity goals also includes a sort of revolving-door practice, which fills statistical voids and brings in new hires to replace faculty who leave voluntarily or who do not earn tenure, while the institution itself maintains the appearance of being diversity compliant. When explanations for the resulting nonretention of the unfortunate hires are given, they usually focus on the departees' failure in areas of scholarship and/or teaching, or in cases of voluntary departure, it is said that the person did not integrate well into the environment. In both of these arguments the fault is assigned to the faculty member who left.

The Diversity Mandate in Higher Education _____

In the pursuit of excellence in education, there is agreement that multiple perspectives are essential and that exchanges among intellectuals from a wide range of communities will yield a proportionally wide variety of knowledge. These desirable conditions are a challenge for most institutions where a dominant ideology and culture creates a bubble-like environment that is out of touch with the realities of the minority communities that are often in their vicinity. Demagogic discourses of inclusion are often betrayed through practices and social norms that continue to exclude faculty, staff, and students whose characteristics are not similar to those of the members of the dominant group. Oftentimes, these institutions neglect their mandates of enhancing the quality of life of citizens in their states even though enormous grants are secured from the government and other entities for exactly that purpose.

In many cases, the grantees who secure these monies go into communities to glean data, implement programs, and influence policy with partners who are like them or who are of their same ideology, and they position themselves in patronizing and condescending stances in communities they are presumably meant to "serve." If they choose to engage those of us who are embedded in the minority community, it is usually just to gain entry and skip over the lengthy rapport-building process and to later report the outcomes and findings as their own. The subtleties of this practice of exploitation might not be evident, but they are part of the everyday experiences of many scholars and faculty of color (De la Luz Reyes & Halcón, 1988). We are asked to participate in brain-picking and idea generating, in student and community recruitment and connecting for studies and initiatives, in committees that legitimize practices related to diversity, and in visibility events (graduations, open houses, and even funding initiatives), yet our names are sometimes omitted or minimized when it comes to leadership and credit-worthy roles. When we question these practices or point out their inherent dishonesty, we are then labeled as "non-team players," "hostile," and even "racist." This response may even serve to legitimize alienation and exclusion from any participation in tenure- and merit-earning endeavors. These practices are evident in nonappointment to relevant committees and nonselection for representation in important bodies within our institutions and at state, national, and international levels.

What is worse, through the mechanism of advisement, students are often "herded" away from our courses with justifications that our courses are elective or that there are scheduling conflicts with required ones. Consequently, the goals of hiring diverse faculty—to afford students the exposure to diverse perspectives— are not met. Unfortunately, there is no serious inquiry to gauge patterns of exclusion and ghettoizing of minority faculty who have left, yet to an insider with minimal observation skills, there are clear patterns that show the devaluing of minority colleagues through the advisement process. An effect of this practice is lower enrollment in minority-taught courses. Another is that minority faculty are often not considered for merit recommendation. Still others include nonselection of minorities to department chair positions, to significant committees such as promotion and tenure review (PTR) committees, to institutional appointments in graduate schools, and others, which enhance the merit and PTR credentials of the faculty who are selected. I believe that a commitment to diversity requires a commitment to undo these patterns of exclusion and truly foster and respect our colleagues of all backgrounds.

Bias and Selectivity in the Hiring Processes

My experience in academia has been informed by my travels through a series of universities, encompassing years as a graduate and undergraduate student and appointments of different kinds, in locations throughout the Northeast and the Southwest (Reyes 2004, 2006). One of the practices I often heard criticized by accreditation teams and hiring committees was that of inbreeding. This practice of hiring faculty from graduates of the same university is tantamount to nepotism. It reproduces the culture and practices of the institution by way of appointments of people educated under the same epistemological and ideological formation. This replication of similar paradigms and values defeats the purpose of what a university education is supposed to offer its students—a richness of diverse perspectives and worldviews.

Spousal hiring presents a similar dilemma. Although having two qualified scholars in a field who happen to be a couple is a desirable and even ideal situation for hiring committees, the appointment of partners would seem to be counter-intuitive when the goal of increased diversity among faculty is considered. Similarly, I have seen cases of inbreeding where a recent graduate with no visible outstanding qualifications is appointed over another candidate who has richer experiences, ethnic and linguistic diversity, and numerous attributes that might satisfy the quest for enhancement of the academic environment to better prepare graduates and serve the greater community. Other situations I have observed include the creation of adjunct and other types of appointments (resident, visiting, etc.) to get around the required search procedures that might allow for the hiring of a valuable minority. In some settings this is described as "getting in through the back door." In these cases, opportunities for visibility are assigned subjectively—denied to one person, often a person of color, because he or she is resident faculty, yet assigned steadily and abundantly to others in the same status. Biased hiring continues, whether it's hiring the mainstream wife or the graduate student, or being rationalized as responding to the need to "preserve the family." In other words, practices once considered nepotistic are currently being revisited with positive arguments (Bellows, 2003) and are now being legitimized.

The vulnerability of the excluded minority members of the faculty is evident to the point that even students of color are prone to align themselves with those faculty members who are favored by the system, lest they too be diverted from opportunities in the setting. There have been Latino and African-American students in my departments in several institutions, some that I or other colleagues of color have even recruited, who distanced themselves once they perceived that we were not as "powerful" in the system as other less experienced and less empathetic colleagues. As indicated earlier, some of the favored colleagues even have the surnames and other characteristics to fill diversity slots, but they are ideologically, racially, socioeconomically, and experientially disconnected from diverse experiences and perspectives. In fact, many are content and thrive in the midst of the alienating and marginalizing dynamics toward other diverse faculty to the point of being complicit in pushing them away.

Righting the Wrongs to Make Diversity Initiatives Work_____

The impact of the failure of diversity initiatives could not be more consequential. The United States has an increasingly diverse population where youngsters of color continue to rise in number and yet are still left behind academically. Some of the factors that affect academic performance are related to the absence of role models among educators who are in these youngsters' lives. It is still typical in many urban or inner-city schools to find the majority of minority adults located in staff positions, such as cafeteria personnel, custodians, security guards, and other nonacademic positions. Thus, there is an absence of people of color in teaching, counseling, and administrative positions. For those students who make it to postsecondary education, these demographics are intensified. The dismal percentages of faculty of color at most universities make the environment very challenging for first-generation college students, especially those who are visibly different from the rest of the population. The presence of federal TRIO programs helps ameliorate the transition processes for students who qualify for such support services and who have been able to access them. But a better solution would be an increase in the hiring and retaining of diverse faculty. The culture of higher education institutions and the characteristics that need to change was best captured by the following statement cited by Turner (2002):

> To be a professor is to be Anglo. . . . As Latina [faculty of color] professors we are newcomers to a world defined and controlled by discourses that do not address our realities, that do not affirm our intellectual contributions, that do not seriously examine our worlds. (pp. 74–75)

According to Trower (2002), some of the features of the traditional academic model affect both women and people of color adversely. Among them she mentions that earning tenure depends on publishing in "appropriate" journals and that full professorship is obtained through approval by tenured faculty, predominantly white males (p. 3). Both of these conditions are subjective and will depend on the ideologies of those who are empowered by the current status of academia. This dominant group will support only the work and advancement of those who will continue to produce scholarship that supports their own ideologies. Moody (2004) makes specific recommendations that must be taken to heart to change these practices and to create the conditions for the more effective recruitment and retention of minority faculty. The list of recommendations includes preparing existing faculty for integrating the new hire. Moody mentions critical lapses pointed out by faculty developer Robert Boice, such as not being invited to lunch by colleagues during the first few weeks, not being mentored in the way of nominations for career-enhancing awards, not chairing conference sessions, and not being invited to submit scholarly manuscripts. She further states that "new colleagues must not be denigrated as affirmative action [or diversity] hires" (p. 2)—department chairs should help newcomers choose committee assignments that will bring them in contact with other faculty members who are important for them to know (p. 4). Another recommendation involves the advancement of women and minorities to leadership positions. Only if and when the process of hiring and retaining minorities is thoughtfully addressed will there be educational conditions that translate into academic excellence.

Conclusion

Those of us who do make it through the system in spite of the odds and who are able to meet tenure and promotion requirements have the opportunity to become the voice of the voiceless. Although doing so implies risks and at times further marginalization, we must challenge practices that are disguised as diversity initiatives but are a mere facade. Narrow views on scholarship and teaching are in place to limit the contributions and possibilities of diverse faculty. On the other hand, there are arguments raised to justify nepotism and privileging some mainstream hires through policy positions, such as a supposed need for supportive environments to retain talented faculty. These initiatives become offensive when the same zeal is not applied to retaining faculty hired to enhance diverse epistemologies, perspectives, and scholarship. We must continue to examine the duplicity in the messages included in our institutions' policies and practices and demand transparency and coherence between theory and practice.

References

Bellows, A. (2003). *In praise of nepotism: A natural history.* New York, NY: Doubleday.

De la Luz Reyes, M., & Halcón, J. J. (1988). Racism in academia: The old wolf revisited. *Harvard Educational Review, 58*(3), 299–314.

Moody, J. (2004, January/February). Supporting women and minority faculty. *Academe, 90*(1), 47–53.

Reyes, X. A. (2004). Transnational nomad in academia: A Puerto Rican perspective. In M. V. Alfred & R. Swaminathan (Eds.), *Immigrant women in the academy: Negotiating borders, crossing boundaries in higher education.* Hauppauge, NY: Nova Science Publishers.

Reyes, X. A. (2005). Dissonance and dialogue in the academy: Reflections of a Latina professor. *Latino Studies Journal, 3*(2), 274–279.

Reyes, X. A. (2006). *How the language and culture of scholars affects their choice of subjects and methods of research: Investigating the researcher's habit of mind.* Lewiston, NY: Edwin Mellen Press.

Reyes, X. A., & Rios, D. I. (2005). Dialoguing the Latina experience in higher education. *Journal of Hispanic Higher Education, 4*(4), 377–391.

Trower, C. A. (2002). Why so few minority faculty and what to do? Diversifying the region's professoriate. *Journal of the New England Board of Education, 17*(2), 25–27.

Turner, C. S. V. (2002). Women of color in academe: Living and multiple marginality. *Journal of Higher Education, 73*(1), 74–93.

Part III

Humanities

13

Introducing Gender and Race Into the Curriculum of Medieval Italian Studies

Dennis Looney

I attended the second faculty seminar organized by the chancellor's Diversity Working Group at the University of Pittsburgh with a bug in my ear. I had always known that LeRoi Jones, who changed his name to Amiri Baraka when he embraced black nationalism in the late 1960s, published an autobiographical work in 1965 loosely modeled on Dante's *Inferno* called *The System of Dante's Hell.* I also knew that the African-American novelist Gloria Naylor had used the *Inferno* as a guiding principle in the design of her second novel, *Linden Hills* (1985). I came to the seminar with the goal of preparing myself to read and eventually teach these two works. I wanted to understand the contexts in which each of these writers of color turned to Dante's poem, a canonical Western work written by— dare I say it—a dead white European male. Additionally, I wanted to read up on cultural history and theory to complement my engagement with the two novels.

At the same time I intended to revamp a course that I regularly teach to freshmen and sophomores every fall at the University of Pittsburgh—Italian 0080, Italian Cultural Heritage I—which includes a month on Dante's *Inferno.* The course, taught in English, is a survey of medieval Italian literature and culture from its beginnings around 1200 to approximately 1400. The syllabus revolves around a trio of writers whom literary historians have canonized as the Three Crowns of Italian literature: Dante (1265–1321), Petrarch (1304–1374), and Boccaccio (1313–1375). It is a good course, well designed, stimulating, and always overenrolled. Why fix it, then, if it wasn't broke?

Suspicious of my own course's lack of noncanonical authors, I used the seminar's discussion of diversity to explore the problematics of canon formation as

70

it related to the three authors at the core of Italian 0080. I explored how I might include the topics of gender and race in a course on medieval Italian literary culture. Gender was easier to tackle first.

For many years my syllabus did not include a single female author—until I came upon a sonnet written by one of Dante's contemporaries, an unidentified Florentine woman whom an earlier generation of Italian scholars dubbed tellingly the Accomplished Maiden (*la Compiuta Donzella*). In the sonnet the speaker protests being forced into an arranged marriage with someone she doesn't love. This poet's predicament, as well as the name critics have given her, have now become points of departure in the course for discussing the status of women in Dante's day and the study of (or rather the relative lack of scholarly attention to) women in medieval Italy. In looking for other women writers to include in this syllabus (and in other courses) and in researching writers like the Accomplished Maiden, I have benefited enormously from Italian Women Writers, an authoritative online resource sponsored by the University of Chicago (2001).

I now see more clearly than I did when I first organized Italian 0080 that under scrutiny even the canonical texts of Dante, Petrarch, and Boccaccio open themselves up to interesting questions of gender. Boccaccio's *Decameron,* one of the sources of inspiration for Chaucer's *Canterbury Tales,* in particular lends itself to a gendered reading through the author's representation of himself in the opening section of the work as an authority on the vagaries of love and on the suffering that Eros often visits upon naive lovers. Along those lines he submits his work primarily to women who have similarly suffered and who have had to do so privately with none of the outlets available to men. Reading fiction, then, becomes a means of consolation and an escape for the afflicted lover. In the medieval courtly tradition, Boccaccio places his idealized lady on a pedestal, but at the same time he alludes to the medieval stereotype of the female's potential for sexual activity, if not downright depravity. More than one tale focuses on the dichotomy of woman as angel/whore. Analyzing Boccaccio's duplicitous rhetoric, which is scandalously risqué while supposedly instructing his female reader in codes of proper behavior, has become another effective way to open up the course to conversations about gender in medieval Italy. Students become very quick to note that there is much to critique in Boccaccio's feminism.

In researching other voices that might provide alternate perspectives on Italian culture in the late medieval period, I discovered the letters of Catherine of Siena (1347–1380). A contemporary of Petrarch and Boccaccio, Catherine is a great writer by any standard. An authoritative history of Italian literature credits her with the "most dynamic Italian prose of the fourteenth century" (Wilkins, 1954, p. 120). Here was a literary artist—forget for a moment that she was a woman—whom I had completely missed in my graduate studies in the 1980s and who was arguably the best writer of her generation! I had missed her, of course, precisely because she was a woman, a woman of religion no less, excluded from the traditional literary canon for both these reasons. I have since made a significant place for Catherine in the syllabus of Italian 0080. But I have done so without attempting to marginalize her even more in the process.

Dittmar (1985) points out the limitations of relegating previously excluded material to a special unit of a course as if the material were "alien to the mainstream but morally important and politically unavoidable" (p. 38). As well intentioned as such course development may be, it inevitably leads to a kind of tokenism in which the material one felt compelled to include is made to appear so marginal that it cannot be taken as seriously as the material to which it has been appended. Dittmar is describing the design of course syllabi, daring educators to imagine the potential a new course, if carried out properly, can have on curricular transformation. To avoid the tokenism that can arise once a missing woman is located to fill an obvious gap in a syllabus like mine, I not only study Catherine in her own right, but I use her inclusion (and the story of how I had failed to notice her sooner) as a means of understanding and questioning the practice and concept of canon formation. I set Catherine in dialogue and debate with the Three Crowns to the delight of the class. Her moral asceticism rivals Dante's; her political activism outshines Petrarch's; and her genuine concern for women as seen in her many letters to nuns, wives, mothers, widows, prostitutes, and family members forces us to read Boccaccio's attention to women by comparison as feigned or at best somewhat less than genuine.

The exercise of finding a way to incorporate the discourse of race into Italian 0080 proved far more challenging, but I came up with a slightly different strategy to introduce students of medieval Italian culture to the problem of race and its representation in literary art. I now offer a separate follow-up course to students who are interested in the topic (at the graduate level but open to undergraduate students): Italian 2200, From Hell to Harlem: African-American Responses to Dante's *Divine Comedy* from 1850 to Today.

In the course I consider an extraordinary period in the reception of Dante in the United States, where the poet has always been an important literary model (his influence on Emerson, Eliot, and Pound come to mind). Several prominent 20th-century African-American writers—Richard Wright, Ralph Ellison, LeRoi Jones/Amiri Baraka, Toni Morrison, and Gloria Naylor, among others, including the independent filmmaker Spencer Williams—created sophisticated imitations of Dante, making them inheritors of a cultural trend to appropriate the canonical poet, which has its origins in the work of 19th-century Anglo-American abolitionists and Italian nationalists. Even Frederick Douglass was a devotee of Dante, as this note suggests:

> Early in January 1889 an unnamed reporter of the Washington
> Press visited Douglass's home. . . . Mr. Douglass invited the re-
> porter into his library, and there the faces of the late Chief Jus-

> tice Chase, William Lloyd Garrison, . . . Dante, Abraham Lin-
> coln, John Brown, and Charles Sumner looked down in smiles
> and respect upon the great Negro sage. (Blassingame,
> 1979–1992/1889, p. 399)

After an intensive reading of parts of the *Divine Comedy* with a focus on the
Inferno, the course moves to track the changing reception of Dante over the past
150 years or so by writers and artists of color, from what I call the Colored Dante,
to the Negro Dante, to the Black Dante, and finally to the African-American
Dante. Examples of each of these unique moments in the appropriation of the
Italian writer take us from slavery and reconstruction in the 19th century, to
segregation in the South in the first half of the 20th century, to the black
revolution of the 1960s, and finally to the tensions between the urban ghetto and
suburbia of our own day.

In the course I explore how these imitations, adaptations, rewritings, and
responses to Dante's *Divine Comedy* call into question the poem's canonical status
and at the same time often reaffirm it. Of particular interest to me is how
canonicity and cultural identity intersect in the reception of Dante in African-
American culture. What happens when a canonical text like the *Divine Comedy*
comes into dialogue with writings and art perceived to be at the margins of the
Western tradition? How has the response to Dante over the past 150 years or so
influenced the development of an African-American identity? How is Dante used
to articulate the boundaries of cultural difference? To what extent has a canonical
European cultural icon like Dante had an impact on theorizing about race? How
does Dante become, to borrow from Stuart Hall (1997), a "floating signifier" in
the discourse of race? Of specific interest to me is this question: How has an
imitation of Dante served as a marker that signals admittance to European culture
and, paradoxically, enabled some form of rejection of it? What commerce can
there be, for example, between Cordelia Ray, one of Joan Sherman's (1974/1989)
Invisible Poets of the 19th century, and Amiri Baraka, who (post-1965)
denounced every attempt, 19th-century or otherwise, of accommodation to the
literary models of white culture? Why does James Baldwin make the outrageous
claim that an illiterate Swiss villager has more purchase on Dante than an erudite
intellectual like himself?

One goal of this more advanced course is to identify imitations of Dante by
artists of color; another goal is to demonstrate how those imitators, some more
than others, excel in their response to the original medieval model. A final goal is
to return to Dante's *Divine Comedy* with these rewritings in mind to assess how
they might affect our interpretation of it and to determine what the
methodological and theoretical implications of this history of reception might be.
What cognitive advantage do we derive in reconsidering Dante's work through
the unique perspective provided by African-American culture? Moreover, what

does the reception of Dante tell us about African-American culture that we might not see otherwise? In what ways has this neglected tradition of response to Dante contributed to the surge in American interest in the Italian poet over the past two centuries?

Through Italian 0080 and 2200, I have introduced a generation of students to the problematics of gender and race in the context of medieval Italian studies, a feat I myself would have never thought possible as recently as a decade ago.

References

Blassingame, J. V. (Ed.). (1979–1992). *The Frederick Douglass papers* (Vols. 1–5). New Haven, CT: Yale University Press. (Original work published 1889)

Dittmar, L. (1985). Inclusionary practices: The politics of syllabus design. *Journal of Thought, 20*(3), 37–47.

Hall, S. (1997). *Race: The floating signifier* [Video recording]. Northampton, MA: Media Education Foundation.

Sherman, J. (1974/1989). *Invisible poets: Afro-Americans of the nineteenth century.* Urbana, IL: University of Illinois Press.

University of Chicago. (2001). *Italian women writers.* Retrieved February 22, 2007, from www.lib.uchicago.edu/efts/IWW/

Wilkins, E. H. (1954). *A history of Italian literature.* Cambridge, MA: Harvard University Press.

14

Black German Studies: Curriculum Initiatives for Diversity in German Studies

Sarah McGaughey

"**A** re there really black Germans? Who are they?"

Such were the student questions after a screening of Oliver Hardt's (Hardt & Brunn, 2005) documentary on blacks living in Germany, *Black Deutschland.* Hardt's German-language film was the first event of a month-long cultural program associated with the international conference "Remapping Black Germany: New Perspectives on Afro-German History, Politics, and Culture," hosted by the University of Massachusetts Amherst (UMass Amherst) on April 21–23, 2006. Though recognition of the existence of black Germans in Germany is a significant goal in increasing the awareness of diversity in German studies, the inclusion of black German studies in research and in the curriculum also illuminates new perspectives on the social and historical forces that contribute to contemporary political discourse on minorities and people of color in both the United States and Germany, while it turns renewed attention to notions of diaspora and culture within the contemporary context of globalization.

The astonishment of the film audience reflects a prevalent assumption that German studies focuses on a white population and its white culture. Although German studies programs now often highlight emerging roles of minorities within Germany, in particular the Turkish minority, these are presented primarily as recent changes to the German population and culture. Thus, even today, German studies in the United States is all too often faced with student and instructor interest that reinforces this racial assumption. The dominance of whites among the student population in postsecondary study of Germany in the United

States underscores this supposition. According to the Modern Language Association's 1996–1997 census of Ph.D. placements, only five of the 85 students awarded doctoral degrees in German were of a racial or ethnic minority, and none of them were black (Welles, 2000). Unwilling to accept this underrepresentation of African-Americans and other minorities, the UMass Amherst Graduate Program promotes German as a field of study for people of all colors. We established connections with colleagues at institutions with a higher representation of minority students and received grant money from the Max Kade Foundation to explore the creation of a Master's of Art in Teaching (MAT) program with the goal of increasing German language programs and opportunities in Massachusetts high schools. This publicity, along with the MAT program development, aims to increase awareness of German language learning and German studies among populations that address and communicate with communities composed largely of minority populations.

By effecting change in the representation of people of color in teaching and research positions, we can contribute to a change in the perception of German studies as a "white" subject. This perception, however, must also be addressed at the content level of our German courses and our German studies curricula—a change that the Department of German and Scandinavian Studies at UMass Amherst works to achieve through its research projects in black German studies and its fundamental revisions to the curriculum of both the graduate and undergraduate programs.

Curriculum Development

Discovering Black German Studies

As a field of academic study, black German studies is still in its early stages of development. Research on the history of blacks in Germany, on the colonial and postcolonial discourse on blacks, on the history of race theories as applied to people of color, and even on the presence of blacks in Germany before the 20th century constitute areas scholars have not yet studied exhaustively. To fill this gap in scholarship—to make the invisible visible—a group of German and American scholars created transnational cooperative research projects. One of these is the project entitled "Black German Studies: An Interdisciplinary and Multi-Perspectival Approach," funded by the TransCoop Program of the Alexander von Humboldt Foundation with matching money from the provost of UMass Amherst. Conceived as a partnership between Sara Lennox of UMass Amherst and Randolph Ochsmann of the University of Mainz, working together with Fatima El-Tayeb of the University of California–San Diego and Peggy Piesche of the University of Mainz, the Black German Studies project is located at UMass Amherst. In collaboration with international research projects, Lennox and postdoctoral fellow Tobias Nagl were able to draw the field's preeminent scholars to UMass Amherst for two 2005–2006 events to discuss the state of black German studies and the role it can play in the field of German studies. The first event, a 2005 National Endowment for the Humanities (NEH) summer seminar "Changing World, Shifting Narratives," focused on the status and role of German studies in a postcommunist Europe and included a weeklong component on black German studies coordinated by Lennox, Ochsmann, Piesche, El-Tayeb, and Nagl and keynoted by Professor Tina Campt of Duke University, author of a study on black Germans during the Third Reich. The week concluded with a panel of African-Americanists, who discussed the role of African-American studies in Germany and elsewhere in Europe. The second event, mentioned earlier, was the spring 2006 international conference "Remapping Black Germany," which hosted more than 18 international scholars of black German studies. The two events provided insight into the contemporary scholarly work under way to reveal and investigate the history, culture, and politics of the black population in Germany.

German and Scandinavian Studies thus began its mission to incorporate black German studies into the curriculum with programs that reach beyond traditional classroom boundaries. The scholars, workshops, and conferences hosted by UMass Amherst introduce and support black German studies' emergence but also call attention to this area of study to enable further discovery and publication of materials about and by Afro-Germans and their participation in German culture. As a second component of the Black German Studies project, Tobias Nagl will be conducting interviews with Afro-Germans living in the United States, particularly the so-called Brown Babies, children of African-American GIs and white German mothers. Many of the films screened in the Remapping Black Germany film series have recently become available on DVD with English subtitles, and the DEFA Film Library at UMass Amherst locates and distributes East German films on African-American and Afro-German topics. Such scholarship and material collections are evidence of a rich history and present of black German culture and eliminate the lack of materials on the subject as a barrier to creating curricular content on black German culture and history.

Graduate Program

Since its initial stages in the 1980s, the project of recovering the black presence in Germany gave way to a whole array of methodological approaches, drawing inspiration from African-American studies, feminism, literary theory, postcolonialist theory, anthropology, and cultural studies. Black German studies, conceived in such an interdisciplinary and transnational way, reflects the current trend at U.S. universities and colleges away from traditional literary- and linguistic-oriented German language and literature programs toward the cultural approach of German studies. With recently established interdisciplinary guidelines in the M.A. and Ph.D. programs at UMass Amherst, our graduate students are able to work in fields related to German studies on issues of race and ethnicity in society as well as historical and theoretical issues related to colonialism, the postcolonial era, and globalization. This allows our graduate students to work in numerous fields with faculty members in history, anthropology, sociology, French and francophone studies, and other disciplines. Such an interdisciplinary approach is central to discovering the transnational context of black German studies and allows for new approaches to illuminate the process of modern racial formation.

Curricular developments within German and Scandinavian Studies underpin our efforts at UMass Amherst to confront the need for a black German studies course. Our program offers upper level undergraduate and graduate-level seminars on topics of German colonialism, racial politics, and the history of racial theories in German nationalism. These courses began to be offered in the 1990s, when the field of black German studies emerged in the United States, and initiated the development of courses on migration, history, and cultural theory.

Undergraduate Program

The undergraduate program benefits from the graduate program's offerings and the scholarly work described earlier. Current work creates a forum for our graduate students and faculty to implement their growing knowledge of black German studies into the undergraduate curriculum. The one-credit undergraduate course that was created as part of the international conference and that began with *Black Deutschland* forms the initial step of this project to integrate black German studies. The 16 enrolled undergraduate students, with the exception of four more advanced German speakers, were native English speakers with less than a year of college-level German language instruction. Their knowledge of German history, culture, and politics was mixed: Most knew 20th-century history, others were more informed about 19th-century nation building, and still others were aware of aspects of contemporary German culture (such as poems, music, and art) from their elementary German coursework. The course was a mix of academic and cultural events and included film screenings, attendance at conference presentations, and an evening of conversation with four black German artists: Daniel Kojo Schrade, an artist; Olumida Popoola, a poet; Chima, a musician; and Branwen Okpako, a filmmaker. With such a broad introduction of historical, theoretical, practical, and social materials and information on black Germans, students formulated complex questions about the nature of the black German community at the final two-hour discussion session in May. Instead of merely asking who black Germans are, students were able to discuss familial relationships within which black German children grew up in post-WWII Germany, race theories of Immanuel Kant and their influence on modern definitions of race in Germany, and the relevance of African-American definitions of community and diaspora in a transnational context.

The initial demand for this course and the excitement of students when faced with the opportunity to discuss both African-American notions of diaspora and the unique situation of black Germans further prove the importance of expanding the horizons of German studies. The students found they were able to approach racial discourse from a new perspective as a result of the course's events and were also engaged in discovering new aspects of the importance and significance of developing communities and cultures.

Future Plans

The success of this short conference course and the students' suggestions for ways in which the materials should be incorporated into the German studies curriculum at UMass Amherst are the beginning of radical change in our language curriculum. A project led by me will collect and assemble black German studies materials for use in classrooms of varying levels of German language learners. Students at the 100 level will have the opportunity to discover contemporary Afro-German art, such as the work of Daniel Kojo Schrade, within the context of active acquisition of descriptive vocabulary or to review the biographies of historical Afro-German figures, such as Hans J. Massaquoi, who grew up in Nazi Germany and later became editor of *Ebony*. For courses at the 200 level and above, literature, poetry, and films by and about black Germans and Germany's colonial past in Africa (e.g., Uwe Timm's *Morenga*) will be included as part of classroom discussion on existing course themes, such as German history.

We also plan to offer pedagogical training on diversity and black German studies. This addition to the already growing number of courses on the subject will allow graduate students to effectively implement their knowledge of black German culture and history in their teaching of language courses. The new curriculum and accompanying instructor training build a broader historical perspective within which our students can analyze contemporary social issues surrounding the role of foreigners, migrants, and guest workers in Germany. Working within current course goals and themes allows us to reject the marginalization of black Germans and other minority populations in Germany and instead locate them as central to German culture.

Outreach initiatives to involve high school, college, and university instructors of German language and culture will continue to complement additions to the UMass German studies curriculum. Two summer NEH seminars for high school teachers in 1996 and 1998 placed attention on current black German associations and cultural production with the assistance of Professors Yvonne Poser and Alphonso Frost, students from Howard University, and an address by the president of the Black German Cultural Society of the United States, Christoph Schneider. This new project on diversity in the language curriculum will continue such outreach projects with articles in journals and presentations at conferences.

Conclusions

The projects described here aim to establish diversity on the curricular and research levels of the discipline. However, the goal of achieving critical awareness of black German studies is a long-term project that needs to take root in German studies programs and high school German curricula across the country. Contributing to the success of this relatively new approach to German studies is a growing number of publications on black Germans or Afro-Germans, including web sites on the history of Africans and black Germans in Germany. In 2005, a new curriculum project supported by the American Association of Teachers of German, Alle lernen Deutsch, created a web site to distribute class plans and information on black Germans online. Such new projects underscore the interest in curriculum developments in German studies and in German language courses. They are encouraging signs of a shift in educators' conception of German studies that recognizes diversity as central to all levels of the profession.

References

Hardt, O. (Director), & Brunn, C. (Producer). (2005). *Black Deutschland.* Germany: HR/Arte.

Welles, E. B. (2000). Employment of 1996–97 PhDs in foreign languages: A report on the MLA's census of PhD placement. *ADFL Bulletin, 31*(2), 6–21.

Resources

Afrikaniche Diaspora in Deutschland (Bundeszentrale für politische Bildung): www.bpb.de/themen/X5FI94,0,0,Afrikanische_Diaspora_in_Deutschland.html

Alle lernen Deutsch: http://ald.aatg.org

Center for Black European Studies at the University of Mainz: www.best.uni-mainz.de/modules/Informationen/index.php?id=13

DEFA Film Library: www.umass.edu/defa/

NEH Summer Institute 2005, Changing Worlds, Shifting Narratives: www.umass.edu/germanic/neh2005/

Oliver Hardt's *Black Deutschland*: www.blackdeutschland.de/

Remapping Black Germany conference: www.umass.edu/germanic/remapping/

15

Afro-Hispanic Studies and Implications for Diversity in the Spanish Curriculum

James Davis

In this chapter I use the terms *Afro-Hispanic, Afro-Latino,* and *Afro-Romance* interchangeably. There is much to be said about the intriguing early history of Afro-Hispanic studies in the United States and in other countries, but I limit my discussion to those pivotal events that have taken place in the area of language, cultural, and literary studies since the 1970s. The discussion is further limited to events in which I have been involved. It recapitulates what I perceive to be the major impact of the scholarship and activism in this area and the implications for future directions. Specifically, I recount the efforts of scholars and educators to integrate nationwide Afro-Hispanic cultural concerns in the curricula of pre- and postsecondary educational institutions, the founding of two major institutes dedicated to the study of Afro-Hispanic studies, and the research and other professional activities of those institutes.

Regarding diversity in the Spanish language and literature curriculum, the prophetic call for the inclusion of Afro-Hispanic studies in the language and literary curriculum was made by Martha Kendrick Cobb over 35 years ago. Cobb (1971) addressed "the issue of race and its heritage of prejudices, conflict, and human divisiveness—all of which are and should be themes in the great dialogue in the humanities" (p. 306). She stated that the "study of Afro-Hispanic literature, like the study of any artistic manifestation of African peoples, can be an act of liberation. Art represents the triumph of the human spirit, and for people who have been oppressed, this triumph is full of significance" (p. 306). In 1972, an article by Miriam DeCosta-Willis with a title that for the times was shocking ("Africanizing the Spanish Curriculum"), appeared in *Dimensions*. DeCosta-Willis declared that "courses and materials dealing with Afro-Hispanic Literature and culture have not been available in most American Colleges, primarily because teachers are unaware of the contributions that Africans have made to Spain and Latin America" (p. 30). Similarly, in 1978, Shirley Jackson, in her article "Afro-Hispanic Literature: A Valuable Cultural Resource," called Afro-Hispanic literature a "special gift" to the humanities because of its potential for teaching positive values and positive self-images and for expanding students' horizons. She wrote:

> The need for a program in Afro-Hispanic culture becomes ap-
> parent when one considers the uniqueness and beauty of the
> Hispanic Heritage. Indeed, the institution of such a program
> should be a major goal of *all* educators in order that modern
> day students may have a more balanced view of the roles various
> ethnic groups have played in the formation of what is today
> known as Hispanic culture. (p. 421)

Regarding curricular development projects, one has to consider the work of Beatrice S. Clark at Hampton Institute who administered, starting in 1977, a multiple-year grant from the National Endowment for the Humanities that would later become known as African Cultural Elements in Language Learning (AFCELL). The project developed out of the concern about the steady decline in foreign language enrollments at many Historically Black Colleges and Universities (HBCUs) in the 1970s. The overall aim of the project was to revitalize the foreign language curriculum at the HBCUs involved in the project. The participation of foreign language faculty, both black and nonblack, from the HBCUs launched a series of research and curriculum development projects designed to infuse the cultures of African-ancestored peoples in the French- and Spanish-speaking worlds.

In 1978, I joined the faculty at Hampton to teach Spanish, to develop and inaugurate a course in Brazilian Portuguese, and to serve as curriculum developer for the project. It was then that I became familiar with some of the major research that had been done in the area of Afro-Hispanic studies. I admittedly focused initially on the work by African-American scholars on the topic. Specifically, I became familiar with Valaurez B. Spratlin's (1938) *Juan Latino, Slave and Humanist,* Miriam DeCosta-Willis's (1977) *Blacks in Hispanic Literature: Critical Essays,* and Shirley Jackson's scholarship. These works, among others, prompted me to redirect my own research focus and my teaching of Spanish as a world language. Indeed, I began to see Spanish in a different light when I began to learn more about the diversity of the Spanish-speaking world. I was suddenly thrown into a new area of inquiry because of the AFCELL project on which I continued to work when, in 1979, I joined the faculty at Howard University, which had a rather long history of promoting and teaching about the black presence in both

Spain and Latin America. Spratlin, the first African-American to be awarded the doctorate in Spanish (at Middlebury in 1931), served as the chair of the Department of Romance Languages at Howard University from 1927 to 1961. When I arrived at Howard, discussions of the formation of the Afro-Hispanic Institute were in progress.

The Afro-Hispanic Institute (in Washington, DC) and the Afro-Romance Institute (in Columbia, MO) were established as an outgrowth of faculty initiatives and activism to diversify curriculum content in Spanish programs and to expand the traditional literary canon in both undergraduate and graduate programs in Spanish language and literature as well in Latin American studies programs. The Afro-Hispanic Institute (AHI) was founded in 1981 by a group of scholars based in a number of universities throughout the United States, Latin America, and the Caribbean. Its major goal was to promote the study of literature and the culture of African-ancestored peoples whose native language is Spanish. One of its greatest accomplishments was launching the first issue of the *The Afro-Hispanic Review* (in January 1982) with Stanley A. Cyrus and Ian I. Smart, both of Howard University, as editor and managing editor, respectively. Billed as "a bilingual journal of Afro-Hispanic literature and culture," *The Afro-Hispanic Review* (*AHR*) offered literary criticism, book reviews, translations of works originally written is Spanish, creative writing, and announcements regarding relevant developments in this area of inquiry. The AHI provided the major first journal in which scholars could publish their research dedicated exclusively to themes on Afro-Hispanism. Among the many significant contributions of the *AHR* was its introduction of English translations of works by upcoming and established writers from the Spanish-speaking Americas. The *AHR* has been published continuously since it appeared in 1982, although its home has changed twice since it was inaugurated. In 1986, the *AHR* was moved to the University of Missouri–Columbia and was coedited by Marvin A. Lewis and Edward J. Mullen, who, like Cryus and Smart, were stalwarts in the promotion and inclusion of Afro-Hispanic literature and cultures in the Spanish curriculum. The *AHR* is now headquartered at Vanderbilt University, where William Luis serves as its editor.

Recognizing the need to expand the scope of Afro-Hispanic studies to embrace all of the Americas and Africa and their official languages, Marvin A. Lewis founded in 1996 the Afro-Romance Institute for the Languages and Literatures of the African Diaspora (ARI) at the University of Missouri–Columbia. As described on the institute's web site:

> The Institute's primary focus is the literature and language of
> selected areas of Africa, the Caribbean, Latin America and the
> United States, and the interrelations between these three poles
> of the African dispersion. It coordinates a number of both inter-
> nal and external programs designed to bring the literature of

black writers of French, Portuguese, and Spanish expression
into the academic mainstream. (University of Missouri–Columbia, 2002)

Since its inception over ten years ago, the ARI has provided incalculable
professional development activities for secondary and university faculty,
graduate students, and scholars interested in the field of Afro-Hispanic
literatures and culture.

With unrelenting efforts and dynamic leadership, Lewis spearheaded and
founded the Afro-Latin/American Research Association (ALARA) in 1996, which
was headquartered at the ARI. The following year, ALARA launched its first issue
of the *Publication of the Afro-Latin/American Research Association* (PALARA) with
Marvin A. Lewis and Laurence E. Prescott, of the Pennsylvania State University,
as coeditors. Complementing the goals of ALARA, *PALARA* is multidisciplinary
in scope and publishes research and creative works relevant to all the geographic
areas of the African diaspora outlined in ALARA's charter constitution. In
addition, ALARA and the ARI have sponsored a series of conferences and
symposia on Afro-Hispanism. One of the standard outstanding features of these
conferences and symposia has been the attendance of notable writers and cultural
artists from the regions studied by the participants. Lewis had started this
tradition when he organized the International Symposium on Afro-Hispanic
Literature (1991) and the International Research Conference on Afro-Hispanic
Literature and Criticism (1993), at which conference attendants were able to
interact with some of the most notable Afro-Romance writers: Quince Duncan
(Costa Rica), Carlos Guillermo Wilson (Panama), Beatriz Santos (Uruguay),
Manuel Zapata Olivella (Colombia), Blas Jimenéz (Dominican Republic),
Yvonne A. Truque (Colombia), Nancy Morejón (Blas Timénez, Cuba), Nelson
Estupiñán Bass (Ecuador), Antonio Acosta Márquez (Venezuela), Luz Argentina
Chiriboga (Ecuador), Cristina Rodríguez Cabral (Uruguay), and Arnoldo
Palacios (Colombia). The conferences, sponsored by the ARI, with financial
backing from other organizations, have been held in Brazil (1996), the
Dominican Republic (1998), Haiti (2000), Panama (2002), and Puerto Rico
(2004). This lineup demonstrates the efforts to take the conferences to the
language groups and cultures treated at those functions.

The teaching of diversity and tolerance of the "perceived other" is a
requirement in today's classrooms. Collectively, the AFCELL project, the AHI,
and the ARI have made an indelible mark on the promotion of diversity in the
Spanish curriculum nationally and internationally. The legacy is apparent in the
growing number of scholars and educators from all over the world who are
promoting and researching the ever-evolving face of Hispanism and Afro-
Hispanism. Today, for example, one has to consider the culture of Equatorial
Guinea, the only sub-Saharan nation in Africa where the official "colonial"

language is Spanish. The ARI, in following its mission, sponsored in 1999 an international research conference around the theme "Spain in Africa and Latin America: The Other Face of Literary Hispanism." The ARI is the first and only research center that focuses on Afro-Romance studies and plays an important role in studying and disseminating the writings of African-ancestored artists who express themselves in French, Portuguese, or Spanish.

Another major impact, direct or indirect, of the AFCELL project and both institutes is that of curricular reform. The teaching of full courses in Afro-Hispanic literature and cultures at colleges and universities has not been around for a long time. A survey of Spanish programs throughout the nation today would reveal a number of new courses on Afro-Hispanic/Latino studies at both the graduate and undergraduate levels. Many of the programs that do not offer full survey courses in the field have revised existing courses to incorporate Afro-Hispanic themes. At Howard University all undergraduate Spanish majors must complete a survey course in Afro-Hispanic literature to complete their degrees. Some years ago, we implemented a course in Afro-Hispanic literature in translation. The University of Missouri offers an undergraduate minor in Afro-Romance literature in translation. The AFCELL project also propelled curricular reform at the secondary levels. In the late 1970s and early 1980s, many secondary school districts purchased and incorporated the instructional materials produced and published by the project. The AFCELL documents need to be updated and disseminated throughout the nation, although there is a variety of appropriate secondary-level materials on Afro-Hispanic culture commercially available from a number of sources. See my now dated "Materials and Sources on Afro-Hispanic Themes" (1995).

A critical shift in instructional materials occurred as a result of the activism of AFCELL, the AHI, the ARI, and individuals. One of AFCELL's goals, for example, was to make available curricular materials that could be used as a supplement to existing course textbooks. When major textbook companies learned of the project and its goals, they quickly moved to include readings and other cultural notes from Spanish-speaking countries with a sizeable black population. It should be noted that although the majority of the students surveyed about the AFCELL project found the course materials interesting and motivating, they overwhelmingly agreed that the Afrocentric materials should be incorporated into their textbooks. That, too, was one of my concerns as a classroom teacher because students often viewed the instructional packets on Afro-Hispanic culture as something above and beyond that which they would normally be taught or required to do. For them, the add-on approach was somewhat discouraging. That sentiment prompted me to write in 1986 that:

> An understanding of Afro-Hispanic culture is important in
> modern foreign language education because it offers greater and

significant insights into the complexities of Hispanic culture.
. . . It must be reiterated that Afro-Hispanic culture should *not*
be presented as an isolated culture, but as an integral part of
Hispanic culture. The overall objective is that students will develop a long-lasting appreciation and awareness of another culture. (p. 30)

To be fair, I should mention that national foreign language associations have
established special initiatives on diversity in the curriculum. These were
prompted, in part, by scholars associated with the AHI, the ARI, and the
AFCELL project. For example, the American Association of Teachers of Spanish
and Portuguese established almost 20 years ago a yearly session on Afro-Hispanic
literature. In the early 1990s, the American Council on Teaching Foreign
Languages formed a special interest group on African-Americans and foreign
language study that explores ways to incorporate diversity into the curriculum.
The College Language Association, founded in 1937 by a group of African-
American language and literature scholars, consistently offers annual sessions on
Afro-Hispanic literature and cultures and, as a result, has amassed an impressive
and growing repository of curricular materials on the topic.

Afro-Hispanic literary and cultural studies are experiencing another boom at
this time. Over these years, the conferences sponsored by the ARI have attracted a
growing number of scholars from all over the world who are discovering writers
who have been marginalized in their countries. The Afro-Hispanic writers have
benefited tremendously from the conferences in that they are getting greater
recognition in the English-speaking world and in their native lands. As a result,
they are beginning to be anthologized. The canon in the Spanish curriculum is
changing, albeit somewhat slowly, but the future will witness greater numbers of
Afro-Romance writers in the canon. The number of doctoral dissertations and
book-length studies on these writers has increased twofold, if not more, in the
past decade. Although AFCELL and the institutes served to facilitate collaborative
research among scholars already working in the field, they also prompted many
scholars who were exploring traditional areas of research in Hispanic literature
and culture to broaden those scholars' research to include Afro-Romance writers.

When one considers the wealth of published materials now available and the
active research on Afro-Romance studies, one might quickly conclude that the
major work has been done. That, however, is not the case. I would say that that it
is imperative to conduct faculty development workshops to engage both pre- and
postsecondary teachers in dialogues not only about instructional materials but
also about how to teach diversity. At this juncture we cannot measure the
effectiveness of the inclusion of these Afro-Hispanic cultural materials because
classroom instructors still make major decisions about what they teach and
include in their courses. Classroom practitioners must buy into and participate

fully in the teaching of diversity across the curriculum. The broader field of Spanish and Hispanic studies has been enhanced by the persistent efforts of individuals and groups who have literally restructured their own knowledge base and our understanding of diversity in the Spanish-speaking world.

I believe that the future of Afro-Romance studies and its incorporation in the Spanish/Hispanic curriculum is quite promising. The efforts described here must be continued and augmented, however. I would like to see the establishment of more study abroad programs in regions where there are significant populations of Afro-Romance groups. I encourage scholars to share their research findings not only through scholarly journals but also in magazines that cater to young people. We must reach them. I further encourage greater collaboration of research and activism among humanists, social scientists, and fine artists so that we can gain even a greater understanding of Afro-Hispanism. We must continue to interact directly with the voices of the artists about whom we research and write.

References

Cobb, M. K. (1971). Spanish and the humanities: Two approaches: A role for Spanish in the humanities program. *Hispania, 54,* 302–307.

Davis. J. (1986). Approaches to teaching Afro-Hispanic culture. *Afro-Hispanic Review, 5*(1), 28–30.

Davis, J. (1995). Materials and sources on Afro-Hispanic themes. *Northeast Conference Newsletter, 38*(5), 28–29.

DeCosta-Willis, M. (1972). Africanizing the Spanish curriculum. *Dimensions: Language, 72*(5), 30–35.

DeCosta-Willis, M. (Ed.). (1977). *Blacks in Hispanic literature: Critical essays.* Port Washington, NY: Kennikat Press.

Jackson, S. (1978). Afro-Hispanic literature, a valuable cultural resource. *Foreign Language Annals, 11*(4), 412–425.

Spratlin, V. B. (1938). *Juan Latino, slave and humanist.* New York, NY: Spinner Press.

University of Missouri–Columbia. (2002). *Afro-Romance Institute.* Retrieved February 22, 2007, from http://afroromance.missouri.edu

16

Diversity and Discipline: Approaching French Literary Studies

Roberta Hatcher

In his 1992 documentary *Afrique je te plumerai* (Africa, I will fleece you), Camerounian filmmaker Jean-Marie Teno explains that he set out to make a film on the written word in Africa ("un film sur l'écrit") when suddenly "the story accelerated in an unpredictable way." The jailing of a journalist and the suppression of his newspaper for publishing an open letter to Cameroun's autocratic president had led to mass demonstrations and violent reprisals that Teno unexpectedly caught on film. These events led Teno to expand his story on writing to engage in a more direct confrontation with Africa's colonial past, with the legacy of what he terms "cultural genocide," and with the ongoing political, social, and cultural effects of this history in present-day Cameroun.

Although the revision of an American university French course in the name of diversity is nowhere equivalent in scope and consequence to Teno's enterprise, I found his reflection on the trajectory of his project helpful in illuminating some of the issues that arise when one starts asking questions about literature. Developments in literary theory over the past several decades—with the emergence of postcolonial studies, cultural studies, new historicism, multiculturalism, and feminist and Marxist analyses—bear witness to the quick entanglement of any question of writing with larger issues of history, power, ideology, resistance, and the institution of literature itself as a social practice. Although this theoretical work has energized the field of literary studies, it has complicated the teaching of literature, particularly at the introductory level. The tension between these theoretical developments and pedagogy is particularly acute, I would argue, in French, with its tradition of close reading and *explication de texte*—ways of reading that as much as the literary corpus itself constitute the specificity of a literary tradition that feels itself increasingly under siege.

My essay will discuss the revision of just such an introductory course under the auspices of the provost's faculty diversity seminar at the University of Pittsburgh. Although much of the discussion will address issues specific to the field of French literary studies, it also relates to a broader lesson concerning questions of curricular change within a disciplinary framework—namely, the realization that it may be possible to create a diversified curriculum by introducing courses with a multicultural orientation yet still leave the fundamental assumptions of the discipline untouched. Just as true course transformation must be considered a multistep process, so too the addition of new or revised courses to a curriculum can be truly transformative only if similar changes are made at the point of entry into the discipline.

I had been asked by my department to revise the intermediate-level Approaches to Literature, a course that, despite its plural title, involved one dominant approach, that of close formal analysis of canonical literary texts. Although the course was not intended as a survey, the syllabus and textbook were organized by genre and were intended to introduce students to the concepts, vocabulary, and practice of literary analysis, focusing on poetry, drama, and prose. Destined for an audience of French majors and minors, the course served as a prerequisite for all advanced coursework in literature, culture, and film. An earlier revision by a colleague had resulted in the addition of two women writers to the syllabus; the course anthology, published over 30 years ago, included none.[1]

As a newcomer to the university, and bringing for the first time to the department a specialization in French language literatures of Africa and the Caribbean, or what is commonly referred to as "francophone literature," I agreed that including francophone texts in the introductory course would not only make it more representative of French language cultural production and the current field of French literary studies but would also prepare students for advanced undergraduate coursework in this area on the same footing as their preparation for other advanced courses focused on metropolitan France. Having devoted significant thought to the place of francophone literatures within a French curriculum, I was delighted with the assignment. I had created and taught courses such as the Francophone African Novel, Caribbean Literature, Francophone Cinema and the Postcolonial, and Black Paris and thus expected the task to be stimulating and challenging but not overly difficult. Yet, in thinking about how to incorporate new works into the syllabus, I quickly fell into a gaping disciplinary divide between a purely formal approach to French literary studies and a more historicized cultural studies approach.[2] (In my advanced courses I work to integrate both. A firm believer in the necessity of close textual readings, I nonetheless include maps, historical documents, visual images, or the layout of the colonial exposition among the texts under consideration; at the same time, I can devote a whole semester to slowly building up context around a historically specific body of works.) To suddenly be called on to teach a selection of texts ranging across five or six centuries, to be responsible for the introduction of basic methodologies and concepts of the discipline, and to try to incorporate multicultural perspectives for students who are for the most part unfamiliar with the history of European colonialism outside the 13 American colonies—this became a daunting charge for a one-semester course.

That I was not able to resolve these issues in a single semester, let alone the two-week framework of the seminar, is not surprising, given that French literary studies as a field has not resolved them still.[3] What the experience brought to light, however, was the particular challenge posed by attempting to transform an introductory course and how a seemingly well-defined objective—incorporating diversity—quickly spilled over into a much larger set of questions that, by working only within my field of specialization, I had been able to avoid. Just as adding a token writer to an existing course does not constitute transformation, simply adding a course to a curriculum and allowing the core courses to remain undisturbed is not fully transformative, either. This is not an indictment of any set of colleagues or of the field at large but rather of my own complacency and the realization that while I was fully engaged in curricular change, I had managed to avoid some of the more difficult disciplinary questions that working in the diversity seminar forced me to confront directly.[4]

My initial revision to Approaches to Literature attempted to go one step beyond what could be perceived as the tokenism of the prior revision. The objective was to introduce questions of race and gender into the course without demanding that women writers and writers of color be included as sole bearers of racial and sexual difference. Simply adding a work by an African writer, for instance, to the already added-on women writers would reinforce the notion that canonical French literary texts transcend issues of race and gender and constitute autonomous aesthetic objects and that works by "others" are of interest for reasons extrinsic to literature. To avoid setting up this relation, I added two texts to the syllabus to supplement the anthology: One, Claire de Duras's *Ourika,* an early 19th-century novella by a French woman writer, features at its central conflict the racism of French aristocratic society; the second, Guadeloupian writer Simone Schwarz-Bart's *Ton Beau Capitaine* was selected not as a representative francophone work but for its formal properties as an example of modernist drama. Both works had the advantage of being short and written in accessible French, important considerations for students at this level. I opted to keep the anthology mostly for its wealth of pedagogical material: glosses, biographical information, reading questions, model texts, critical vocabulary, and extensive introductions to method, all written in French. I optimistically thought, too, that the datedness of certain elements, such as the absence of women writers, might provide an occasion to discuss literary analysis as a socially constructed, historically shifting field.

Theorists of multicultural course change define this level of course transformation—adding new content and analyzing reasons for its historical exclusion—as inclusive (Kitano, 1997, p. 23) or as additive infusion (Banks, 1991; Donath, 1997, p. 164). As a first step it was somewhat productive but not entirely satisfactory. Despite my efforts to avoid a central versus marginal relationship between the noncanonical texts and those of the anthology, it became increasingly apparent that what was needed to truly transform the course was to abandon the textbook and rethink the act of reading from the ground up. What do students need to know to make sense of a literary text? What do we want them to get out of the course? How can an introduction to literature more accurately reflect the types of questions addressed in the field of literary studies today? How can the unsettled nature of these questions be communicated without turning the course into one on theory? Beyond the narrow goal of initiating students into a discipline, why should they read these texts at all? What is at stake in the act of reading and writing literature?

It is this last question that I find most profoundly transformative. The goal of an approaches to literature course can no longer be articulated solely in terms of acquiring disciplinary skills, nor even in terms of integrating new perspectives into an otherwise stable discipline; rather, it forces the formulation of a compelling rationale for engaging with these texts at all and necessitates that the instructor possesses a clear sense of what is significant about them. Asking what is at stake in a text means approaching literature as a set of responses to, and interventions in, situations of cultural conflict and crisis. Viewed from this perspective, a play by Racine could be taught alongside a poem by Aimé Césaire or a film by Jean-Marie Teno, for that matter, not as canonical/noncanonical texts, but each constituting a highly structured, formal response to a complex set of historical circumstances. This argument is not new; thinking about how it might be presented to a group of fifth- or sixth-semester undergraduates in the foreign language classroom has not been widely discussed, at least in the field of French.

Implementing this next level of transformation is still a work in progress, but some useful models from the field of English were provided by the collection *Practicing Theory in Introductory College Literature Courses* (Cahalan & Downing, 1991). Strategies such as pairing texts (Kafka, 1991) and the judicious use of historical documents (Thomas, 1991) seem particularly adaptable to a foreign language classroom.[5] Other changes require thinking not only about content but also about students and the perspectives they bring to the classroom. Some of these can be built on, such as their understanding of speech genres as an entry into a literary text (Bialostosky, 1991); others need to be demystified, such as the notion that a literary work expresses a writer's unique individuality and/or reflects unproblematically the historical period in which it was produced (Lanier, 1991). This last question, in my view, provides the most compelling and achievable goal for an introductory course: to complicate students' notion of literature and cultural production through a fuller, more honest introduction to what readers do when they engage in the act of reading. It also argues, perhaps, for the validity of keeping literature as the primary object of study (an assumption I came to seriously doubt over the course of this journey). Felman (1993) argues it is just this capacity of literary texts to exceed the intentions of their authors and the ideologies that inform them that constitutes the definition of literature itself. Felman's own journey—from deconstructive readings of male-authored texts to coming to understand "the impossible autobiography" articulated in women-authored texts—provides, at a theoretically sophisticated level, a fascinating model of the trajectory of transformation I hope to achieve in the introductory course. At the moment I've come up with more questions than answers, but the questions themselves reveal the need for a conversation on pedagogy that can translate the theoretical transformations of the past several decades into a teaching practice that more accurately reflects what teachers of French do and why.

Endnotes

1. The date of this widely used textbook is more indicative of the current state of publishing in the field of French rather than a lack of change in a particular department.

2. The special issue of *Diacritics* (Culler & Klein, 1998) devoted to "Doing French Studies" provides an overview of this debate.

3. A particularly stunning example of this divide can be found in Antoine Compagnon's (1998/2004) *Literature, Theory, and Common Sense,* which abruptly ends its thoughtful discussion of theoretical interrogations into categories of literature, author, and reader with the publication in 1978 of Edward Said's *Orientalism,* which ushered in approaches he deems extrinsic to literature. Although Compagnon's study claims to address the brief period of French "high theory" of the 1960s and 1970s, it stretches back to Plato and Aristotle and draws heavily on 19th- and early 20th-century thinkers such as Kant, Taine, Sainte-Beuve, and Lanson, making the end of the conversation all the more startling. Needless to say, it offered little help for addressing the questions I was confronting here.

4. For a broader discussion of the place of francophone literatures within the field of French literary studies, see Songolo (2003).

5. Another example of a more comprehensive rethinking prompted by the incorporation of noncanonical texts into an American literature survey can be found in Sullivan (1993). Because she comes to draw more heavily on her students' own experience in the American context, some of these strategies, although instructive, seem less transferable to a foreign language classroom.

References

Banks, J. A. (1991). *Teaching strategies for ethnic studies*. Needham Heights, MA: Allyn & Bacon.

Bialostosky, D. (1991). From discourse in life to discourse in poetry: Teaching poems as Bakhtinian speech genres. In J. B. Cahalan & D. B. Downing (Eds.), *Practicing theory in introductory college literature courses* (pp. 215–226). Urbana, IL: National Council of Teachers of English.

Cahalan, J. B., & Downing, D. B. (Eds.). (1991). *Practicing theory in introductory college literature courses*. Urbana, IL: National Council of Teachers of English.

Compagnon, A. (1998/2004). *Literature, theory, and common sense*. Princeton, NJ: Princeton University Press.

Culler, J., & Klein, R. (1998). Doing French studies [Special issue]. *Diacritics, 28*(3), 3–4.

Donath, J. R. (1997). The humanities. In A. I. Morey & M. K. Kitano (Eds.), *Multicultural course transformation in higher education: A broader truth* (pp. 161–175). Needham Heights, MA: Allyn & Bacon.

Felman, S. (1993). *What does a woman want? Reading and sexual difference*. Baltimore, MD: Johns Hopkins University Press.

Kafka, P. (1991). A multicultural introduction to literature. In J. B. Cahalan & D. B. Downing (Eds.), *Practicing theory in introductory college literature courses* (pp. 179–188). Urbana, IL: National Council of Teachers of English.

Kitano, M. K. (1997). What a course will look like after multicultural change. In A. I. Morey & M. K. Kitano (Eds.), *Multicultural course transformation in higher education: A broader truth* (pp. 18–34). Needham Heights, MA: Allyn & Bacon.

Lanier, D. (1991). Less is more: Coverage, critical diversity, and the limits of pluralism. In J. B. Cahalan & D. B. Downing (Eds.), *Practicing theory in introductory college literature courses* (pp. 199–212). Urbana, IL: National Council of Teachers of English.

Songolo, A. (Ed.). (2003). Littératures francophones: Un corp(u)s étranger? *Présence Francophone, 60*, 5–77.

Sullivan, S. (1993). Transforming the American literature survey course. In B. E. M. Chmaj (Ed.), *Multicultural America: A resource book for teachers of humanities and American studies* (pp. 201–206). Lanham, MD: University Press of America.

Teno, J.-M. (Director). (1992). *Afrique je te plumerai* [Motion picture]. San Francisco, CA: California Newsreel Distributors.

Thomas, B. (1991). The historical necessity for—and difficulties with—new historical analysis in introductory literature courses. In J. B. Cahalan & D. B. Downing (Eds.), *Practicing theory in introductory college literature courses* (pp. 85–100). Urbana, IL: National Council of Teachers of English.

17

Keeping Up With Current Demographic Changes: Responsive Course Content in Foreign Language Departments

Flore Zéphir

The past 30 years have brought about significant changes in the fabric of American society. One only needs to take a look at any American city—large or small, including college towns—to realize that the United States of the 21st century is completely different from the country it was at the beginning of the 20th century. Indeed, contemporary immigration has forever altered the racial, ethnic, and religious texture of the nation. Nowadays, the majority of immigrants no longer come from Europe but mostly from Asia and Latin America. Banks (2006), who consulted figures available through the U.S. Census Bureau, reports that "between 1991 and 2000, 82 percent of the documented immigrants to the United States came from nations in Asia, Latin America, the Caribbean, and Africa." Moreover, he goes on to indicate that "the U.S. Census Bureau projects that ethnic groups of color will increase from 28 percent of the nation's population today to 50 percent in 2050" (p. xvii). Although all of these changes are occurring with immigration patterns and are creating additional challenges with regard to how to make a pluralistic democratic society really work, one must not forget that 50 years ago, America faced the challenge of creating structures of opportunities for another group of American citizens—namely, African-Americans. The 1954 *Brown v. the Board of Education of Topeka* decision to end racial segregation in the schools, as well as the civil rights movement of the 1960s and 1970s, certainly brought to the fore issues of racial and social justice in America. Decades later, these issues are being debated with the same intensity and even with added complexity, because the nonwhite population has sharply increased, owing to an influx of the "new" immigrants.

The educational sector certainly took the lead in providing a meaningful response to the challenges of pluralism when it formulated the concept of multicultural education. In 1995, James Banks, arguably the founder and chief proponent of multicultural education in the United States, and Cherry McGee Banks published the *Handbook of Research on Multicultural Education,* "a watershed event" in the field, as they would later refer to this monumental work in the introduction of the second edition, published in 2004. Indeed, in the past 10 to 15 years, this emerging discipline has received and continues to receive a great deal of scholarly attention (e.g., Ball, 2006; Banks, 2002, 2006; Banks & Banks, 2004; Gollnick & Chinn, 2006; Knaus, 2006; Ladson-Billings & Tate, 2006; Nieto, 2004; Sleeter & Grant, 1999; Turner, Garcia, Nora, & Rendón, 1996). The principles of multicultural education outlined in Banks (2004)—content integration, knowledge construction, prejudice reduction, equity pedagogy, and empowering school structure and social structure—serve as a guide for the educational reforms that have taken place in higher education to meet the needs of an increasingly diversified American society. Banks (2006) defines multicultural education as "a reform movement designed to make major curricular and structural changes in the education of students in schools, colleges, and universities" (p. 52).

This widespread reform movement has penetrated almost every academic program at the university level in one form or another. Buzzwords such as *multiculturalism, cultural pluralism,* and *diversity,* which are oftentimes used interchangeably to refer more or less to the "dewhitening" or the "browning" of America, permeate academic discourse. There seems to be a consensus that institutions of higher learning need to be more in sync with contemporary demographic trends and to prepare all citizens to function effectively in society by removing ethnic and cultural blinders that keep citizens encapsulated and unable to appreciate and deal with other cultural, racial, linguistic, and ethnic perspectives.

Departments of foreign languages and literatures are not impervious to social changes. Many professors in these departments are involved in modifying some of their courses to include content that is more representative of the wide range of themes that permeate the pluralistic society that America has become.

In the remaining pages, I would like to discuss how I have modified the content and structure of two of my courses to incorporate more contemporary issues that are important to the so-called minority segments of the population.

Content Modification

I have had the privilege of teaching in the Department of Romance Languages and Literatures at the University of Missouri–Columbia for almost 20 years. Our department offers courses in the area of language, literature, linguistics, and foreign language education. In addition to teaching French courses at all levels, I coordinate the foreign language teaching program in the department, and I also direct the interdisciplinary program in linguistics. In that capacity, I teach such classes as Foreign Language Teaching Methods and a seminar, Bilingualism and Language Contact, which all graduate students pursuing a master of arts in language teaching take. Moreover, I teach every now and then an undergraduate course called Survey of Minority and Creole Languages of the U.S. and the Caribbean that is used for general education purposes.

Course I: Bilingualism and Language Contact

The graduate seminar I teach, Bilingualism and Language Contact, provides a global analysis of the study of bilingualism from a combined psycholinguistic, sociolinguistic, and sociocultural perspective, based on current research. First, it examines the development and measurement of bilingualism and various cognitive theories of bilingualism. Second, it explores various phenomena of language contact—such as interference, code-switching, and mixing—in terms of their social functions for particular speech communities. Finally, the course examines a variety of social and educational issues related to bilingualism, such as language status, language attitudes, language planning, and bilingual education. In recent years I have somewhat shifted the emphasis of the course to give more weight to the last section because many of the social and educational issues covered in the course were making headline news. Moreover, I have added more readings on these issues and encourage students to research them in greater depth. Such issues include the so-called Ebonics controversy that surfaced in December 1996, after the Oakland Unified School District in California passed a resolution to allow African-American English in the classroom as a means of helping students bridge the gap between their vernacular language and standard American English. This resolution caused such an uproar that it constituted the object of a congressional hearing before a subcommittee of the U.S. Senate Committee on Appropriations (1997). The issue of African-American student education is certainly far from over, and prospective teachers need to be well versed on these matters. Therefore, students enrolled in my bilingualism seminar had an opportunity to watch the *Ebonics in Education* video (available at www.c-span.org or through 1-877-ONCSPAN) and hear firsthand the testimony of Oakland Superintendent Carolyn Getridge, as well as the testimonies of Congresswoman Maxine Waters, leading American sociolinguist William Labov, and psychology professor Robert Williams, who coined the term *Ebonics* in 1973. Students also heard opposing points of view from other witnesses, such as Reverend Amos C. Brown, from the Civil Rights Commission of the National Baptist Convention, and Armstrong Williams, a well-known conservative syndicated columnist.

Other issues covered in the seminar were bilingual education and the English-only movement (see www.usenglish.org/inc/), which, like Ebonics, have been at the forefront of major controversial decisions involving language policies. In the course students had ample opportunity to read about the various arguments for and against bilingual education from a wide range of perspectives, including those of scholars, politicians, and prominent Americans (for a concise reference for such arguments, see Krashen, 1999). They learned about legislation that has been proposed with regard to bilingual education. Such legislation included California's Proposition 227, spearheaded by millionaire entrepreneur Ron Unz to dismantle bilingual education programs and replace them with an English-immersion curriculum; and subsequently Proposition 203, also proposed by Unz, that advocated what he called "English for the Children" (for more on these propositions, see Wiley, 2004). These propositions passed in June 1998 and November 2000. However, the dismantling of bilingual education in California and in other parts of the country does not seem to have resulted in higher academic achievements on the part of *all* immigrant children. Some are still left behind. Consequently, the issue of immigrant education remains as critical as ever, and university students preparing for a teaching career will undoubtedly have to deal with the challenge of finding the best educational models to meet the needs of the pluralistic student population. Therefore, it becomes imperative that they gain a solid understanding of these very important language issues and policies while at the university.

Discussions about the English-only movement were also incorporated in the bilingualism seminar. Students researched the genesis of the movement and its development to the present day in an attempt to assess the merits of such a proposal and the proposal's consequences for society. Thorny questions, such as whether English should be law and how the English-only movement fits with U.S. civil rights traditions, were intensely debated in the class.

Course II: Survey of Minority and Creole Languages of the U.S. and the Caribbean

The undergraduate course I teach explores the state of minority languages of the United States and Creole languages of the Caribbean. With regard to the United States, the languages that constitute the focus of attention include Black English, Spanish, native American Indian languages, and the three varieties of Creole—namely, Gullah, Louisiana Creole, and Hawaiian Creole. For the Caribbean we look at both the English- and French-based pidgins and Creoles found in the region. The following questions are addressed: What is the social status of these languages? What is their relationship with the standard language of the country and/or the community? What makes them "minority" languages? What is the mainstream attitude toward these so-called minority languages? Are these attitudes reflected in social institutions? How are these languages used to reinforce social boundaries? What are the speakers' attitudes toward their own languages or varieties? What is the relationship between language and ethnic, national, or cultural identity?

In recent years the languages that students have been more interested in covering in their oral presentations and projects are Spanish/Spanglish, Louisiana Creole (and other French Creoles), African-American English, and Gullah. Consequently, I have somewhat modified the course to include more information on the structure of these languages and their functions for their speakers. The objective is to help students make an informed decision about whether there is something inherently deficient or impoverished with these languages that could prevent them from being used in certain domains, such as education, politics, the media, and the world of literature. Moreover, the topics of regional dialects and the role of language in ethnic identity formation receive more coverage than before as a result of students' interests. Indeed, students appreciate reading selections from John Rickford (1999), Geneva Smitherman (2000), and John Baugh (2000, 2004) for African-American English; from Ana Celia Zentella (2000, 2004) and others for Spanish/Spanglish; and from Albert Valdman (1997) for Louisiana Creole. (Other good references to consult include Finegan & Rickford, 2004; Klingler, 2003; and McKay & Wong, 2000). In addition, they enjoy and learn a great deal from the video *Family Across the Sea* (South Carolina ETV Network, 1991), which deals with the connection between the Gullah speech community of South Carolina and the Krio speakers of Sierra Leone. Students also find the video *American Tongues* (Alvarez & Kolker, 1986), which portrays the dialectal richness of American English as well as Americans' attitudes toward this dialectal diversity, very informative.

Outcomes

Students have explicitly expressed a real interest in these sociolinguistics and language policy issues, which is documented in student evaluation forms. During the course of the semester, students told me that they were genuinely enjoying these classes, because they were able to find real connections between our classroom readings and discussions and current societal challenges. Many indicated that they were happy that such content was covered in courses offered by the department; otherwise, they would not have had the opportunity to learn about such topics. In fact, some students continued investigating these issues on their own and presented their research at regional conferences. For example, one student did a research paper on Louisiana Creole and presented her findings at a conference on teaching foreign languages. Another student, who was very interested in issues of language and identity, presented the paper that he developed in the bilingualism seminar at a conference at the University of Miami.

Another student called me after graduation to say that she was involved in an ethnographic project about health issues with the Brazilian community. She went on to say that she was witnessing firsthand, with her Brazilian informants, some of the questions about linguistic insecurity that were raised in my bilingualism class. This experience prompted her to get in touch with me for additional references on the subject.

Perhaps the most rewarding story is that of the undergraduate student who took my minority language course in her senior year. After she graduated, she joined the Peace Corps and went to Guinea (Conakry). There she was exposed to issues of African vernacular languages in education and people's attitudes toward these indigenous languages. Indeed, some of the same questions we debated in class were African realities, which she was experiencing herself. She would on several occasions email me from Guinea just to say how useful this course was to her, now that she was in the real world. After spending two years in Africa, she came back to the University of Missouri–Columbia and enrolled in the master's program in language teaching. All of these stories go a long way to document that student responses to this sort of content have been highly positive.

Moreover, in my advanced French classes, I have begun to include readings and more discussions on current events in France with regard to its immigrant populations. Once again, I find that students do respond favorably to being exposed to real-world problems, because they choose to research these issues further for their papers and oral presentations. In a similar fashion, in my modern French class I include a section on French dialectology in which students gain some familiarity with regional varieties of French—that of Quebec, Haiti, and parts of Africa.

Raising multicultural and multilinguistic awareness is the only responsible path for foreign language departments. The curriculum cannot be disconnected from the multiple challenges that society faces. It is my fervent hope that language professors will continue to recognize the need to modify the traditional curriculum to respond to current societal changes and to provide students with the knowledge and training necessary for succeeding in the global village of the 21st century and for reducing prejudice.

References

Alvarez, L., & Kolker, A. (Producers). (1986). *American tongues* [Motion picture]. United States: Center for New American Media.

Ball, A. F. (2006). *Multicultural strategies for education and social changes.* New York, NY: Teachers College Press.

Banks, J. A. (2002). *An introduction to multicultural education.* Needham Heights, MA: Allyn & Bacon.

Banks, J. A. (2004). Multicultural education: Historical development, dimensions, and practice. In J. A. Banks & C. M. Banks (Eds.), *Handbook of research on multicultural education* (pp. 3–29). San Francisco, CA: Jossey-Bass.

Banks, J. A. (2006). *Cultural diversity and education: Foundations, curriculum, and teaching* (5th ed.). Needham Heights, MA: Allyn & Bacon.

Banks, J. A., & Banks, C. M. (Eds.). (1995). *Handbook of research on multicultural education* (1st ed.). New York, NY: Macmillan.

Banks, J. A., & Banks, C. M. (Eds.). (2004). *Handbook of research on multicultural education* (2nd ed.). San Francisco, CA: Jossey-Bass.

Baugh, J. (2000). *Beyond Ebonics. Linguistic pride and racial prejudice.* New York, NY: Oxford University Press.

Baugh, J. (2004). Ebonics and its controversy. In E. Finegan & J. R. Rickford (Eds.), *Language in the USA: Themes for the twenty-first century* (pp. 305–18). Cambridge, UK: Cambridge University Press.

Finegan, E., & Rickford, J. R. (Eds.). (2004). *Language in the USA: Themes for the twenty-first century.* Cambridge, UK: Cambridge University Press.

Gollnick, D. M., & Chinn, P. C. (2006). *Multicultural education in a pluralistic society* (7th ed.). Upper Saddle River, NJ: Prentice Hall.

Klingler, T. A. (2003). *If I could turn my tongue like that: The Creole language of Pointe Coupee Parish, Louisiana.* Baton Rouge, LA: Louisiana State University Press.

Knaus, C. (2006). *Race, racism and multiraciality in American education.* Bethesda, MD: Academica Press.

Krashen, S. D. (1999). *Condemned without a trial: Bogus arguments against bilingual education.* Portsmouth, NH: Heinemann.

Ladson-Billings, G., & Tate, W. F. (Eds.). (2006). *Education research in the public interest: Social justice, action, and policy.* New York, NY: Teachers College Press.

McKay, S. L., & Wong, S. C. (Eds.). (2000). *New immigrants in the United States: Readings for second language educators.* Cambridge, UK: Cambridge University Press.

Nieto, S. (2004). *Affirming diversity: The sociopolitical context of multicultural education* (4th ed.). Needham Heights, MA: Allyn & Bacon.

Rickford, J. R. (1999). *African American Vernacular English: Features, evolution, educational implications.* Malden, MA: Blackwell.

Sleeter, C. E., & Grant, C. A. (1999). *Making choices for multicultural education: Five approaches to race, class, and gender.* New York, NY: Wiley.

Smitherman, G. (2000). *Talkin that talk: Language, culture, and education in African America.* New York, NY: Routledge.

South Carolina ETV Network (Producer). (1991). *Family across the sea* [Motion picture]. United States: California Newsreel.

Turner, C. S. V., Garcia, M., Nora, A., & Rendón, L. I. (Eds.). (1996). *Racial and ethnic diversity in higher education*. Needham Heights, MA: Simon & Schuster.

U.S. Senate Committee on Appropriations. (1997). *Ebonics special hearing*. Washington, DC: U.S. Government Printing Office.

Valdman, A. (1997). *French and Creole in Louisiana*. New York, NY: Plenum Press.

Wiley, T. G. (2004). Language planning, language policy, and the English-only movement. In E. Finegan & J. R. Rickford (Eds.), *Language in the USA: Themes for the twenty-first century* (pp. 319–338). Cambridge, UK: Cambridge University Press.

Zentella, A. C. (2000). Puerto-Ricans in the United States: Confronting the linguistics repercussions of colonialism. In S. L. McKay & S. C. Wong (Eds.), *New immigrants in the United States: Readings for second language educators* (pp. 134–164). Cambridge, UK: Cambridge University Press.

Zentella, A. C. (2004). Spanish in the Northeast. In E. Finegan & J. R. Rickford (Eds.), *Language in the USA: Themes for the twenty-first century* (pp. 182–204). Cambridge, UK: Cambridge University Press.

18

Diversity in the Linguistics Classroom

Shelome Gooden

The linguistic classroom presents a unique opportunity for raising students' awareness about diversity and multiculturalism. This is especially true in sociolinguistics classes in which students learn how and why different social groups speak different languages and dialects and how speakers convey social relationships and social identities through the way they speak. In this chapter I will refer to changes and developments in one undergraduate course, Aspects of Sociolinguistics, taught at the University of Pittsburgh. The course in some sense represents a fusion of elements from undergraduate courses I have taught over the past five years at two different universities in the Midwest. Some of the courses themselves separately emphasized diversity as well as theoretical issues in linguistics. However, the Aspects of Sociolinguistics course satisfies several general education requirements and is therefore geared toward the nonspecialist student population and not just linguistics majors. In this chapter I focus on teaching linguistic awareness vis-à-vis linguistic diversity rather than on the inequities facing speakers of minority dialects in the classroom (Siegel, 1991; Smitherman & Villanueva, 2003). I show how students can be taught to view language as more than just a communicative device—that is, as a social practice through which people channel cultural and social identities (Eckert, 2000).

With respect to diversity, the main goals for students in the course are as follows:

- To understand the reasons for language variation (dialects)

- To appreciate differences in language use as legitimate

- To understand that linguistic differences also reflect differences in class, race, ethnicity, gender, sexuality, and, by extension, culture

- To reflect on how social inequalities are manifested through language attitudes

Implementation

Since one of the requirements that the course fulfills is a writing requirement, the evaluation materials are structured so that students develop critical writing and thinking skills that are not only important for linguistic analysis but that are applicable to other areas of study as well. Listening and speaking are essential when discussing issues of linguistic diversity, so students are asked to make in-class presentations of their own work as well as to lead discussions on selected journal articles and web sites on specific topics. During lectures and in-class presentations, students are asked to comment on their peers' contributions to class discussion. In the latter part of the course, they also comment on their peers' poster presentations, which are based on the students' own research. To cover the material, I combine lectures, classroom discussions, student presentations, classroom exercises, and guest lecturers. The diversity-oriented topics include language and social class, language and gender, language and ethnicity/race, and sociocultural differences in language use. Here is a synopsis of the latter two topics with some detail on implementation.

Language and Ethnicity/Race

Some of the subtopics covered that relate to language and ethnicity/race include:

- *African-American Vernacular English (Ebonics).* Students are introduced to differences in the use of English among African-Americans (Siegel, 1991). Discussions include linguistic differences and differences in the historical development of the variety as opposed to other varieties of American English. In addition, students learn that persons of other ethnicities (e.g. whites, Asians) use the variety as well (Sweetland, 2002).

- *Linguistic profiling.* It is often the case that embodied in perceptions of a speaker's dialect are attitudes (positive or negative) toward the speaker himself or herself. Students are familiarized with sociolinguistic methodologies for getting at speaker attitudes, such as the matched guise technique (Purnell, Idsardi, & Baugh, 1999). In this study one speaker uses different dialects (Ebonics, Chicano English, Standard English) to ask about the availability of apartments and judges landlords' responses. The fact that the Standard English voice received the most responses generated lots of discussion among students. I connect the discussion to current events and popular media by having them review and discuss CNN and NPR reports on the issue and relate those news pieces to the classroom discussion.

- *Linguistic stereotypes and how they are portrayed in film and animation.* Here students review how nonstandard dialect speakers are portrayed in Disney animations, in cartoons in printed media, and in popular film. The main idea is that speakers of nonstandard dialects are typically portrayed negatively as villains and foolish and that Standard English speakers are generally portrayed positively.

- *Language use among Americans of different heritages.* The main point here is that English is not the only language used in the United States and that many Americans are bilingual or even multilingual. In this way students learn about the language varieties used by historically underrepresented groups (in this case, linguistic minorities). Perhaps the most shocking realization for students is that English is not the official language of the United States (at least not at the federal level).

Sociocultural Differences in Language Use

On the topic of sociocultural differences, the class discusses culture-specific norms of language use and general discourse. For example, among African-Americans, the ritualistic insults of "Yo' Mama" games are often foreign to the typical undergraduate student. From an African-American cultural perspective, such games are normal; to others they seem offensive. The class also discusses conversation politeness strategies among the Navajo, where indirectness is highly valued.

Exercises

As an icebreaker and for getting at the idea that dialect differences are systematic and rule governed rather than linguistic aberrations, I usually have students complete an exercise on a-prefixing (Wolfram & Schilling-Estes, 2006). For example, "She was a-hollering" and "They make money a-building houses" are acceptable, but "A-hollering is fun" and "They make money by a-building houses" are not. I use this exercise because the Appalachian variety is very salient for students from the Midwest or Pennsylvania and because a-prefixing is also used in familiar American folk songs (e.g., "Oh Susanna"). By working through the exercise, students come to the realization that there is a correct way to use a-prefixing—that is, there are certain contexts in which it is not appropriate. The larger lesson is that all dialects are similarly rule governed.

A second exercise is one I call "Language/Dialect Myth Busters." In this exercise students are asked to contribute their views on dialects, which are then critically assessed by their peers. For example, it's a myth that a dialect is something someone else speaks; the reality is that everyone who speaks a language speaks some variety (or dialect) of that language. Here's another example: It's a myth that a dialect results from unsuccessful attempts to speak the standard, or "correct," form of a language; the reality is that dialect speakers acquire their language by adopting the speech of those around them, not by failing to adopt standard language features (Wolfram & Schilling-Estes, 2006).

A third exercise I do in class involves the recognition of dialects. Students are asked to give their opinions on differences and similarities in the speech of places surrounding Pittsburgh. They are then asked to compare their judgments with dialect maps of the Midwest and Northeast. Invariably, they are better able to judge the varieties in regions closest to them and at the same time either have negative opinions or no opinions of dialects farther away from them. For example, one student suggested that because in the past Pittsburghers competed with Ohioans (especially those from Steubenville and other areas close to the Pennsylvania border) for steel and coal mining jobs, they may have over time perceived that Ohio dialects sounded odd.

Guest Lecturer

As a way of broadening and enriching the students' multicultural experience with language, I invited an American Sign Language (ASL) instructor to give a lecture. The experience was very rewarding for students because the instructor herself used ASL in everyday interaction. She gave an overview of the history, development, and use of ASL and also shared personal experiences with the students. An ASL interpreter worked with the class for the entire period, which was many students' first experience interacting with an ASL speaker.

Outcomes

Perhaps the best way to judge outcomes is by the quality of the work produced by the students. Several students investigated issues of multiculturalism and diversity in research papers. For example, some students researched minority languages spoken in the United States; others looked at language variation in ASL and language use among African Americans. One student looked at differences in the local variety of English spoken in Pittsburgh. Along the lines of forensic linguistics and language attitudes, one student did a paper called "Identifying Discrimination Through Use of Language." Another student looked at the portrayal of language diversity in the media in a paper titled "Ali G: Perceptions of Ethnic Minorities and the Use of Language in Satire." The main results of these research papers were presented in conference-style poster sessions during the final week of classes. Students were able to share their insights on the different topics and increase their peers' understanding of the subject matter. Here are samples of students' comments from the Survey of Student Opinion of Teaching, specifically in references to this question: What aspects of this course were most beneficial to you? The comments strongly suggest that educational goals were attained.

- "This course provided a greater understanding of the socioeconomic differences between cultures, and it has forced me to consider more critically the assumptions and prejudices concerning linguistic variations from society to society."

- "I found a new way of seeing my own language use, as well as viewing the language of others. This class destigmatized and redefined words like *slang*."

- "[This class] allowed for an open mind and showed that language differences are not bad."

Conclusions

I trust that I have shown that a linguistic class such as this one can create an environment in which students gain knowledge and appreciation for their own linguistic and cultural backgrounds as well as that of others. Of course, there are lots of other topics, exercises, and so forth, that I would like to add or exchange, (as is the case with any course every time I teach it) but I came away from this course pleased that the lessons learned went beyond sociolinguistic theory and improved students' writing and oratory skills. I felt strongly that I was able to positively affect the student's attitudes toward language differences and thereby cultural differences.

References

Eckert, P. (2000). *Linguistic variation as social practice.* Oxford, UK: Blackwell.

Purnell, T., Idsardi, W., & Baugh, J. (1999). Perceptual and phonetic experiments on American English dialect identification. *Journal of Language and Social Psychology, 18*(1), 10–30.

Siegel, J. (1991). Creoles and minority dialects in education: An overview. *Journal of Multilingual and Multicultural Development, 20*(2), 508–524.

Smitherman, G., & Villanueva, V. (2003). *Language diversity in the classroom: From intention to practice.* Carbondale, IL: Southern Illinois University Press.

Sweetland. J. (2002). Unexpected but authentic use of an ethnically marked dialect. *Journal of Sociolinguistics, 6*(4), 514–538.

Wolfram, W., & Schilling-Estes, N. (Eds.). (2006). *American English.* Oxford, UK: Blackwell.

19

Latin American Film and Culture

María Cristina Saavedra

Although it may seem at first glance as if any course on Latin America already includes issues of diversity by the very nature of the subject matter and would therefore not require any tweaking to incorporate elements of diversity into its framework, the reality is not so simple. It is easy to assume that discussing another culture implies a discussion of diversity, but for many students, the Latin American reality is as utterly foreign and distant as life on another planet. Diversity, then, is seen as something "they" have but something completely irrelevant to "us." This is especially true on a socially conservative, rural campus, where there is very little diversity in the student body and where most students have had little, if any, direct exposure to other cultures. Unless students explore and understand Latin American reality as informing the cultural identity of the United States and, therefore, their own realities, Latin America remains a distant "other."

One of the first goals of Latin American Film and Culture, a course taught at the University of Pittsburgh–Johnstown was to make that reality and the cultural production of Latin America relevant to students. This is a particularly important goal given the current heated debates surrounding immigration in the United States. More and more, Latin America is informing who Americans are and helping reformulate a sense of individual and collective identity in the United States.

Adapting the Original Course to Suit Specific Needs _____

The course Latin American Film and Culture (LAFC) grew out of an original course called Latin American Literature in Translation (LALT), which was designed either to fill a general education requirement or to substitute for the foreign language requirement for several majors, especially those in the humanities. Many students enrolled in this class because they needed the credit hours and/or because, given the choice between studying a language or taking literature in translation, the latter seemed more appealing or at the very least less daunting. Although some students of literature or humanities were specifically drawn to the course, the majority of students enrolled were not primarily interested in the content. The first challenge of this class, then, was to make the subject matter engaging enough to pique students' interest. There was also no danger of replacing Latin American literature with Latin American film because the original course continued to be taught almost every semester by other faculty members. Generally, it surveyed a collection of texts by major writers of Latin America with some variations, depending on the specific likes and/or preferences of the professor teaching the class. LAFC was easily added on as a subtitle to the original title, or it was offered as a special topics course.

If the goal of LALT had been to expose students to literary and cultural traditions from Latin America, then LAFC could achieve similar goals and do so employing a medium that most students are drawn to—namely, film. After trying several other approaches, I decided to focus specifically on geographic areas that I felt would help students connect with Latin America, both because of their physical proximity to the United States and because of the United States' historical and political interactions with them. These included Central America, Mexico, and the Caribbean. The idea was to help students redefine the term *American* to include all the Americas as an intimately connected whole.

Most of the films studied in this course have accompanying readings and some suggestions for further reading, so the class could easily be adapted to a film and literature course with minor changes. Although the films can be varied and substituted with many other choices, the following are typical examples of works that fit well with the overall concept of the course.

The Films

John Sayles's well-known film *Men With Guns* (*Hombres armados;* Gonda, Patton, Sloss, & Sayles, 1997) is an ideal first film for a course like this because part of its premise deals with U.S. involvement in Latin America. The protagonist of the film is an aging physician who initiated a program for young doctors to bring medical care to the rural areas of his (unnamed) country. The film implies that the program is facilitated through a U.S. initiative of the 1960s, the Alliance for Progress. Before viewing the film, students read about and discuss the goals of the Alliance for Progress and the political turmoil that prompted it in the early 1960s when the Kennedy administration feared the spread of communism in the region. The film is also multilingual. Sayles purposely places the English-speaking audience in the uncomfortable position of not understanding much of the dialogue except through the voice of an interpreter or through subtitles and, as such, displaces the dominant position of the English language for a primarily English-speaking audience. As the protagonist uncovers the truth about the fate of his students, viewers are also forced to question where their responsibility lies with regard to knowledge about the world around them. This film thus sets the tone for a reading of the films that follow by uncovering the somewhat arbitrary lines that divide "us" from "them," lines established by ever-more tenuous physical borders.

The film *El Norte* (Black, Navarro, Thomas, & Nava, 1983), about two Guatemalan siblings who flee their country for fear of being killed by death squads, touches on issues of U.S. involvement in Guatemala and allows students to explore the debates surrounding the struggle of undocumented immigrants in the United States.

The section on Mexico includes the films *Like Water for Chocolate* (*Como agua para chocolate;* Castillo & Arau, 1992), *Danzón* (Kuri & Novaro, 1991), and *Amores perros* (*Love's a Bitch;* Iñárritu, 2000). The first takes place during the Mexican Revolution. It is an excellent film for discussing border issues between the United States and Mexico, the role of women in Mexican culture and the role of the *soldaderas* during the revolution, and the use of magical realism as a filmic and literary device. María Novaro's *Danzón* also serves to introduce issues about women in Mexican society. Finally, *Amores perros,* a popular film with students, is not only visually dramatic and fast paced; it is also useful for initiating a discussion of class, race, and the implications of the global economy on poor regions of Latin America.

The section on the Caribbean includes the classic of Cuban cinema *Memories of Underdevelopment* (*Memorias del subdesarrollo;* Mendoza & Gutiérrez Alea, 1967). This film is a good introduction to the complex issues surrounding the Cuban Revolution. It also ties into the discussion of U.S. policy toward Latin America begun with *Men With Guns.* Another film that sheds light on the era is *I Am Cuba* (*Soy Cuba;* Kalatozishvili, 1964), an example of socialist realism in film and one that opens up discussion on the topic of propaganda and cultural hegemony both in socialist countries and in the West. Finally, films such as *Strawberry and Chocolate* (*Fresa y chocolate;* Balzaretti, et al., 1994) and *Guantanamera* (Vives, Felsberg, Gutiérez Alea, & Tabío, 1995) shed light on different stages of the Cuban Revolution up to the Special Period of the 1990s. There are a great many excellent Cuban films to choose from, many of which can be used to discuss further the ongoing conflict between the United States and Cuba. This section also includes the Dominican film *Nueba Yol* (Céspedes, Lluberes, Martí, Muñiz, & Muñiz, 1995), about an émigré's difficulties and disappointments as he struggles to survive in New York City.

Outcomes_____

Confronting Challenges

As anyone who has ever taught a film in a course that is not designed primarily for majors, one of the biggest challenges is helping students view films critically. Watching movies is, after all, what most students do for fun, and having to "read" films as texts is an entirely different experience. This reorientation of viewing practices is facilitated by books that help students view critically. But in addition, introducing films with readings by figures such as Che Guevara, whom a number of students find intriguing and trendy (a screening of *The Motorcycle Diaries* [Redford, Webster, Yelham, & Salles, 2004] is optional), helps draw them into a discussion of related topics and themes in the films.

Another of the principal challenges in any course on Latin America is broaching the thorny issue of U.S. involvement in the region. The United States' historical legacy in Latin America is not always a very positive one. On a campus where most students are from rural, politically conservative areas, any presentation of ideas that may place the United States in a negative light may be met with some degree of resistance. It is helpful to include readings that present the historical record in a more or less objective fashion. In this way, students come to an understanding on their own about the political and social circumstances in which filmmakers and writers are producing these works, and everyone comes to class discussions prepared with the same background information.

It is also helpful to proceed slowly into the themes and questions surrounding issues of identity and immigration. Questions that lead to reexamining one's own identity or one's national identity (e.g., "what does it mean to be an American?") can be threatening and disorienting. These questions often provoke lively discussion in class.

Variations

As already mentioned, this course lends itself to variations that include pairing some, or all, the films with literary texts. The most obvious choices would be adaptations of novels into films, such as *Like Water for Chocolate* or *Memories of Underdevelopment,* but other pairings are also possible. Mexican writer Elena Poniatowska's (1969/2001) book *Here's to You, Jesusa!* could be read along with the film *Like Water for Chocolate* to discuss, among other ideas, several different aspects of the Mexican Revolution and the importance of *testimonio* in Latin America.

The course could also have a more specific focus, such as migration. Here there are many possibilities. In addition to the films included in the course outline, the following might be useful: the Spanish documentary *Balseros* (*Cuban Rafters;* Roca, Solera, Bosch, & Domènech, 2002), about the Cuban rafters of the

1990s; *Things I Left in Havana* (*Cosas que dejé en La Habana;* Herrero & Gutiérrez Aragón, 1997), a good film to discuss Cuban and/or Latin American migration and xenophobia in a European context; *Maria Full of Grace* (*María, llena eres de gracia;* Mezey & Marston, 2004), about a young Colombian woman who becomes a drug mule. Indeed, there are many ways to structure this course.

Conclusion

Courses on film or literature are sometimes taught without much or any consideration for the political or historical contexts in which the texts were produced. But unless the works are grounded in an understanding of the social conditions under which they are produced, part of their meaning is lost to a reader or viewer who is not familiar with the region. This issue speaks to the question of individual and collective responsibility, touched on earlier in this discussion, through which we explore what it means to be not only a responsible citizen of the United States but also a responsible citizen of the world. Communicating a sense of the interconnectedness of the United States with the rest of the world and the importance of social responsibility and justice on a global scale may be the most important pedagogical goal.

References

Balzaretti, G., Cabrera, F., Cobo, N., Muñoz, J., Vives, C. (Executive Producers), Gutiérrez Alea, T., & Tabío, J. C. (Directors). (1994). *Strawberry and chocolate* (*Fresa y chocolate*) [Motion picture]. Cuba/Mexico/Spain: Miramax.

Black, T., Navarro, B., Thomas, A. (Producers), & Nava, G. (Director). (1983). *El Norte* [Motion picture]. United States/UK: PBS.

Castillo, Ó. (Executive Producer), & Arau, A. (Director). (1992). *Like water for chocolate* (*Como agua para chocolate*) [Motion picture]. Mexico: Buena Vista.

Céspedes, R., Lluberes, J., Martí, L., Muñiz, M. Á. (Executive Producers), & Muñiz, Á. (Director). (1995). *Nueba yol* [Motion picture]. Dominican Republic: Cigua Films.

Gonda, L., Patton, J., Sloss, J. (Executive Producers), & Sayles, J. (Director). (1997). *Men with guns* (*Hombres armados*) [Motion picture]. United States: Sony Pictures.

Herrero, G. (Executive Producer), & Gutiérrez Aragón, M. (Director). (1997). *Things I left in Havana* (*Cosas que dejé en La Habana*) [Motion picture]. Spain: Alta Films.

Iñárritu, A. G. (Director). (2000). *Amores perros (Love's a bitch)* [Motion picture]. Mexico: Nu Vision.

Kalatozishvili, M. (Director). (1964). *I am Cuba* (*Soy Cuba*) [Motion picture]. USSR/Cuba: Gosudarstvenii Komitet po Kinematografii & Instituto Cubano del Arte e Industrias Cinematográficos.

Kuri, D. (Executive Producer), & Novaro, M. (Director). (1991). *Danzón* [Motion picture]. Mexico/Spain: Instituto Mexicano de Cinematografía.

Mendoza, M. (Producer), & Gutiérrez Alea, T. (Director). (1967). *Memories of underdevelopment* (*Memorias del subdesarrollo*) [Motion picture]. Cuba: Instituto Cubano del Arte e Industrias Cinematográficos.

Mezey, P. (Producer), & Marston, J. (Director). (2004). *Maria full of grace* (*María, llena eres de gracia*) [Motion picture]. United States/Colombia: Fine Line Features.

Poniatowska, E. (2001). *Here's to you, Jesusa!* (*Hasta no verte Jesús mío*) (D. Heikkinen, Trans.). New York, NY: Farrar, Strauss, & Giroux. (Original work published 1969)

Redford, R., Webster, P., Yelham, R. (Executive Producers), & Salles, W. (Director). (2004). *The motorcycle diaries* [Motion picture]. United States: Focus Features.

Roca, T., Solera, M. J. (Executive Producers), Bosch, C., & Domènech, J. M. (Directors). (2002). *Balseros* [Motion picture]. Spain: Bausan Films.

Vives, C., Felsberg, U. (Executive Producers), Gutiérrez Alea, T., & Tabío, J. C. (Directors). (1995). *Guantanamera* [Motion picture]. Cuba/Spain/Germany: Alta Films.

20

Reframing the Reference: Diversity in Modern Design Culture

Linda Lindroth

In 1962, when H. W. Janson's *History of Art* first appeared in colleges and universities across America, it contained not a single example of artwork by a woman or an artist of color. Those of us assigned to read this seminal text in subsequent editions were to believe that there were only white male artists in the Western canon. It wasn't until decades later that Lucy Lippard (after dedicating 25 years to writing feminist art history) published *Mixed Blessings: New Art in a Multicultural America* (Lippard, 1990), bringing together in one volume the work of Latin American, Native American, Caribbean American, and African-American artists. By 1994, a copy of Janson's book weighed in at ten pounds. In the introduction to the fifth edition, Anthony Janson, son and editorial heir, seems to have embraced feminism and states almost reluctantly, "The representation of African-American artists has been significantly increased" (Janson & Janson, 1995, p. 14), while at the same time excluding nontraditional, non-Western, and ethnographic art. If the *History of Art* hardly examined the role of the "other," multicultural art was being produced across the country, and educators introduced this work to their students via magazines, museums, and field trips to art galleries. Today it takes but a click of the mouse to peruse diverse art collections online and to download images to a computer desktop or to a PowerPoint presentation. RSS (i.e., Really Simple Syndication) feeds provide an exhaustive amount of old and new material, and nimble fingers and clever phrasing pull up gems that only a few years ago would require airplane travel and grants to research.

By offering Modern Design Culture, the Department of Interactive Digital Design at Quinnipiac University wanted to address the origins of design in the 20th century. Young designers effortlessly Google images on any subject without a

113

care about where or how they came to be. A concern of the faculty was that a pull-down menu could substitute for even the briefest history of typography; there was an obvious need to introduce the roots of design and to show how they travel throughout the United States' multicultural society.

Students in the Interactive Digital Design Program at Quinnipiac are confident and entrepreneurially active before setting foot in the computer lab. The digital design department educates students from progressive elementary and secondary schools who create PowerPoint presentations and web sites as alternatives to term papers and who, as early as preschool, frequently demonstrate more savvy than their parents with software programs and video games. To engage such students in the history of their diverse visual culture without boring them with standard art slide shows, I needed to tap into what they already knew and cared about and to connect it with interesting anecdotal evidence. It needed to be quick and associative like Internet travel. (For example, what is public art? It's easily ignored—a public fountain is a place to sit and eat ice cream on a sunny day.) Establishing a personal relationship to the art was a first step. Through the examination of open design competitions, Percent for Art programs, and art exhibitions, monuments and memorials came alive.

We begin in nearby Boston where an equestrian figure tied to the classical Roman standard provides an important historical link to the United States' multicultural society. At a corner of the Boston Common stands Augustus Saint-Gaudens's *Robert Gould Shaw and the Fifty-Fourth Regiment Memorial* (1900). Here is an equestrian figure, a white man on horseback. What is noteworthy, however, is that it is the black men walking beside him in this bronze relief who are memorialized for their own heroism in a Civil War battle of 1863; they are volunteer soldiers, some former slaves, fighting in the Massachusetts regiment of the Union Army. Shaw and most of his men were killed at Fort Wagner and buried in a mass grave, but as we view the artist's sketches and models and review clips from *Glory* (Zwick, 1989), an Academy Award–winning film of young colonel Shaw and his men, they become living history. By incorporating these examples into Modern Design Culture, I create openings for students to comment and to build on previous knowledge. An African-American student volunteers how she first encountered Saint-Gaudens's memorial to the black soldiers on a field trip in middle school. Now the bronze relief is a source of pride for her, and her classmates listen as she describes where to look for the monument near the swan boats and the site of another piece of artwork, *Make Way for Ducklings,* based on the children's book classic (McCloskey, 1941).

Emotionally involved now in the connection between diverse groups and visual culture, we move to Maya Lin, the Asian-American designer of the Vietnam Veterans Memorial. In Freida Lee Mock's (1995) documentary film *Maya Lin: A Strong Clear Vision,* Maya Lin describes her ordeal as a young college student whose anonymous entry won an open design competition and the prejudice and hostility she endured as a woman and an Asian selected to memorialize a war in Southeast Asia that, in some circles at the time, still raised anger. How quickly the students begin to relate to the process of creativity in a multicultural world with a Maya Lin as their guide.

Modern Design Culture covers a period bookended by Mackintosh (the turn-of-the-19th-century Scottish architect of the Glasgow School of Art and other art nouveau buildings and decorative arts) and Macintosh, the 20th-century manufacturer of the computers used by the students in the class. These students learn differently than past generations. Glued to screens both mobile and fixed, their fingers get them from fantasy to reality and back again. As they refine their abilities to use search engines, they locate information in seconds, and it is teachers who have to help them discriminate and filter the results and who guide them to .edu and .org web sites and then cautiously help them ascertain the relevance and credibility of the .coms and the Wikipedia-style web sites. And oh, the wonders they find. If one merely types "first black artist" into Google, the invaluable database of Long Island University's *African Americans in the Visual Arts: A Historical Perspective* (Sylvester, n.d.) appears.

A web site of the American Society of Magazine Editors (2005) selects the top 40 magazine covers from the past 40 years. We learn that in 1968, *Glamour's* college issue introduced a new face to us, and it was not white—for the very first time a black female model appeared on the cover of a fashion magazine. Another 1968 highlight is a cover called "The Passion of Muhammad Ali." Refusing to be drafted and risking imprisonment and the loss of his heavyweight title, Ali is depicted by *Esquire* with an over-the-shoulder glance at Andrea Mantegna's *The Martyrdom of Saint Sebastian* (1480) included in the *History of Art* (Janson & Janson, 1995). Art directors, I tell my students, would be lost without ART 101.

Each week Modern Design Culture provides evidence that the contemporary visual world was formed not yesterday but gradually as artists, designers, photographers, and marketers have been mining the visual arts over the past century, creating a diverse melting pot of sources for every style and subject. By dividing the lectures into subject areas like advertising, architecture, film, drawing, and icons, I am able to reframe the familiar with modern insight and student involvement.

Students witness the power of the pen through political cartoons depicting Boss Tweed, Alfred Dreyfus, and anti-Semitism; through Dr. Seuss's World War II war bonds posters, and through Art Spiegelman's (1993) *Maus*. Children's drawings from Terezin (a concentration camp) and Sarajevo provide a window into the real lives of the victims of oppression and genocide through pictures (Volavkova, 1993). Discussions provoke questions like these: Is there such a thing as a benign political cartoon, or is it bound and gagged in cruelty? Why are there so few African-American cartoons in the *New Yorker?*

Modern design culture and history lie before these students in a smorgasbord of images and sounds. Like any good tour guide, I provide them with context and background, urging them to use what they have learned in exercises like designing a magazine spread on the subject of cloning and incorporating some historical visual reference as an illustration. Another exercise, inspired by an exhibition at New York's Museum of Modern Art entitled *The Humble Masterpiece,* asks students to explore the history of some commonplace household object. It is not unusual to discover, as in the case of the ironing board, that the designer is a black woman, Sarah Boone.

When it comes to multiculturalism in TV advertising, we all have our favorites: Alka Seltzer's speecy spicy meatball, Mean Joe Green's Coca-Cola, "You don't have to be Jewish to love Levy's Kosher Rye." By combining these historic campaigns with one contemporary artist's view of the world of brands—Nina Katchadourian's *The Genealogy of the Supermarket*—students see the relationship and pattern of corporate logos in a clever, manipulative, and hip way: a sort of family tree of Aunt Jemima, Chef Boyardee, and the Jolly Green Giant. Their minds are spinning, and their contributions to the class no longer need to be coerced. It is easy now for them to identify Cinderella's castle as a quasi-Gothic cathedral and the queen in *Snow White* as Gothic horror. Current events stimulate classroom discussion: within the past year the identity of the white man in the black suit sitting behind Rosa Parks in the famous bus photo was revealed by the man's family after Parks's death. He is a reporter, and a discussion evolves in class about the role played by the famous photograph and its use as propaganda. Other photographs in this discussion include one by Gordon Parks's (the only black photographer in the FSA) 1942 portrait of Ella Watson, a black cleaning woman standing with the mop and broom she used to clean the floors of the nation's capitol. Parks called it *American Gothic,* a reference to the iconic Grant Wood painting of the same name. We compare each work of art, easily accessed from the Internet in our computer lab classroom. A Holocaust survivor reveals his identity in Margaret Bourke White's famous photograph *Prisoners at Buchenwald, 1945,* significant not only because he is alive and well but because he is living in New York City. These revelations put a human face on the visual history available to students from which they will create future campaigns through illustration, photojournalism, and graphic design.

We begin to examine images of ourselves through other artists' work. Pioneering computer artist Nancy Burson's *Human Race Machine,* which Quinnipiac brought to campus in March 2005, allowed students to view themselves in a different ethnic or racial group. After the reflection and observation prompted by such exhibitions, we took the discussion further, to consider the Rodney King video; the duplicate O. J. Simpson mug shot covers on *Time* and *Newsweek* (one "Photoshopped" and the other presented without being touched up); Andy Warhol's silk screens of celebrity icons, including Jackie

Kennedy, Elizabeth Taylor, Elvis, and Michael Jackson; Mathew Brady's images of P. T. Barnum's family of Tom Thumb, albinos, and giantesses; the horrific photographs from Abu Ghraib, Kent State, and Vietnam; and Tibor Kalman's *United Colors of Benetton* magazine layouts on the subjects of race and AIDS. The class structure allows for easily inserting the events of the moment: a front-page photograph, an op-ed piece, a Danish cartoon depicting Mohammed wearing a headdress shaped like a bomb, and a photograph of New Orleans devastated by Hurricane Katrina. By the end of the course, we have assembled—teacher and student—our own textbook of URLs, and one of the students' final assignments is to take that research and turn it into an illustrated book called *Modern Design Culture*. Which sections they choose to illustrate their design style reveal to me what they have learned and which things have become part of their inventory, the elements of their visual and multicultural toolbox that they will take with them into their future professions—a vast storeroom to inform their work.

References

American Society of Magazine Editors. (2005). *ASME's top 40 magazine covers from the last 40 years.* Retrieved February 28, 2007, from www.magazine.org/Editorial/Top_40_Covers/

Janson, H. W., & Janson, A. F. (1995). *History of art* (5th ed.). New York, NY: Harry N. Abrams.

Lippard, L. R. (1990). *Mixed blessings: New art in multicultural America.* New York, NY: Random House.

McCloskey, R. (1941). *Make way for ducklings.* New York, NY: Viking.

Mock, F. L. (Director). (1995). *Maya Lin: A strong clear vision* [Film]. United States: Ocean Releasing.

Spiegelman, A. (1993). *Maus I: A survivor's tale: My father bleeds history.* New York, NY: Pantheon.

Sylvester, M. R. (Ed.). (n.d.). *African Americans in the visual arts: A historical perspective.* Retrieved February 28, 2007, from www.liu.edu/CWIS/CWP/library/aavaahp.htm

Volavkova, H. (1993). *I never saw another butterfly: Children's drawings from and poems from Terezin concentration camp, 1942–1944* (2nd ed.). New York, NY: Schocken Books.

Zwick, E. (Director). (1989). *Glory* [Motion picture]. United States: TriStar Pictures.

21

Introduction to Dance

Susan Gillis Kruman

Dance exists in almost every society, even at different levels of society, and is a basic form of aesthetic expression. Introduction to Dance is designed to provide students with a comprehensive overview of dance as an art form, religious expression, and social activity. A broad historical overview of dance is presented, as well as information on the important roles of the dancer, choreographer, and audience. Specific dance genres—such as ballet, modern dance, jazz, and world dance—are also the focus of this course. Instruction includes lectures, discussions, viewing performances on video and film, attending live dance events, and movement experiences in a variety of dance genres and historical periods in the dance studio lab.

The format of the class is a weekly three-hour class. The class is divided into lecture-discussion, movement lab, and viewing videos and films.

The rationale for this course is to enhance the knowledge of, and bring to life, the performing and visual art of dance. By looking at dance in the context of history and the actual experience of dance through movement, students can gain a deeper understanding of the art form in the context of cultural history. The making and comprehension of dance reveal the art form in a cultural and historical context and give students an understanding of art and humanity. Students are encouraged to view, analyze, and find solutions for intellectual, aesthetic, and technical problems by experimentation and informed, guided analysis.

Course Objectives

By the conclusion of Introduction to Dance, students should be able to:

- Articulate, verbally and/or in written form, an understanding of dance as an art form, a type of entertainment, and a social or recreational activity

- Demonstrate the knowledge and behaviors necessary to be a responsible, well-educated audience member

- Demonstrate the capacity to intelligently critique live dance performances from an informed point of view

- Demonstrate an understanding and appreciation of the role of the choreographer and the elements of dance used within a composition through movement and lecture

- Incorporate the elements of dance in original choreography and/or movement projects

- Demonstrate an understanding and appreciation of the role of the dancer as an artist

- Demonstrate a basic knowledge of the history of dance and its role in global cultures

- Describe and articulate, verbally and/or in written form, a basic knowledge and understanding of dance forms and genres

- Demonstrate a knowledge of past and current dance artists and their philosophies of, and impact on, dance career opportunities within the dance field and their importance in a contemporary global society

- Understand and appreciate the role of dance in education, dance as a performing art, and dance as a healthy, lifelong social and recreational activity

Impetus for Changing the Course

Providing a diverse representation of courses in the arts at the University of Pittsburgh was my primary motivation for creating the Introduction to Dance course. A secondary motive was to help men, women, and physically challenged students enjoy a class in dance in which they did not have to wear leotards and tights, a nonthreatening environment in which they would be able to experience dance and learn about the art form.

The University of Pittsburgh had introductions to art, writing, music, and theater, but there was no course that included dance as a subject that merited its own history, philosophy, literature, and culture. To remedy what I considered a large omission in the arts offerings at the university, I created the Introduction to Dance course in 1998. Initially, it was offered as a general studies course, and one year later it was offered as a regular undergraduate course that could fulfill the creative process requirement for the undergraduate liberal arts distribution.

In the past, undergraduate students could take technical dance courses in modern dance, jazz, or ballet, but I understood there was a very large student population that would be interested in taking a more theoretical dance course in which physical ability was not the primary source for grading. Not many men or women would be thrilled with the prospect of taking a dance class in which leotards and tights were required. With that in mind, Introduction to Dance was offered so that all students, regardless of their physical limitations or expertise, could participate.

Implementation

Consider this quotation from Mary Wigman (1983), an early German modern dance performer, choreographer, and philosopher: "The dance is one of many human experiences which cannot be suppressed. Like music, the dance is a language which all human beings understand" (p. 305).

Dance, by its nature, is a phenomenon that happens in almost every culture and country in the world. Because of the content of the course, it is not difficult to incorporate numerous traditions, ceremonies, and practices of dance in historical and contemporary contexts. There are dances of religion, dances for personal expression and social interaction, and dances that are performed in theaters and that are meant to be viewed by audiences. This class looks at the historical evolution of dance in various world cultures. From hip-hop to Native American Kachina dances, hula, West African dance, court dances of the Renaissance, contemporary modern dance, and classical Indian dance, we attempt to discover the historical and contemporary influences of society on dance and of dance on society.

One in-class activity that I do is to go around the class and ask students whether they have had any experiences in dance that were indicative of their cultural heritage. The responses are numerous and varied. This is almost always a springboard for discussion about the global nature of dance and how a particular frame of reference affects each student. I've found that this is an excellent entrée to a discussion about culture and dance and what class members share—or do not share—culturally.

Unlike a traditional dance class where there is an expectation of a physical performance in a specific genre like ballet or jazz, in this class we have experiences in a variety of dance types that do not call for a specific expertise in performance. Students in wheelchairs or walkers or students with physical constraints are easily able to access the movement assignments and experience dance performance at some significant level. Some in-class projects have included re-creations of historical dance in which the students created court dances based on their readings of dance history. In another project they created a primitive religious dance based on readings about the earliest beginnings of dance. Other projects had students creating their own line dances or folk dances or trying to interpret poetry in a 1900s soiree. Dancing in the shoes of a different class, a different time, a different culture, or the opposite sex makes a significant impact on student learning.

Outcomes

A performance in class can be as stressful to some students as a performance on stage. When planning Introduction to Dance, I initially assumed that the men would be more stressed than the women because they were not as inclined to dance or express themselves as much as women. What I discovered was that both male and female students were equally stressed by the prospect of a physical performance in class. To alleviate this pressure, early in the semester we now do physical warm-up activities with the whole group and conduct many class discussions with the whole group. As we continue through the semester, the group divides into smaller discussion and performance groups. This way, students get used to the idea of performing for each other and viewing each other. I have clear rules for critiquing performances, and students generally are both positive and constructive in their critiques. Usually by the fourth week of the semester, students are much more comfortable with the physical performance aspect of the course, and both male and female students seem to enjoy the physical aspect of the class. I have also discovered that sometimes the students who were not so verbally articulate in discussion have no problem expressing themselves physically. In class the physical expression of a student, limited or not, gives me great insight into his or her personality. The students themselves seem to appreciate the honesty of the physical performances, and the increasing ease of relating to group members in various in-class projects becomes visible.

Conclusions

Given the scope of this course, which includes several historical periods and many genres of dance, the inclusiveness of dance easily incorporates a multitude of dance forms based on religions, ethnic diversity, and individual points of view. The practical dance aspect of the class can accommodate all individuals regardless of their physical abilities. The movement assignments are simple but meaningful and support the lecture aspect of the course. Those students who are reluctant to verbally articulate their ideas or points of view in class have access in the performance part of class to express themselves physically. I have not had a visually impaired student take this course yet, but I believe that such a person could be easily accommodated and I look forward to that challenge.

References

Wigman, M. (1983). The philosophy of modern dance. In R. Copeland & M. Cohen (Eds.), *What is dance?* (pp. 305–306). New York, NY: Oxford University Press.

Resources

My web site for the tutorial on the early history of modern dance: www.pitt.edu/AFShome/ g/i/gillis/public/html/dance/disp.html

Part IV

Health Sciences

22

Diversity Curricula in Medical Education

Jeannette E. South-Paul

M edical educators realize the importance of exposing students to a dynamic curriculum so that they may meet future population needs. In the late 1990s, faculty and staff of the Minority Affairs Section of the Association of American Medical Colleges (AAMC) recognized the absence of a requirement for curricula related to culture and health disparities. In 2000 their advocacy resulted in the institution of a diversity requirement by the Liaison Committee on Medical Education (LCME), a joint representative body of the AAMC and the American Medical Association that accredits allopathic medical schools. The requirement says:

> The faculty and students must demonstrate an understanding of the manner in which people of diverse cultures and belief systems perceive health and illness and respond to various symptoms, diseases, and treatments. Medical students should learn to recognize and appropriately address gender and cultural biases in health care delivery, while considering first the health of the patient.

Following the establishment of this requirement, it was clear that the desired curricular content needed to be identified. A multidisciplinary group of faculty under the auspices of the AAMC, led by Vanessa Northington Gamble and Deborah Danoff and funded by a grant from the Commonwealth Fund, administered a project to describe the essential elements of a cultural competence curriculum for medical students. The group determined that a comprehensive cultural competence curriculum should contain elements of each of five domains:

1. Cultural competence—rationale, context, and definition

   • Definition and understanding of the importance of cultural competence, of how cultural issues affect health and health care quality and cost, of the consequences of cultural issues

   • Definitions of race, ethnicity, and culture, including the culture of medicine

   • Clinician self-assessment, reflection, and self-awareness of his or her own culture, assumptions, stereotypes, and biases

2. Key aspects of cultural competence

   • Epidemiology of population health

   • Patient/family-centered versus physician-centered care: emphasis on the healing traditions and beliefs of patients and their families (e.g., ethnomedical healers)

3. Understanding the impact of stereotyping on medical decision-making

   • History of stereotyping, including limited access to health care and education

   • Bias, stereotyping, discrimination, and racism

   • Effects of stereotyping on medical decision-making

4. Health disparities and factors influencing health

   • History of health care design and discrimination

   • Epidemiology of specific health and health care disparities

   • Factors underlying health and health care disparities, including access-related, socioeconomic, environmental, institutional, and racial/ethnic factors

   • Demographic patterns of health care disparities, both local and national

   • Collaborating with communities to eliminate disparities through community experiences

5. Cross-cultural clinical skills

   • Knowledge, respect, and validation of differing values, cultures, and beliefs, including sexual orientation, gender, age, race, ethnicity, and class

   • Eliciting a culturally valid social and medical history

   • Communication, interaction, and interviewing skills

   • Understanding language barriers and working with interpreters

   • Negotiating and problem-solving skills

- Diagnosis, management, and patient-adherence skills that lead to patient compliance

The content of those five domains should be augmented by careful communication training. Effective communication is intrinsic to the delivery of satisfactory health care. Good communication plays several roles in health care. It ensures the sharing of key information (diagnosis). It prevents medical accidents (protecting patients). It helps build consensus between providers and patients so that treatment regimens lead to better outcomes (compliance or concordance). Furthermore, good communication improves the use of preventive services (health promotion; Johnson, M. R. D., 2004).

It is logical to assume that communication problems will adversely impact health care delivery. Racial differences in the quality of patient-physician interactions helped explain the observed disparities in satisfaction, but not in the use of health care services, in a study of data from the Commonwealth Fund's Health Care Quality Survey (Saha, Arbelaez, & Cooper, 2003). African-American patients who visit physicians of the same race rate their medical visits as more satisfying and participatory than do those who see physicians of other races (Cooper, 2003). A cohort study comparing patient-physician communication in race-concordant and race-discordant visits demonstrated that race-concordant visits are longer and characterized by more patient positive affect (Cooper, 2003). Previous studies link similar communication findings to continuity of care. The association between race concordance and higher patient ratings of care is independent of patient-centered communication, suggesting that other factors, such as patient and physician attitudes, may mediate the relationship.

Another study found that patient-physician communication during medical visits differs for African-American patients versus European American patients. This investigator examined the association between a patient's race or ethnicity and patient-physician communication during medical visits, using audiotape and questionnaire data. He found that physicians were 23% more verbally dominant and engaged in 33% less patient-centered communication with African-American patients than with European American patients (Johnson, R. L., 2004). Furthermore, both African-American patients and their physicians exhibited lower levels of positive affect than European American patients and their physicians did.

Communication barriers are only one outcome of physician-patient cultural discordance. The recognized lack of attention to cultural issues in the medical school curriculum, as well as obvious disparities in health and health care that seemed to be worse in the face of culturally discordant clinicians and patients, stimulated the addition of more culturally focused instruction in medical school curricula. One of the greatest barriers faced at medical schools across the country is the lack of space in the curriculum for new material. In addition to the need for adding instruction in cultural factors that relate to health and illness, schools are faced with the need to add instruction in genetics, pharmacogenomics, information technology, quality care, patient safety, and bioterrorism. Therefore, it has become clear that cultural sensitivity training must be woven throughout coursework that already has an established place in the curriculum.

Implementation

Experiential sessions related to cultural differences have been incorporated into the medical school curriculum during orientation at the University of Pittsburgh School of Medicine for a number of years. Incoming first-year medical students participate in three half-day sessions during the first week of orientation. One session each is devoted to gender issues, race and ethnicity issues, and gay/lesbian/transgender issues. No further formal didactics were incorporated into the required curriculum thereafter. Recognizing that students who enter medical school undergo a personal and professional transformation during the four-year educational process, a change that rapidly accelerates as they transition from the basic science years to the clinical years, we elected to go beyond just increasing awareness of differences to introducing the clinical environment and its impact on the delivery of health care. This instruction has been provided as three two-hour sessions during the second semester of the first year in the Health, Illness, and Behavior course and as a formal presentation during the third-year Family Medicine clerkship.

The first session offered in the second semester of the first year is titled "The Family and Illness" and describes the influence of chronic illness on the family. A patient with a chronic illness that has required multiple medical encounters and/or hospitalizations is interviewed before the class with close family members. Students are encouraged to query the family regarding their experiences as well as their perceptions of the health care environment. The second session, "Race, Ethnicity and Health," spotlights the subtle and not-so-subtle ways that race and ethnicity influence interactions between patients and clinicians. Videos of problematic interactions between patients and the health care system are used to stimulate discussion and guide problem solving. The third session, "Language Literacy and Illness," demonstrates, through a clinical case, why linguistic competence is critical to the delivery of quality care and patient satisfaction.

Additional educational exposure is provided for students in the clinical years. A one-hour session on cultural competence and health disparities is presented as part of a daylong didactic at the beginning of the required third-year Family Medicine clerkship. Evidence of clinician bias, communication difficulties associated with physician-patient racial or ethnic discordance, and the clinical consequences are presented. Clinical cases are then presented and analyzed by students to identify opportunities for, and to learn strategies for, changing provider behaviors.

Outcomes_____

The experiential sessions that the students attend during orientation require total participation. It's almost impossible to sit on the sidelines. The structure of the sessions, however, is designed to promote self-reflection rather than a critical atmosphere toward one another. By the time students begin the Health, Illness, and Behavior course in the second semester of the first year, they have been heavily immersed in basic science courses (such as anatomy, physiology, and biochemistry) and, therefore, sometime find "soft" courses a distraction. Attendance is light, and some students question why they must devote two hours per week to subjects of such "limited" importance. Feedback from student leaders varies from year to year—sometimes reflecting a disagreement regarding the importance of this material and other times embracing its importance to the degree that they feel attendance should be required.

However, by the time students reach the clinical years and actually become immersed in a patient care environment, a transition is seen. Not only do they seem to accept the importance of the material, but they also often share stories of their own experiences in this area. An assessment of the cultural competence modules in the third-year Family Medicine clerkship over three years showed 1) that most students do not identify with underrepresented or vulnerable groups (more than 70% are European Americans from stable, if not affluent, socioeconomic backgrounds); 2) that they want to be good clinicians and recognize the association between cultural competence and eliciting a good history and caring for the patient; 3) yet this material is still considered "soft" science and less important than "hard" science.

It is clear that the breadth of diversity must be taught and discussed, rather than limiting training to one or two vulnerable groups. To prepare future physicians for the population for whom they will be providing care, the following are important: 1) increased instruction in cultural competence must be placed in the curriculum; 2) this material should be presented in multiple formats and places over time, both in the basic science years and clinical years; 3) instructions should include the link between personal clinician decision-making and the delivery of patient care; 4) faculty must be trained in this content; and 5) more research is needed to expand and clarify the association between cultural competence and health disparities.

References

Cooper, L. A. (2003). Patient-centered communication, ratings of care, and concordance of patient and physician race. *Annals of Internal Medicine, 139*(11), 907–915.

Johnson, M. R. D. (2004). Cross-cultural communication in health. *Clinical Cornerstone, 6*(1), 50–52.

Johnson, R. L. (2004). Patient race/ethnicity and quality of patient-physician communication during medical visits. *American Journal of Public Health, 94*(12), 2084–2090.

Saha, S., Arbelaez, J. J., & Cooper, L. A. (2003). Patient-physician relationships and racial disparities in the quality of health care. *American Journal of Public Health, 93*(10), 1713–1719.

23

Diversifying Medical Ethics

Anita Silvers

A distinctive feature of early 21st-century American society is the great importance assigned to both the triumphs and the failures of the health care system. There is a rarely a day when stories about health care are absent from the nation's newspapers. And encounters with the health care system occur in almost everyone's lives. Some people are in the role of professionals who provide care, but many more are in the role of patients (and their family members) who seek care.

Another distinctive feature of the early 21st century is the diversification of perspectives from which these engagements are portrayed. It is commonplace now for published accounts of particular health care situations to specify sex, age, race or ethnicity, religion, economic status, or other varieties of group identity. These characteristics and affiliations of patients are treated as relevant to the ethical conduct of individual health care professionals and to the justice (or absence of justice) of the health care system in general.

Reflection about the values that should guide decision-making in medicine, and the virtues that should prompt the conduct of professionals and patients (and their families) toward one another, educates students by preparing them for their experiences in the health care system. The main goal of teaching medical ethics, thus, is to prepare students for problematic or challenging situations in which decisions about allocating, withdrawing, or refraining from offering medical intervention have to be made. For this reason, courses in medical ethics should be anchored by the facts of the health care system, both by the clinical details of how modern medicine is practiced and by the concepts and values that shape community standards of medical practice.

Of course, political, social, cultural, and economic conditions that influence the delivery of health care alter precipitously and profoundly, making systematic, ethical decision-making challenging for health care professionals and patients

130

alike. Studying medical ethics mediates students' encounters with the evolving system by helping them reflect on how both general moral values and specialized medical values apply to the complex and often cloudy situations that have become familiar in the provision of health care. By doing so, students learn to stabilize their moral compasses, even when rocked by the uncertainties and terrors of making decisions about their own or other people's medical care.

Medicine has been revolutionized twice in the past 50 years. On the practical side, research and technology have created new capabilities to intervene in human biological processes. To mention just a few such innovations, almost unimaginable in earlier times, physicians now jump-start reproduction outside the human body, replace failing organs, turn previously terminal conditions into chronic ones, and predict with greater and greater precision who will become symptomatic of inherited diseases. Possibly the most challenging expansion of medicine's power has been the ability to preserve life indefinitely in patients with head injuries so severe that they are incapable of interpersonal interaction.

Just as revolutionary, but more on the conceptual side, has been a major shift in thinking about the patient's proper conduct. Expectations of the patient's role have evolved from passive recipient of medical paternalism to autonomous executor of responsibility for deciding about one's own medical care. Even the autonomy of unresponsive patients is respected with a well-developed practice of appointing surrogate decision-makers qualified to represent what the patient herself would, if competent, decide.

It would be presumptuous to suppose that either of these revolutions is at its end. And given the impact of the medical system on people's lives, universities should enable students to understand the challenge of these revolutionary changes to the delivery of medical care. Students should reflect preemptively on what health care decisions their own values recommend, for there is almost no chance that any student will escape involvement with the medical system, whether as a professional, a patient, or a decision-maker for a family member or friend who is a patient.

This focus on individual decision-making requires us to acknowledge the diversity of standpoints. Religious diversity is the most commonly recognized reason for different viewpoints on the benefits of medical interventions. For example, some religions prohibit certain life-saving procedures, such as blood transfusions, and courts recognize the right of competent citizens to sacrifice saving their own lives if it means to them saving their souls. Others promote the sanctity of life over all other considerations. Yet others focus on the responsibility of each person, through the free exercise of will, to choose religious commitments.

Concerns about the ethics of imposing a uniform idea of the good on a diverse population, and about the equality of different groups' participation in various aspects of the health care system, are also central to sensitizing medical practice to the differences of viewpoints attendant on gender, race, and ethnicity. Usually, diversifying medical ethics courses with considerations of gender, race, and ethnicity begins by appealing to the historical treatment of women and minority groups in the medical system. Such study shows students that Western medicine in the past worked with the paradigm that patients were male and white.

As a result, women's common biological differences from men were medicalized—that is, imagined to be pathological. And actual pathologies commonly found in women but infrequent in men were dismissed as imaginary manifestations of excessive female emotionality. Designing pharmaceutical and surgical interventions for men and testing them on men is another result of making men the paradigmatic patient. Until recently, adjusting dosages or techniques to suit physical differences in women has been little more than guesswork.

Medical ethics courses can incorporate material presented from women's perspectives to counter the bias of presumptions about the paradigmatic patient's being male. Female students can contribute to constructing these perspectives by, for example, commenting on historical documents that construe the processes associated with the female reproductive cycle as illnesses or physical defects. Or the syllabus can include critical analyses of the usual reasons for selecting only men as the subjects on whom experimental pharmaceuticals and innovative techniques are tested. Or attention can be drawn to how frequently in medical discourse women are used to illustrate the kind of individual whose life is supposed not to be worth living or who is least deserving of scarce health care resources.

For example, in the early days at some liver transplant centers, men were assigned priority to receive organs on the ground that families needed the income fathers brought home and that hired housekeepers could replace the homemaking that mothers contribute. Understanding that on such nonmedical criteria the women in a medical ethics class would receive inferior care to the men effectively convinces students of both sexes how important diverse perspectives are. Occasionally, a student attempts to defend the bias by hypothesizing that women are less successfully transplanted than men. A lesson about the importance of establishing, rather than speculating about, facts can be taught here. When students are told to search for supporting medical data showing sex to be a factor in liver transplantation success, they discover there are no dispositive facts. They also discover the insidious ease with which plausible-sounding, but undocumented, claims about human biology can be used to rationalize social bias.

Minority racial and ethnic perspectives can be introduced in similar ways. Here it is useful for students to learn about the historical victimization of minority groups that were used as laboratory subjects to facilitate the advancement of medical knowledge. African-American women in the antebellum United States were subjected to brutal procedures to gain information for improving obstetrics and gynecology, syphilitic African-American men in the postbellum United States went untreated to prolong their use as research subjects, and Jews and Gypsies were substituted for laboratory rats by Nazi concentration camp physicians. Recognition that some medical professionals may place certain kinds of people beyond the protection of the Hippocratic prohibition against doing harm gives students an important insight—namely, that being identified with minority groups can make patients especially vulnerable to disregard by, or danger from, the medical system.

The diverse perspectives described so far can be integrated fairly readily into a medical ethics course, and a large amount of reading material has been developed to support this effort. After all, women and racial and ethnic minority members who contribute to the bioethics literature generally accept the conceptual framework that has come to be known as "the medical model." Their main issue is access for their groups to the system governed by the model.

On this model, medical practice presumes that diagnosing pathologies, that identifying the causes of pathological symptoms or sequelae, and that eliminating or mitigating either the causes or their results are the system's goals. No inherent difficulty defies benefiting women and ethnic and racial minorities in pursuit of these goals. Doing so is mostly a matter of exercising moral sensibility and political will to give them equitable access to the system's resources.

The perspectives of another important minority group are not so easily integrated into medical ethics courses, however. Many people with disabilities, as well as the majority of scholars of disability studies, condemn the medical model as discriminatory. The focus on curing patients, on making them seem as normal as possible if no cure is available, or on applying medical knowledge to prevent people with higher risk of illness or disability from even being born devalues individuals with chronic illness or disabling conditions. Individuals like these frustrate health care practiced according to the medical model because they inherently defy attaining what the model presumes to be medicine's goals.

Traditional medical ethics courses embrace the medical model because it captures the values on which the current health care system appears to rest. Health care has been promoted as being specially placed to command a large share of resources not just because it is able to save lives (comparatively few health conditions are imminently life threatening) but because life with illness or disability is judged not worth living, or significantly less worthwhile than a perfectly healthy life. Resources might be less readily directed to medicine if it were not for the idea that the health care system saves people from death or from a life of illness or disability that is worse than death. In the same vein, the risks attendant on medical intervention would be less readily accepted or downplayed if people who could not be cured, or at least altered enough to pass as normal, nevertheless were seen as living acceptable lives.

Both perspectives possess some legitimacy, for some people can be disabled or chronically ill and yet thrive and others wither from stress and loss. It can be difficult to introduce the minority view, however, because so much of the literature of medical ethics assumes the medical model. Essays by individuals with various chronic conditions or disabilities are enormously stimulating to students' reflection, for they force reevaluation of how social as well as biological factors contribute to well- or ill-being when people experience health or other physical or mental deficits. These writers often question whether resources should be focused so uniformly on biological rather than on social interventions.

There are many essays by such authors that show that maintaining social participation, despite having a physical or mental deficit, in identity-building areas of life (such as family and friends, employment, and education) is crucial to thriving. The presence of class members with experiences of chronic illness or disability may contribute additional perspectives to this conversation. For instance, my own classes' discussions about whether to maintain life in preterm neonates who are at high risk of physical disability are nuanced by there being a professor with a serious physical disability in the classroom.

Appreciating the perspectives of the disabled and chronically ill prompts students to consider the organization of the medical system itself—to question, for example, whether the delivery of health care should be made compatible with maintaining ordinary activities or whether receiving medical care should become, for those who need it, life's dominating or exclusive pursuit. The thoughtfulness of community responses to questions like this will influence the future of health care. And in an age when enhanced understanding of the mechanisms of biological inheritance can mark out individuals who are at heightened risk for disease even when they are not, and possibly may never become, symptomatic, community responses to questions about the value of lives lived with chronic illness or disability may determine how much opportunity, including opportunity to obtain continuing health care, will be afforded to the many individuals identified with one of the genetically compromised groups.

Having for more than a decade taught a medical ethics course organized around the perspectives of vulnerable populations, with special attention to the disabled and chronically ill, I know some students cannot convince themselves that life's satisfactions can be achieved in the absence of undiminished health, whereas others are equally impervious to persuasion about the preeminent importance of full health. But the point of teaching medical ethics from multiple group standpoints is not to proselytize students into changing their perspectives, but rather to make them aware of perspectives that may not be their own. Recognizing different perspectives facilitates ethical decision-making in medicine by deterring the imposition of health care choices on those who would not make the same choices for themselves. Moreover, when those with a role in determining what medical intervention to pursue—health care professionals, patients, and family members and friends with different degrees of relationship to the patient— differ about the morally right thing to do, a first step to mediation, and sometimes to reconciliation, is to appreciate the differences of perspective that inspire differences of choice. Diversifying medical ethics courses is, therefore, not only the right thing to do, but also the prudent thing to do. For a citizenry more open to biological difference will be more prepared for the emerging ethical challenges that are sure to press us as the medical system continues to change.

24

Transforming a Public Health Curriculum for the 21st Century

*Martha Ann Terry, Robert M. Goodman,
Ravi K. Sharma, Kenneth J. Jaros*

Public health, by its nature, is concerned with diversity because it addresses conditions and situations that afflict some of the United States' and the world's poorest and most underserved populations. These are, in many cases, people of color, people with alternative lifestyles, women, and the very young and the very old. Concerns regarding the link between health disparities and diversity are codified in *Healthy People 2010: Objectives for the Nation* (U.S. Department of Health and Human Services [HHS], 2000), the HSS's latest ten-year plan, which makes the reduction of health disparities a top priority. Similarly, other contemporary policy pronouncements regarding modern public health training programs assert that students should be exposed to a curriculum that integrates issues of diversity and cultural competence (e.g., Association of Schools of Public Health [ASPH], 2006; Institute of Medicine, 2003).

The Institute of Medicine (IOM) report (2003) details strategies for reducing the gap by taking an ecological, or multifaceted, approach to public health actions. It requires health professionals in training to attain an interdisciplinary education that focuses on the health of populations and an understanding of social determinants of health, such as poverty, age, race, ethnicity, access to health care, and quality of education, to name a few. The ecological approach also holds that complex health issues require multiple linked interventions across social strata—the individual, the family, social networks, the community, organizations, and policy (McLeroy, Bibeau, Steckler, & Glanz, 1988). Thus, training programs must require an understanding that effective interventions entail not only biological causal factors and behaviors but also the social, cultural, economic, and environmental contexts within which populations live.

The IOM report (2003) additionally emphasized community-based participatory approaches to program planning, implementation, and evaluation to reduce the distance between professional planners and community members. Working with communities to determine their needs and help build capacity requires public health professionals who not only have a strong educational foundation but also have training in working with diverse communities, including an awareness of, and respect for, cultural differences.

The community-based participatory approach is but one of several areas that the IOM report recommends as innovative for training in the 21st century. Others include communication, informatics, genomics, policy and law, global health, cultural competence, and public health ethics. In concert, the ASPH (2006) developed a set of professional competencies for master of public health (MPH) candidates to attain before graduation that are based largely on the areas included in the IOM report.

In accordance with the movement toward greater focus on diversity, health disparities, and ecological and community-based approaches, the Department of Behavioral and Community Health Sciences (BCHS) at the University of Pittsburgh's Graduate School of Public Health embarked on a curriculum revision of its entire MPH degree program. The process began in 2002, at which time the BCHS curriculum committee began to review requirements in the behavioral and social sciences at other schools of public health. The arrival in 2003 of a new department chair, hired from another school of public health, provided additional impetus to approach curriculum renewal with a critical view from the outside. By 2007, the process resulted in several innovations, including an entirely revamped set of core requirements for the MPH program, professional certificate programs in important areas of concentration, renting space at a multiservice community agency from which to operate service-learning and other educational approaches, and organized community field experiences that occur outside the classroom. This paper highlights why and how the curriculum changes were made, and how, in combination with other educational innovations, the newly structured program addresses diversity and health disparities.

Curriculum Revision and Development

Table 24.1 indicates the required courses, or core BCHS curriculum, before and after revisions were made. On the surface, the following changes are of note. Two previously required courses were retained: Theories of Health Behavior and Education and Community Health Assessment (in italics, Table 24.1). And both courses were raised from two to three credit hours (in bold, Table 24.1), along with all the new requirements. Other courses were dropped from the requirements and became electives (Health Survey Methods and Political and Legal Factors in Public Health). Health Program Evaluation and Ethnographic Methods of Evaluation were combined into the new Introduction to Applied Research Methods. Community Development Approaches to Public Health, Health Program Planning, and Health Communication were newly developed and added to the core.

Table 24.1

Core Curricula Comparison

Former Curriculum	New Curriculum
Health Behavior and Education Theories (**2 credits**)	*Health Behavior and Education Theories* (**3 credits**)
Health Survey Methods (2 credits)	Introduction to Applied Research Methods (3 credits)
Health Program Evaluation (2 credits)	
Community Health Assessment (**2 credits**)	*Community Health Assessment* (**3 credits**)
Ethnographic Methods of Evaluation (3 credits)	Health Communication (3 credits)
	Health Program Planning (3 credits)
Political and Legal Factors in Public Health (2 credits)	Community Development Approaches to Public Health (3 credits)

The deeper reasons behind such changes stem from a reorientation of the BCHS department from a combined focus with the health services. Before 2000, BCHS was a unit of the Department of Health Services Management within the School of Public Health. At the last accreditation review of the school (in 1999), the Council on Education for Public Health, the accrediting body, called for an independent department in the social and behavioral sciences, thus resulting in BCHS. Some of the changes, including turning the survey research and policy courses into electives, resulted from a shift in orientation when BCHS separated from Health Services. Although the curriculum committee recognized the importance of these courses, it felt that, within the confines of a limited number of credit hours devoted to required courses, other courses took priority to focus more on diversity and health disparities. Thus, a new course in community public health was developed to expose students to methods for working cross-culturally with diverse community groups. The new program planning course emphasizes social (and not solely quantitative) representations of health and quality of life in different cultures, teaches techniques of eliciting diverse framings of community needs and strengths, and joins forces with a local partner in a minority community. The new communication course emphasizes techniques in cross-cultural communication and in conveying public health concerns in culturally appropriate ways.

Revised courses, such as applied research, were altered to incorporate a foundation for participatory research approaches—that is, those approaches that involve community members in defining the research objectives and participating in all aspects of the research. The theory course was expanded to become more comprehensive in covering not only approaches to changing human behavior but also theories around community and policy change with a focus on health disparities, thus becoming more ecological in orientation. Similarly, the health assessment course began to incorporate real-world data collection methods based on requests from groups like a local alliance for the homeless. In all, core curriculum revisions were geared to providing all MPH students with a corpus of knowledge that is oriented to reducing health disparities in cross-cultural settings.

To develop the curriculum revisions, faculty were assigned to committees corresponding to each of the courses to be designed and based on faculty expertise and interest. Also, students were asked to join each of the four committees to enrich faculty perspectives. Each committee developed a syllabus for one of the new courses, which was then approved by all BCHS faculty, who were given several opportunities to provide feedback before the submission of the revised curriculum for the necessary approval at the school and university levels.

Once approved, the new core curriculum necessitated a review and restructuring of teaching assignments, with decisions about teaching responsibility based on faculty expertise and interest. But even using existing faculty, the department recognized that it would need to add to its numbers to effectively implement many of the new courses. The BCHS department was fortunate to obtain 10 new faculty slots through different funding mechanisms to revamp its program. Expertise in areas addressed by core courses was a critical consideration in making new faculty hires.

As we made course revisions, we also considered strategies for paying attention to different learning styles and emphasizing various skills, such as comprehension, abstraction, synthesis, presentation, and written analysis. Faculty were encouraged to consult with the university's instructional design support for ways to address learning styles and to incorporate skills into course learning objectives.

We also considered the ASPH (2006) core competencies for departments in social and behavioral sciences to ensure the relevance of the core curriculum and to be more accountable for the training and education that students receive (see Table 24.2). We are developing the format for a student portfolio, which students and their advisors will use to monitor progress through the program and to identify both areas in which students have had the opportunity to acquire skills and competencies and areas in which they need additional training.

Table 24.2

Competencies and Relevant Courses

Social and Behavioral Sciences Competencies	Relevant BCHS Course(s)
Describe the role of social and community factors in the onset and solution of public health problems	
Identify causes of social and behavioral factors that affect health of individuals and populations	Health Behavior and Education Theories
Identify basic theories, concepts, and models from a range of social and behavioral disciplines that are used in public health research and practice	Health Behavior and Education Theories
Apply ethical principles to public health program planning, implementation, and evaluation	Health Program Planning
Specify targets and levels of intervention for social and behavioral programs and/or policies	Health Behavior and Education Theories Health Program Planning
Identify individual, organization, and community concerns, assets, resources, and challenges	Community Health Assessment
Apply evidence-based approaches in developing and evaluating social and behavioral interventions	Introduction to Applied Research Methods
Describe merits of social and behavioral science interventions and policies	
Describe steps and procedures for planning, implementing, and evaluating public health programs, policies, and interventions	Health Program Planning Community Health Assessment Introduction to Applied Research Methods
Identify stakeholders for planning, implementing, and evaluating public health programs, policies, and interventions	Community Development Approaches to Public Health Community Health Assessment

Certificate Programs and the Practicum

Along with revisions in the core curriculum, BCHS extended its learning approach by developing professional certificate programs. The University of Pittsburgh has a provision for specialized programs at the graduate level that consist of 15 credit hours. A certificate can be taken in conjunction with a degree program (although attaining one requires additional credit hours), or it can be taken for career advancement by those who qualify for entry into a graduate program but may already hold a professional position. The certificate represents the attainment of an area of specialization. BCHS already offered a certificate in public health and aging. Considering the present emphasis on health disparities and diversity, BCHS partnered with the Center for Minority Health (CMH) at the Graduate School of Public Health, which has a mission to provide leadership in working with diverse communities. Together, BCHS and CMH developed a certificate in Minority Health and Health Disparities that focuses on cultural diversity and competence in doing public health work in communities that experience health disparities. Similarly, BCHS developed a certificate program in Evaluation of Public Health Programs that provides students with a skill set in assisting community service organizations with evaluation data to help improve local programming, which often serves those communities of greatest need. In addition to the current certificates, others are planned for Community-Based Participatory Practice and Lesbian/Gay/Bisexual/Transgendered Health Issues, the first of its kind to be offered through a school of public health. A common thread among these programs is the emphasis on embracing methods that contribute to the health and well-being of diverse population groups.

Those MPH students who are not enrolled in a certificate program must participate in a practicum experience. The practicum is designed to give students an opportunity to apply knowledge and skills that they have learned in the classroom in a real-life public health setting. But, unlike the certificate program, the practicum currently requires 120 hours of service, a relatively short duration. Among the projects students have completed include the following:

- Design and implement a telephone survey of clients of western Pennsylvania well-baby clinics to determine where clients sought health care subsequent to the clinics' closing

- Develop and implement an educational sexually transmitted disease or HIV prevention curriculum for homeless women

- Develop and implement an educational nutrition and exercise program for pregnant teens

- Evaluate an HIV/AIDS prevention and treatment program in rural Tanzania using ethnography

- Plan and coordinate a conference on schizophrenia for rural mental health care providers

- Design, facilitate, and analyze focus groups evaluating an internship program

- Prepare an educational CD on community health assessment

- Interview Haitians about their use of traditional healers and assess barriers to accessing hospital services

- Develop progress and outcome measures for clients of a program that provides housing and support services to homeless women

- Design and conduct a process evaluation plan for an intervention program for pregnant women with developmental or mental disabilities

As a result of the curriculum revision, practicum requirements have been made more rigorous by increasing the number of contact hours (potentially to 400 hours), instituting more formal evaluation procedures, and requiring a final paper. In addition, a full-time coordinator of community affairs has been hired, who directly oversees students fulfilling the practicum requirement, among other responsibilities. She is establishing relationships with new agencies and strengthening those with agencies already in our network, many of which serve minority and underserved populations. Her work has significantly increased opportunities for practicum experiences with these groups.

Community Relationships

Core education and certificate programs provide, respectively, a basis for practicing public health in diverse settings and a deeper set of practice skills in partnering with community organizations and groups. Ultimately, to be effective in training, the educational experience must transcend the classroom and occur in diverse community settings. The ASPH (2004) advocates that a service-learning approach be incorporated into professional training. Service-learning entails the coupling of classroom-based learning with on-the-job real-world experience for students who are assigned to work part-time in service organizations as part of the degree experience. To facilitate a service-learning approach, the BCHS department contracted with Hosanna House, a community-based social service organization located in an economically underserved community about five miles west of the university. This collaboration has resulted in an initiative to "bring the university to the community and the community to the university." That goal is accomplished in a number of ways. First, Hosanna House provides 3,000 square feet of rental space to BCHS for BCHS to offer its required community public health and needs assessment courses to MPH students. Thus, as part of the core learning experience, students are placed in a diverse community setting that is multiethnic and largely poor. Additionally, the BCHS space at Hosanna House contains a bank of office modules for students working within the certificate programs, carrying out other service-learning activities, or working with faculty on community-partnered projects. The space also includes a lounge and drop-in area where students can meet with community members. In essence, by actually living in rental space within a community organization, students' classroom education is augmented by immersion into actual community enterprises.

Organized Community Field Experiences

Because public health is an applied discipline, much of contemporary training is focused on the health of population groups, reducing health disparities, working with diverse groups, and being highly participatory. To integrate these areas into training, the BCHS faculty coupled curriculum revision of formal courses with experience in applied community settings. To augment the experiential aspects of learning, the BCHS department initiated organized field experiences as extracurricular activities. The department contracts with a former president of a local health care philanthropic foundation who has worked on community health issues across the region for the past 40 years. Because of his contacts, he is able to arrange informal sessions with heads of local philanthropic foundations, elected officials, spiritual centers, and others who are influential. The activities take place twice a month, usually alternating between a field trip to a relevant organization in the region and an after-dinner meeting with an important local political figure at the department chair's house. Students and faculty attend on a voluntary basis. The purpose of these sessions is to provide opportunities for the students to meet in diverse community settings and with leaders who can serve as role models for professional practice in a manner that is not possible within the classroom. The sessions have become quite popular and are attended by 15–20 students on average.

Discussion and Conclusion

The process of curriculum revision in BCHS has had several positive results:

- The curriculum is more integrated and purposeful.

- Coursework and experiential learning train master's students in core skills and values that align with the department's mission of working with communities to improve their health and with the department's commitment to social justice.

- Students are exposed to issues about diversity and disparities through several opportunities for community-based apprenticeships and field experiences.

Several lessons can be taken from BCHS's experience in curriculum revision for diversity. First, guiding policy documents can be a strategic catalyst for curriculum reform. Having reports from influential bodies like the IOM and the ASPH created a climate in which innovation could take place. Second, having a receptive faculty, one engaged in the process, facilitated active participation, ownership, and implementation. Third, support for curriculum innovation is critical both at the department chair level, which championed many of the new extracurricular innovations, and at the dean's level, which paved the way for growth in faculty positions. Fourth, adding components to the curriculum that are not course bound exposes students to a diverse mix of public health issues and to people who grapple with such issues.

In conclusion, the curriculum revision process in BCHS took several years to complete, and it is questionable whether it can ever be totally finished. Public health is a discipline that engenders constant and dynamic change. Three decades ago, the world had no inkling of HIV and AIDS. Our current concerns about bioterrorism were hardly a matter for national debate. The methods for rapid communication like the Internet were only a dream. To stay current in an ever-changing world, public health professionals must be trained to be responsive and flexible. Well-trained public health professionals in the 21st century are imbued to be responsive to emergent and diverse public health issues that are approached differently in different community settings. The focus on flexibility is to ensure that, when working with diverse groups, the trained professional applies innovative solutions to health concerns based on local conditions. Thus, the changes incorporated into the curriculum are calculated to produce practitioners who may be versatile in applying their skills to a broad range of health issues in diverse community settings.

References

Association of Schools of Public Health. (2004). *Demonstrating excellence in practice-based teaching for public health.* Washington, DC: Author.

Association of Schools of Public Health. (2006). *Master's degree in public health core competency development project.* Retrieved February 22, 2007, from www.asph.org/competency

Institute of Medicine. (2003). *Who will keep the public healthy? Educating public health professionals for the 21st century* (K. Gebbie, L. Rosenstock, & L. M. Hernandez, Eds.). Washington, DC: National Academies Press.

McLeroy, K. R., Bibeau, D., Steckler, A., & Glanz, K. (1988). An ecological perspective on health promotion programs. *Health Education Quarterly, 15,* 351–377.

U.S. Department of Health and Human Services. (2000). *Healthy people 2010.* Retrieved February 22, 2007, from www.healthypeople.gov

25

Dialogues on Diversity in Speech-Language Pathology: Not a Job for the Faint of Heart

Shelly S. Chabon, Dorian Lee-Wilkerson

Our role as educators is to help our students to understand their role as inter-preters of the culture who are, in the process, regenerating that culture. As we move toward a multicultural society, the demands on those generating that new culture are indeed bewildering. This challenge is not a job for the faint of heart. (Cone & Harris, 2003)

Approximately 20 years ago, the American Speech-Language-Hearing Association (ASHA) adopted a resolution that "encouraged undergraduate, graduate and continuing education programs to include specific information, course content and/or clinical practica which address the communication needs of individuals within socially, culturally, economically and linguistically diverse populations" (Committee on the Status of Racial Minorities, 1987). By 1994, ASHA strengthened this position and required accredited programs to provide evidence of multicultural/multilingual content in the academic and clinical curricula (Committee on the Status of Racial Minorities, 1987). As might be expected, this mandate led to an increase in the number and variety of pedagogical approaches and educational models used to prepare communication sciences and disorders (CSD) students for work in a multicultural society (Stockman, Boult, & Robinson, 2004). In 2004, ASHA described the knowledge and skills needed by speech-language pathologists and audiologists to provide culturally and linguistically appropriate services (ASHA, 2004). These acts were stimulated in large part by the recognition that the demographic composition of this country has diversified and will continue to diversify, even though the percentage of ASHA members from culturally and linguistically diverse groups has remained low. Zeichner (1992) acknowledged this population shift and asserted that although the growing disparity between teachers, teacher educators, and students is the area that has received the most attention in the literature, it is the quality of instruction offered by these teachers that should be the focus of scholarly work.

Energized by our profession's commitment to diversity and our own personal experiences and convictions, both of us began discussions about how best to educate our students to be culturally aware and responsive. We had both taught courses of a theoretical and/or applied nature that addressed, to varying degrees, multicultural/multilingual issues. As observed by others (e.g., Zeichner, 1992), our classes at Rockhurst University and Hampton University were distinctly different in their homogeneity. The Rockhurst University students were primarily white, monolingual, and female, whereas the Hampton University students were primarily African-American, monolingual, and female. Our obligation was clear, but our plan was uncertain. Thus, the courses Dialogues on Diversity I and II, which are described in this chapter, emerged from our awareness of the need to educate our students about multicultural issues to best serve a growing diverse population, from our dissatisfaction with the lack of campus diversity and with traditional lecture-based methods, and from our desire to move information about working with diverse populations from a marginal to a central position in our students' education.

Course Description

Dialogues on Diversity (DOD) is offered as an inter-institutional, two-course sequence by the CSD departments at Rockhurst University and Hampton University. The first course, DOD I, focuses on developing awareness of self and others and on fostering cultural responsiveness. Students from the two institutions engage in in-class and online discussions, participate in diversity training activities, and complete reflection journals as they learn more about their own and each other's cultural heritages, feelings, beliefs, and experiences. The second course, DOD II, focuses on the application of skills and knowledge acquired during the first semester. Problem-based learning is used to promote collaboration among inter-institutional teams in active case analyses involving clients of culturally diverse backgrounds.

Course Design and Course Objectives

We designed Dialogues on Diversity to foster significant learning among students about cultural sensitivity and cultural responsiveness. According to Fink (2003), significant learning is often related to six broad goals: 1) foundational knowledge, 2) skill development, 3) integration of knowledge, 4) responsiveness to human relations 5) professional and ethical competency, and 6) skill in self-directed learning. The course objectives for DOD I and II related to these learning goals are listed in Tables 25.1 and 25.2.

Table 25.1

Dialogues on Diversity I: Course Objectives

Foundational Knowledge	Explain basic concepts and terminology required for understanding and learning from other cultures and apply skills and concepts learned in discussions.
Responsiveness to Human Relations	Critically examine stereotypes, prejudices, discrimination, and racism. Identify the unique characteristics of diverse individuals while becoming more cognizant of the characteristics, cultural views, customs, and history of a variety of groups. Describe and explain how different cultural histories, values, beliefs, and languages influence perceptions of, and participation in, the clinical process; and discuss ways to learn from and appreciate different perspectives.
Professional and Ethical Competency	Identify the qualities and skills needed to be successful in working with diverse populations. Reflect on discussions, readings, learning, and personal experiences in relation to diverse populations through open, constructive dialogue with multiple challenging perspectives, and through writing assignments.
Skill in Self-Directed Learning	Be interested and confident enough to increase opportunities for, and skills, in cross-cultural communication.

Table 25.2

Dialogues on Diversity II: Course Objectives

Foundational Knowledge	Describe cultural competence as officially defined in the ASHA (2004) document, *Knowledge and Skills Needed by Speech-Language Pathologists and Audiologists Providing Services to Culturally and Linguistically Diverse Clients/Patients.*
Skill Development	Identify steps involved in developing cultural competence. Apply successful cross-cultural communication with peers. Apply the knowledge and skills required for planning treatment for individuals from culturally and linguistically diverse backgrounds. Describe and apply the knowledge and skills important in the training of, and in collaborating with, interpreters and translators in the assessment and intervention of individuals from culturally and linguistically diverse backgrounds.

Class Outline

The sequence of course content in DOD I included discussions of the concepts of culture, race, and ethnicity. We talked about and searched for examples of the ways cultural values and beliefs guide how we interact with others in all settings, focusing the major portion of our discussions on the clinical context. We explored the origins and impacts of stereotypes, institutional racism, test bias, and culture shock. We ended the course with discussions about the need for developing cultural competence and suggested steps for doing so. In DOD II, students spent the majority of course time in asynchronous online threaded discussions about a diverse client with a communication disorder. Inter-institutional teams of Rockhurst University and Hampton University students met online with course instructors to consider aspects of the case as well as the cultural sensitivity and responsiveness of the clinician. Discussion proceeded from analysis of the referral, the intake process and the case history, and the gathering and interpreting of assessment data; it culminated with an analysis of the treatment plan and the exit interview with the client and client's family. Every three weeks, Rockhurst University and Hampton University students met in class with their respective instructor to reflect on the team's functions and the results of the threaded discussions.

Content and Methods/Instructional Strategies

Our challenge in designing DOD I and II was to select course content and instructional strategies that would meet course objectives and student learning goals. Our courses needed to stimulate real dialogue about multicultural issues among students, to prompt students to engage in meaningful research and reflection about multicultural issues, to encourage students to examine their personal beliefs, and to assist students with gaining the knowledge and skills needed for working with culturally and linguistically diverse (CLD) populations. We realized that our students formed two homogenous groups, one predominately Caucasian and one African-American, and that if engaged in discussion about multicultural issues, they might find it difficult to offer, view, and understand multiple cultural perspectives. By linking our students over the Internet, we were able to form a diverse learning community that encouraged open dialogue about culture, cultural differences, cultural sensitivity, cultural responsiveness, and the impact of these factors on clinical processes. Our use of the online learning environment allowed students to engage in conversations with diverse peers; to view themselves and their diverse peers as having valued information to be shared; to view themselves and their diverse peers as change agents that questioned and challenged existing assumptions about race, ethnicity, and culture; and to collaborate with diverse team members and make connections with one another (Hewett & Ehmann, 2004).

Although an online learning environment allowed us to offer course content from multiple cultural perspectives and stimulate dialogue about diversity, it was not used to simulate all the nuances that characterize intercultural interactions as they naturally occur. Consequently, we required that students complete home assignments, encouraging them to immerse themselves in cultures different from their own and reflect on those experiences. We also engaged students in scientific inquiry so they could interpret and critique the existing literature on clinical practice with diverse communities and could construct new knowledge about the roles culture plays in diverse clinical settings as suggested by Archbald and Newmann (as cited in Micheller, 2002). Finally, we used in-class learning activities to help students to make connections between what they were learning online, in the community, and through lectures, discussions, readings, and videos and to express their feelings about the educational process.

In DOD I, inter-institutional teams of African-American and Caucasian students used online discussion threads to learn about the principles of effective intercultural communication and to apply those principles during asynchronous interactions with one another as they discussed values, beliefs, stereotypes, and bias. Instructor-posted threaded discussions also prompted students to share their culture, cultural histories, how their cultural histories may have shaped personal views, and how their personal views may influence professional practice. Students also shared best and worst moments of intercultural encounters and their reflections about these activities.

In DOD I, students' at-home learning projects included completing an ethnographic investigation of their own cultures, and of professionals whose cultural backgrounds were different from theirs, and participating in immersion experiences in a culture different from their own. Home activities also involved viewing videos or reading books written by or about members of cultural groups different from their own, attending a religious service different from their own faith, eating at an ethnic restaurant, and/or visiting diverse communities. In-class learning experiences engaged students in real and simulated intercultural encounters. Exercises were used that helped students to discover their unique values as well as those shared with one another, to learn more about their own cultural histories, and to reflect on feelings associated with culture shock. Students discussed videos, books, and articles to better appreciate and understand multiple perspectives in problem solving and decision-making.

In DOD II, we selected exercises focused on problem-based learning, research, and self-reflection to develop knowledge and skills in approaching the clinical intervention process with cultural competence using online, in-class, and at-home learning environments. About half the course was devoted to the use of online problem-based learning. Using the WebCT, inter-institutional teams collaborated in active case analyses involving individuals with communication disorders from culturally and linguistically diverse backgrounds. Each week, instructors posted a summary of information online based on actual clients and one or more discussion threads addressing a problem about the case for the team to solve. At the end of each week, a student (the group "reporter") summarized the results of the team's collaboration, and the instructor provided feedback about the clarity, cultural sensitivity, and cultural responsiveness of team communications. Threaded discussions prompted students to collaborate when addressing the clinical problems posed, such as client access to services, acceptability of services for different cultural groups, culturally biased assessment and treatment approaches, alternative approaches for assessment and treatment of CLD populations, and use of best evidence for planning assessment and treatment of CLD populations. In-class learning activities in DOD II were more limited than in DOD I. Students heard from persons with communication disorders, from disability experts, and from professional interpreters about the unique experiences of, and special challenges faced by, CLD persons with communication disorders. Students also engaged in in-class group reflection about each of these presentations.

At-home learning activities for DOD II involved maintaining a journal. Over the course of the semester, students submitted a minimum of three (approximately one per month) written reflections about the threaded or class discussions and activities, course-embedded events, or relevant interactions that occurred outside the classroom. Students then rated their own and each other's reflections using a rubric created by the course instructors and students in previous DOD classes.

Students were also required to complete three research projects as at-home learning activities. First, each student researched the need for the profession of speech-language pathology to strengthen its database to support evidence-based practice when working with culturally and linguistically diverse populations. Each student selected a communication disorder to develop a file of useful clinical evidence relevant for a particular cultural/linguistic group. Students gathered evidence of etiologies, incidence, and prevalence and how these data may vary, as well as how characteristics of the communication disorder (including articulation/phonology, voice/resonance, fluency, and language characteristics) may be expressed for the group selected. Information about the physical, cognitive, social, and emotional impacts of the communication disorder within the population studied was also included. Students also sought evidence of efficacious assessment and treatment strategies and of documented treatment outcomes. The last section of the file contained a needs statement listing areas where support for evidence-based clinical practice was lacking. The second at-home research activity required that each student complete a critical incident study. Students interviewed two practicing CSD professionals about perceived behaviors associated with culturally sensitive and culturally insensitive professional practice. Students then collaborated with one another to develop a list of culturally competent clinical skills for comparison with the ASHA (2004) knowledge and skills document. Students also reviewed the existing literature in health and education on the cultural appropriateness of treatment plans to devise an evaluation rubric as a research application at-home learning activity. (See ASHA, 2004; Coleman, 1999; Cummings-James, 2000; Lynch & Hanson, 2004.)

Evaluation and Indicators of Learning

Among the most important aspects of these courses was developing good indicators of learning. According to Newmann and Associates (as cited in Micheller, 2002), "authentic" learning occurs when students are able to interpret and evaluate knowledge, formulate new ideas, engage in scientific inquiry, and value their learning beyond the classroom. We believe that the four indicators of learning selected not only assessed student outcomes as they related to course objectives but also fostered "authentic achievement" as defined by Newmann and Associates. Indicators of learning (see Tables 25.3 and 25.4) included pre and post surveys and several learning products, including reflection journals, student-produced original artifacts, and active engagement in online threaded discussions.

Table 25.3

Dialogues on Diversity I: Assessment of Student Learning

Course Objectives	Learning Indicator	Assessment Criteria
Explain basic concepts and terminology required for understanding and learning from other cultures and apply skills and concepts learned in discussions.	• Ethnographic investigations • Reflection journals • Participation in online threaded discussions	• B or better on course projects • Timely completion of all online assignments, journal entries, and inter-institutional activities • Active participation
Critically examine stereotypes, prejudices, discrimination, and racism.	• Book or video review • Reflection journals • Participation in online threaded discussions	• B or better on course projects • Timely completion of all online assignments, journal entries, and inter-institutional activities
Identify the unique characteristics of diverse individuals while becoming more cognizant of the characteristics, cultural views, customs, and history of a variety of groups.	• Ethnographic investigations • Reflection journals • Participation in online threaded discussions	• B or better on course projects • Timely completion of all online assignments, journal entries, and inter-institutional activities
Describe and explain how different cultural histories, values, beliefs, and languages influence perceptions of, and participation in, the clinical process; and discuss ways to learn from and appreciate different perspectives.	• Ethnographic investigations • Reflection journals • Participation in online and in-class discussions	• B or better on course projects • Timely completion of all online assignments, journal entries, and inter-institutional activities
Be interested and confident enough to increase opportunities for, and skills in, cross-cultural communication.	• Immersion experience • Reflection journals • Participation in online and in-class discussions	• B or better on course projects • Timely completion of all online assignments, journal entries, and inter-institutional activities
Identify the qualities and skills needed to be successful in working with diverse populations.	• Ethnographic investigations • Reflection journals • Participation in online and in-class discussions	• B or better on course projects • Timely completion of all online assignments, journal entries, and inter-institutional activities
Reflect on discussions, readings, learning, and personal experiences in relation to diverse populations through open, constructive dialogue with multiple challenging perspectives and through writing assignments.	• Reflection journals • Participation in online and in-class discussions	• B or better on course projects • Timely completion of all online assignments, journal entries, and inter-institutional activities

Table 25.4

Dialogues on Diversity II: Assessment of Student Learning

Course Objectives	Learning Indicator	Assessment Criteria
Describe cultural competence as officially defined in the ASHA (2004) document titled *Knowledge and Skills Needed by Speech-Language Pathologists and Audiologists Providing Services to Culturally and Linguistically Diverse Clients/Patients.*	• Participation in online and class discussion	• Active participation
Identify steps involved in developing cultural competence.	• Participate in online and class discussion • Completion of critical incident surveys and summary report	• Active participation • Timely and appropriate completion of critical incident survey report
Apply successful cross-cultural communication with peers.	• Completion of online case analysis via active collaboration with inter-institutional team • Participation in online threaded discussions	• Timely and successful completion of inter-institutional activities and online assignments. • Active participation
Apply the knowledge and skills required for planning treatment for individuals from CLD backgrounds.	• Completion of online case analysis via active collaboration with inter-institutional team • Completion of a needs assessment • Development of a treatment plan evaluation rubric • Participation in online discussions	• Timely and appropriate completion of treatment plans. • Timely and appropriate completion of a needs assessment project and development of a treatment plan evaluation rubric • Active participation
Describe and apply the knowledge and skills important in the training of, and in collaborating with, interpreters and translators in the assessment and intervention of individuals from CLD backgrounds.	• Participation in online and in-class discussions; completed readings; meetings with interpreters/translators; successfully adapted clinical interpretations or recommendations to families • Complete needs assessment	• Active discussion and collaboration • Timely and appropriate completion of needs assessment project

Pre and Post Surveys

Students completed a self-confidence rating scale at the beginning and end of each course to assess their growth in comfort when working with clients and families of CLD backgrounds. On this scale, students reported their level of confidence in working with CLD populations, ranging from extremely low to extremely high, and described factors that contributed to their selected rating.

Students also described their best and worst moments in class and their past and future challenges in developing cultural competency. This post-assessment discussion provided evidence, albeit in anecdotal form, that cultural competence can be taught and that diversity training works.

Online Threaded Discussions

In DOD I and II, online threaded discussions were used both to support and evaluate learning (Newmann & Associates, 1996). As a learning product, our evaluative criteria for grading participation in online discussions included:

- Weekly postings of two or more responses to discussion threads

- Using assigned readings, course lectures, and/or class discussions to support posted statements during threaded discussions

- Using clinical or personal experiences to support posted statements during threaded discussions

Varied Learning Artifacts

As a third indicator of learning, we evaluated the original artifacts students produced in DOD I and II. These artifacts included written ethnographic reports, summaries and analysis of critical incident studies, development of a treatment plan evaluation rubric, and a summary of a needs assessment for the profession.

Reflection Journals

We also used the critiques of the reflection journals students submitted in DOD I and II as a fourth indicator of learning. In DOD I, instructors critiqued reflections about course experiences and learning according to cognitive level (i.e., descriptive, empathic, analytic, and metacognitive) and achievement level (i.e., emerging, proficient, and advanced), using a grading rubric created through student-instructor collaboration (see Table 25.5). In DOD II, both students and instructors critiqued the reflections using the rubric.

Table 25.5

Rubric Used to Evaluate Reflection Journals

This rubric allows course instructors to capture data related to students' expression of cultural competence in four dimensions of reflection. It is anticipated that, as students are exposed to content about diversity, their ability to incorporate diversity awareness, sensitivity, and knowledge in clinical practice will evolve.

	Degree/Level of Expression of Cultural Competence		
Dimensions of Reflection	**Emerging Level:** *Relies on unsupported beliefs or one aspect of the situation*	**Developing Level:** *Provides insights, perceives difference in viewpoints*	**Advanced Level:** *Uses multiple perspectives, recognizes broader context in which actions occur*
Descriptive			
Clearly identifies diversity terms and concepts relevant to clinical practice			
Empathic			
Openly expresses recognition of beliefs, values, and attitudes of self and those of others			
Thoroughly elaborates on diversity terms and concepts by commenting on personal reactions, making references, and sharing points of agreements/ disagreements			
Analytic			
Appropriately considers and uses course content to appraise, compare and contrast and/or contemplate new or alternative actions			
Metacognitive			
Explicitly acknowledges an awareness of a change in behavior as a result of exposure to course content			

Scoring and Grading	
Descriptive state of reflection Emerging level: 1 Developing level: 2 Advanced level: 3	*Analytic stage of reflection* Emerging level: 7 Developing level: 8 Advanced level: 9
Empathic stage of reflection Emerging level: 4 Developing level: 5 Advanced level: 6	*Metacognitive stage of reflection* Emerging level: 10 Developing level: 11 Advanced level: 12

Source: Adapted from Fink (2003) and Bradley (1995).

Conclusion

An examination of this instructional model reveals several important findings. First, the course focus is not on information about specific cultures. This was a deliberate decision based on our awareness and concern that culture-specific content may lead to the development of stereotypic perceptions. We strongly believe that students need to understand the cultural and linguistic backgrounds of those individuals with whom they work. We agree, however, with Cazden and Mehan (as cited in Zeichner, 1992) and others that students should be encouraged to gain this information from their own clients or students and from their own local communities. We are convinced that, in this way, these individuals become resources rather than challenges and that the relationship between service provider and service receiver becomes more reciprocal. Second, we have found that there needs to be continuous emphasis on, and instruction in, diversity and a means to view students' development over time. This might include a series of courses, such as those described in this chapter, or a continuum of structured experiences. Third, it is not only possible but plausible to use a web-based approach to promote conversations about diversity. Several students indicated that they participated in this course more than they did in others and that the nature of the online discussions did not inhibit their expression of feelings (Chabon, Cain, & Lee-Wilkerson, 2001). Fourth, it is important, if not imperative, to include CLD individuals in the discussions about diversity if these discussions are to be truly meaningful and motivating. Fifth, students of color should not be considered representatives of their culture. Although at times they may serve as cultural mediators, it should not be assumed that they are cultural experts. Sixth, assessment of learning, however difficult, is necessary. It provides an occasion to be creative in selecting indicators of diversity learning through the use of such means as journals, portfolios, and oral reflection—all of which have strong theoretical bases. Finally, no matter how much time, thought, and dedication are involved in preparing for and executing this type of class, it is likely to be the most rewarding opportunity teachers will have to learn about and from students and engage in their personal and professional growth.

Zimphor and Ashburn (as cited in Zeichner, 1992) assert that the most significant thing we can do as teachers is to use an approach that enables our students to think and talk together about the various kinds of problems they encounter related to cultural diversity and how they are addressing such problems. Our hope is that Dialogues on Diversity I and II will provide a tested, practical, and replicable instructional model to do just that for those who are engaged in diversity education and who are not faint of heart.

References

American Speech-Language-Hearing Association. (2004). *Knowledge and skills needed by speech-language pathologists and audiologists providing services to culturally and linguistically diverse clients/patients.* Rockville, MD: Author.

Chabon, S., Cain, R., & Lee-Wilkerson, D. (2001). Diversity and technology: Strange bedfellows or virtual partners? *ASHA Leader, 6,* 10.

Coleman, T. J. (1999). *Clinical management of communication disorders in culturally diverse children.* Needham Heights, MA: Allyn & Bacon.

Committee on the Status of Racial Minorities. (1987). *Multicultural professional education in communication disorders: Curriculum approaches.* Rockville, MD: American Speech-Language-Hearing Association.

Cone, D., & Harris, S. (2003). Service-learning practice: Developing a theoretical framework. In Campus Compact, *Introduction to service-learning toolkit: Readings and resources for faculty* (pp. 27–39). Providence, RI: Author.

Cummings-James, N. (2000). When Miss America was always white. In A. Gonzales, M. Houston, & V. Chen (Eds.), *Our voice: essays in culture, ethnicity, and communication.* Los Angeles, CA: Roxbury Publishing Company.

Fink, L. D. (2003). *Creating significant learning experiences.* San Francisco, CA: Jossey-Bass.

Hewett, B., & Ehmann, C. (2004). *Preparing educators for online writing instruction: Principles and processes.* Urbana, IL: National Council of Teachers of English.

Lynch, E., & Hanson, M. (2004) *Developing cross-cultural competence: A guide for working with young children and their families* (3rd ed.). Baltimore, MD: Paul H. Brookes.

Micheller, J. (2002). *Curry/Samara model curriculum, instruction, and assessment: A tool to transfer scientific research on authentic assessment to the classroom.* Retrieved February 22, 2007, from www.curriculumproject.com/CSM-Researchbasis.htm

Newmann, F. M., & Associates. (1996). *Authentic achievement: Restructuring schools for intellectual quality.* San Francisco, CA: Jossey-Bass.

Stockman, I. J., Boult, J., & Robinson, G. (2004). Multicultural issues in academic and clinical education: A cultural mosaic. *ASHA Leader, 20,* 6–7.

Zeichner, K. M. (1992). *Educating teachers for cultural diversity.* East Lansing, MI: Michigan State University, National Center for Research on Teacher Learning.

26

Cultural Diversity as More Than a Lecture Topic: Bridging the Divide Between School and Real Life

Kris English

One day in class, a student presented the following case from her current clinical placement:

About 24 hours after their daughter was born, a family was informed that she did not pass a routine hearing screening. They were given instructions on how to follow up with more comprehensive testing. The parents kept the appointment, and those tests were conducted. The professional (an audiologist) informed the family that the tests indicated their baby had a mild hearing loss in both ears. Because hearing loss adversely affects a baby's speech development and language skills, the clinic's standard recommendation was to fit the baby with very small hearing aids. In the interest of saving time, the audiologist suggested the process begin immediately by making impressions of the baby's ear canals. The parents were visibly upset but agreed.

Three days later, the mother called and asked the audiologist for another appointment. She wasn't going to bring the baby this time; she just wanted to discuss some concerns. The audiologist was not surprised, because most parents have many questions about hearing problems and child development.

The audiologist, however, could not have anticipated the discussion that followed. At the appointment, the mother said, "Ma'am, you have explained to us why our baby needs hearing aids. I want to explain to you now that this is a problem: Our culture does not permit us to put things on our heads. It is taboo. We are not permitted to wear hats, wigs, ribbons, or earrings. You can see now why we are distressed about the recommendation to put hearing aids on our baby."

The audiologist replied, "With all due respect, you'll have to get over that taboo. You are in the United States now, and this is best for your child."

The mother left and did not keep the next appointment, when the hearing aids would have been provided. The clinic attempted several times to reschedule, leaving messages with tentative appointment times on the family's message machine, but received no confirmation from the family. The parents had become "chronic no-shows."

Class Discussion

The student concluded the case presentation with this question: What can the clinic do to make sure it doesn't lose this family?

The instructor waited for her classmates to point out that the clinic had *already* lost this family. Instead, they jumped into problem-solving mode and made a range of suggestions, including contacting appropriate agencies to report child abuse. Finally, the instructor asked everyone to consider the following question: Around the globe, what do other countries commonly object to regarding U.S. policies? The students seemed uncomfortable with this challenge, but finally someone offered, "Because we think we know how other people should live?" Other students nodded their heads in agreement but looked perplexed. What was the point?

The instructor acknowledged that the United States does tend to be perceived this way. And couldn't this case presentation be described as a microcosm of that perception? The entire class objected: Surely, this was different! This was a parent who was not putting her child's interests first. One student insisted, "Making sure this baby can hear overrides all other concerns."

Considerations for the Instructor

The topic was debated for the remaining class time, but the instructor thought about it for days afterward. Two concerns came to mind.

First, these students had addressed cultural diversity in at least three other classes in their graduate program. On paper, at least, it would seem that the topic of diversity had been sufficiently covered. Yet, clearly, the students had not made the connection from theory to practice; they had not considered how cultural differences could impact their own clinical practices.

Second, the student presenting the case was herself a first-generation American. When cultural differences had been discussed in the previous classes, she had made a point to describe her experiences growing up with two languages in the home and how expressing herself still tended to be problematic. She described being shaped by her parents' culture and by American culture and how those two influences were at odds more often than not. She described herself as working as a broker between the two cultures and how that role caused a kind of stress that her classmates could not begin to appreciate. From her background, then, one would expect her to be particularly sensitive to the challenges of the family being discussed. However, she was wholeheartedly in agreement with the position taken by the clinic: Cultural differences were not relevant; the family needed to adhere to the recommendations made by experts.

Teaching Implications

Why did students, especially the student presenting the case, not apply their previous exposures to cultural differences to the family presented in this case? Two possible explanations come to mind.

Transferring abstractions to reality. Just talking about cultural diversity in class probably makes little impact on attitudes or behaviors. Classroom instruction likely followed the traditional approach described by Barrera and Corso (2003), wherein features of two cultures are listed in two vertical tables, usually contrasting Western culture to others. For instance, in column A, Western culture perceives human life as more important than nature, and individuals are expected to find solutions to problems using scientific methods. In column B, many non-Western cultures perceive humans as a part of nature, which cannot be modified, and problems are predetermined by fate, so they can't be solved by human intervention.

This compare-and-contrast approach provides only a superficial understanding of cultural differences and also subtly implies that one set of cultural values is superior to the other. If left at that, there is no opportunity to consider any applications to real life. Although discussion questions might challenge students to consider diversity in general terms, using *case-based learning* (National Research Council, 2000) can help students grapple with some very specific implications. For instance, given the case presented at the beginning of this chapter, did this mother actually say that she would never consider hearing aids? Or was there a possibility that this was an issue that had to be presented to an elder or other authority in her cultural group? Are exceptions allowed, and if so, how are they managed? Why didn't the audiologist take time to find out? Was there the possibility of developing some common ground? If so, how could that have happened? Should we be surprised that the family effectively fired the clinic? Is this a predictable outcome, and if so, why would the professionals involved not change their approach?

Broadening the definition of culture. The student presenting the case was probably shaped by another culture that had never been discussed in class. Without realizing it, she was influenced by the culture of the *medical model,* a model that carries much prestige and authority in the United States. The medical model's cultural values include a respect for objective test results and an expectation of patient adherence (Stewart, Brown, & Freedman, 2003). This model is highly appropriate when a patient presents with disease, injury, or pain; a diagnose-and-treat approach directly and efficiently addresses the cause for concern.

Although most hearing loss and many other disabilities cannot be cured, they can be managed. In those circumstances, a *rehabilitation model* of service delivery is more appropriate, wherein the patient and family members are supported over time as they assume ownership of, adjust to, and learn to manage the disorder. A rehabilitation culture values patient-professional relationships and patient autonomy (Clark & English, 2004). The role of the professional is not one of authoritative healer but of supportive facilitator. The relationship between patient and professional includes and works with cultural differences (Groce, 2005).

The differences between the medical and rehab models are typically not mentioned in class but are assumed to be picked up by students as they rotate through various settings. However, if not given a working vocabulary, students may not see those differences—just as author Amy Tan (2003) once wrote that until she learned the word *mauve* in her mid-20s, that color didn't exist for her—she did not "see" it. Once she learned the word, however, mauve suddenly seemed be everywhere. Seeing the differences is a prerequisite to understanding their implications.

Conclusion

Each profession has its own culture. But if one asks colleagues to describe that culture, they will likely be hard pressed to do so—*living it* can prevent us from *seeing it*. The culture of audiology does value hearing—but why do students believe hearing "overrides all other concerns"? A new goal for this instructor is to use case-based instruction specific to the goal of exploring cultural diversity (not only medical anomalies or complicated management issues). Students will be asked to consider their professional culture as well as their patients' cultures. Students will be asked to present cases that demonstrate cultural acceptance as well as cultural misunderstandings. They will be asked to interview patients specifically to ask, "What would you like me to know?" Perhaps then they may be able to cross the bridge between school and real life and work with Barrera and Corso's (2003) proposition that each patient and each professional hold only one piece of a multifaceted truth.

References

Barrera, I., & Corso, I. (2003). *Skilled dialogue: Strategies for responding to cultural diversity in early childhood.* Baltimore, MD: Paul H. Brooks.

Clark, J., & English, K. (2004). *Counseling in audiology: Helping patients and families adjust to hearing loss.* Needham Heights, MA: Allyn & Bacon.

Groce, N. (2005). Immigrants, disability, and rehabilitation. In J. H. Stone (Ed.), *Culture and disability: Providing culturally competent services* (pp. 1–13). Thousand Oaks, CA: Sage Publications.

National Research Council. (2000). *How people learn: Brain, mind, experience, and school.* Washington, DC: National Academies Press.

Stewart, M., Brown, J. B., & Freedman, T. (2003). *Patient-centered medicine: Transforming the clinical model* (2nd ed.). Oxon, UK: Radcliffe Medical Press.

Tan, A. (2003). *The opposite of fate.* New York, NY: Putnam.

27

Preparing Culturally Responsive Practitioners in Occupational Therapy

Jaime P. Muñoz

There are compelling reasons to integrate multicultural training into health professions education. Recent U.S. census figures suggest that ethnic and racial minorities are becoming numerical majorities in our society (Office of Minority Health, 2006). Research demonstrates that levels of health care, health care outcomes, and general health status are typically poorer for racial and ethnic minorities and economically disadvantaged populations (Smedley, Stith, & Nelson, 2003). The accrediting bodies that govern health care professional education have established standards that include specific criteria for multicultural content and training (Accreditation Council for Occupational Therapy Education, 2006). However, allied health programs continue to struggle with the question of how best to expose students to a curricular examination of multiculturalism and its influence on health and illness (Ekelman, Dal Bello-Haas, Bazyk, & Bazyk, 2003), and the goals and processes of multicultural education remain elusive both in theory and in practice (Banks & Banks, 2001; Duarte & Smith, 2000; Morey & Kitano, 1997).

Research in multicultural education spans a wide variety of topics, including the best preparation for educators, effective teaching strategies, optimal curricular content, and diversity in student learning styles (Laubsher & Powell, 2003). My own teaching methods are shaped by my theoretical views as a student and scholar of multiculturalism and cultural competency, by my perspectives as an educator and experiences as a clinician in an allied health profession, and by my personal life experiences, including my status as a minority. This chapter describes one course in an occupational therapy curriculum at Duquesne University in Pittsburgh, Pennsylvania. I have taught this course for 10 years to a student body that consists largely of middle-class European Americans. The structure and

163

content of this course have been continuously modified to reflect my understanding of best practices in multicultural training.

The Course: Sociocultural Systems and Networks_____

Description

Sociocultural Systems and Networks considers issues and implications of multicultural diversity in health care. Two general categories of diversity are explored: intercultural and intracultural diversity. Intercultural diversity includes such issues as culture, ethnicity, migratory history, race, and racism. Intracultural factors include age, gender roles, socioeconomic status, religious orientation, sexuality, disability, and lifestyle choices.

Objectives

There are three primary course objectives.

1. Students will demonstrate awareness of their own cultural values and biases. They will:

   • Develop a greater understanding of their own cultural heritage with its inherent values and beliefs

   • Explore environmental (social and physical) factors that contributed to or shaped their values, biases, and system of ethics

   • Recognize that judgments such as "right" and "wrong," as well as what is "normal" and "abnormal," are culturally specific and the product of a person's own background and experiences

   • Understand how these values and biases can negatively (or positively) impact the cross-cultural clinical encounter

2. Students will demonstrate an increased understanding of worldview as it is perceived by persons with culturally different backgrounds (this refers to both inter- and intracultural diversity). They will:

   • Articulate specific knowledge and information about cultural groups, including their historical background and cultural heritage, and examine the historical and environmental factors that shape these various cultures

   • Explore how inter- and intracultural differences can influence a person's choices in life—in terms of family, vocation, lifestyle, personal interrelationships, and approach to health and wellness

   • Understand how cultural differences may lead to miscommunication between the therapist and the client that can impede treatment

- Demonstrate an awareness of factors (social, economic, political) that may impinge on the life experiences of persons from diverse backgrounds and that may influence the therapeutic process

3. Students will demonstrate an increased knowledge of and ability to apply culturally appropriate intervention strategies. They will:

- Demonstrate an ability to engage in a variety of culturally appropriate verbal and nonverbal helping responses

- Demonstrate an awareness of the cultural limitations of clinical assessments, and use procedures and interpret findings while keeping in mind the clients' cultural and linguistic characteristics

- Describe strategies for collaborating with interpreters, traditional healers, and religious and spiritual leaders

- Demonstrate an increased awareness of institutional barriers that may prevent persons from diverse backgrounds from accessing health or rehabilitation services

Educational Processes

This course employs a variety of educational strategies to develop multicultural competencies. The most fundamental strategies focus on helping students generate knowledge of their own and others' worldviews and understand those sociopolitical influences that often impact the lives of people from diverse cultural groups. The course is taught from a theoretical perspective that holds that culture and cultural practices are dynamic and socially, historically, and contextually constructed (Giroux, 1992).

Course content includes a survey of models of multicultural competency, a review of racism and racial identify formation, and exploration of health care disparities, social justice, and cultural issues that may influence therapeutic relationships. This content is delivered using a wide variety of educational strategies. Awareness- and affect-oriented strategies focus on encouraging students to recognize their own cultural heritage, their biases, and their capacities and limitations for treating culturally diverse persons. Self-assessment and guided reflection; the use of cooperative base groups; simulations; small- and large-group discussion of readings, art, films, and poetry; and the development of a personal portfolio are all methods that support the development of cultural awareness of self and others. Educational strategies that allow for the practice of skills are a prominent aspect of the teaching methods. In particular, skills used in clinical assessment and intervention strategies, including capacities required to forge an interpersonal connection with persons from culturally diverse backgrounds, are emphasized through simulation, role play, interviewing assignments, and support for cross-cultural encounters.

Lectures are kept brief, and learning activities are planned to encourage students to understand, value, and respect similarities and differences between themselves and their clients. Ideally, this course is meant to be a discussion course, one in which the discussions emerge from the assigned readings and the experiences of the students themselves. The richest dialogue develops when students give voice to their reactions, personal experiences, and perspectives. Some learning events are scheduled outside the regular class meeting times and occur in the surrounding community.

This course employs cooperative base groups as a method of instruction to enhance learning and to build community in the classroom (Johnson, Johnson, & Smith, 1991). A cooperative base group is a heterogeneous group of people with a stable membership that serves as a learning community, providing each member the academic and personal support to develop individually and professionally. Early in the semester, students are organized into three- to four-member base groups, which they retain throughout the semester. Frequent in-class meetings are scheduled to provide a forum where members can personalize the learning experience. Base group members discuss and debate assigned readings, share experiences and expertise, and plan group projects. The structure of base groups allows an efficient and effective mechanism whereby small-group discussion can occur.

Reflective portfolios are the primary evaluation method used in this course. A portfolio is a collection of evidence or artifacts that demonstrate the continuing acquisition of skills, knowledge, attitudes, understanding, and achievements (Nagayda, 2005; Seung-Yoeun, 2001). In this class the portfolio functions as a repository that documents a student's personal and professional growth and movement toward becoming a more culturally responsive practitioner. Students complete a learning contract early in the semester and define specific portfolio exercises they want to complete from a menu of activities provided by the instructor. The menu includes learning activities—from those that require predominantly individual reflection and self-assessment to those that require significant cross-cultural encounter and even activism. For example, students might complete a self-assessment of cultural competence, spirituality, or their beliefs and values relative to sexuality and gender roles. They then reflect on their answers and relate the assessment results to course content and concepts in assigned readings in a scholarly paper submitted to their portfolio. Other options require students to trace their cultural heritage through interviews with family members and the creating of a family genogram. Assignments that emphasize cross-cultural encounter include phenomenological interviewing of a person with a significant disability, self-selected cross-cultural encounters in which the student experiences being a minority, mini-ethnographies of community-based health centers, and the exploration of, and participation, in community organizations—such as agencies that focus on disability rights, health care activism, homelessness, or refugee services. Students also have the option to create their own assignment focused on multicultural education. They present a learning proposal to their instructor and negotiate evaluation criteria for their self-defined activity.

Lessons Learned

Those descriptions outline the educational pedagogy I have employed to prepare occupational therapists as culturally responsive practitioners. My personal perspective is that multiculturalism is a journey and that the course I teach is but one educational intervention in the process of becoming a more multicultural person. At best, one course in one academic semester is but a few steps in that journey. Wurzel (1988) has suggested that educational interventions in multicultural learning often give rise to disequilibrium—a form of cognitive dissonance brought on by questioning ideas, concepts, and even one's own values and beliefs. A successful outcome is having each student feel disequilibrium at some point in the semester as a result of critical thinking about multicultural issues. The following are a collection of some of the most important lessons I believe I have learned.

Cooperative base groups are an effective strategy for getting students to talk about difficult issues such as racism, disability, health disparities, social justice, stereotypes, culture, and privilege. Conversations that occur in a small group often provide a point of entry for discussing uncomfortable topics. A small-group context often facilitates a level of disclosure, debate, and dissent that students may be uncomfortable voicing in the larger group first.

Students comes to this course at a unique place in their own multicultural journey, and they continue that journey at their own pace. I have learned that it is important to recognize that one student's next step in this journey can simultaneously be regarded by others as a baby step toward multiculturalism or a significant emotional risk. Allowing students to share experiences and ideas, rather than forcing self-disclosure, and providing a menu of assignments from which to pick and choose allows students to challenge themselves at their own pace.

Attend to the needs of the individuals as well as the dynamics of the class. As an educator, I need to be diligent in honing my skills of attending, validating discomfort, sharing my own struggles, providing accurate information, and challenging disinformation in a way that does not totally silence or shame the source. It is essential that as part of the classroom dynamic, I model self-disclosure and transparency in my thinking and reasoning and help students create linkages between concepts in readings and their experiences and biographies.

Recognize that a current of tension is an inherent part of the teaching dynamic. I am mindful that students' capacities and willingness to explore such issues as bias, prejudice, privilege, or health care disparities and to engage in a thoughtful process of self-exploration will vary. On one end of the continuum, I have had students in my office discussing eye-opening or soul-rendering experiences. Such students explain that they have become better at reading between the lines and that they have learned to consider a broader variety of factors that may impinge on the lived experience of future clients. Themes of transformative thinking are common in the portfolio entries of these students. On the other end, I have had students who steadfastly resist the idea that privilege and power afford opportunities for some while denying others those same opportunities or that social structures can and do influence health care access and treatment. These same individuals may also deny they have any capacity to hold bias or prejudice. In a course with multicultural content, there is a tension that exists between challenging students to explore issues such as bias, privilege, health disparity, and social inequality and not being able to force them to do so.

Cross-cultural encounters are powerful vehicles for learning. In her model of cultural competency, Campinha-Bacote (2002) identifies five components: cultural awareness, cultural knowledge, cultural skills, cultural desire, and cultural encounters. My own teaching pedagogy is strongly influenced by this perspective. The course I teach provides opportunities for students to develop awareness, expand their knowledge base, and learn and practice skills. The motivation to know self and others as cultural beings is cultural desire, which I believe has to come from the student and cannot be taught or learned in a traditional sense. When students have cross-cultural encounters, they can use those encounters to build awareness as they reflect on these interactions. They are able to test their knowledge and, provided the opportunity, to identify the gaps in that knowledge. They can test and develop skills, and such encounters may feed a desire to know and understand the worldviews of others, especially if those encounters are supported with guided reflection methods. Cultural encounters link affective learning and cognitive learning, and opportunities for cross-cultural encounters should be considered as an integral component of any course in multicultural training.

References

Accreditation Council for Occupational Therapy Education. (2006). *ACOTE standards and interpretive guidelines.* Retrieved February 22, 2007, from www.aota.org/nu/docs/acotestandards 107.pdf

Banks, J. A., & Banks, C. M. (2001). *Handbook of research of multicultural education.* San Francisco, CA: Jossey-Bass.

Campinha-Bacote, J. (2002). The process of cultural competence in the delivery of healthcare services: A model of care. *Journal of Transcultural Nursing, 13,* 181–184.

Duarte, E. M., & Smith, S. (2000). Multicultural education: What for? In E. M. Duarte & S. Smith (Eds.), *Foundational perspectives in multicultural education* (pp. 1–24). New York, NY: Longman.

Ekelman, B., Dal Bello-Haas, V., Bazyk, J., & Bazyk, S. (2003). Developing cultural competence in occupational therapy and physical therapy education: A field immersion approach. *Journal of Allied Health, 32,* 131–137.

Giroux, H. A. (1992). *Border crossings.* New York, NY: Routledge.

Johnson, D. W., Johnson, R. T., & Smith, K. A. (1991). *Active learning: Cooperation in the college classroom.* Edina, MN: Interaction Book Company.

Laubsher, L., & Powell, S. (2003). Skinning the drum: Teaching about diversity as other. *Harvard Educational Review, 73,* 203–224.

Morey, A. I., & Kitano, M. K. (1997). *Multicultural course transformation in higher education: A broader truth.* Boston, MA: Allyn & Bacon.

Nagayda, J. (2005). *The professional portfolio in occupational therapy: Career development and continuing competence.* Thorofare, NJ: Slack.

Office of Minority Health. (2006). *Racial and ethnic populations.* Retrieved April 3, 2007, from www.cdc.gov/omh/Populations/populations.htm

Seung-Yoeun, Y. (2001). Using portfolios to reflect on practice. *Educational Leadership, 58,* 78–81.

Smedley, B. D., Stith, A. Y., & Nelson, A. R. (2003). *Unequal treatment: Confronting racial and ethnic disparities in health care.* Washington, DC: National Academies Press.

Wurzel, J. S. (1988). The multicultural world. In J. S. Wurzel (Ed.), *Toward multiculturalism: A reader in multicultural education* (pp. 2–10). Yarmouth, ME: Intercultural Press.

28

Threading Diversity Through an Occupational Therapy Curriculum

Denise Chisholm

O ccupational therapists, like all health professionals, need to be skilled in addressing cultural and diversity issues. As a profession, occupational therapy has long acknowledged the influence of culture on an individual's selection of, and participation in, activities for everyday life. The standards for an accredited master's-level educational program for the occupational therapist include specific requirements and expected student outcomes that reference diversity and cultural factors (American Council for Occupational Therapy Education, 2006). Faculty are required to develop learning activities and evaluation methods to document that students achieve these outcomes. Therefore, occupational therapy education must prepare culturally skilled occupational therapists. *Occupational Therapy Practice Framework: Domain and Process* (American Occupational Therapy Association [AOTA], 2002) defines culture as "customs, beliefs, activity patterns, behavior standards, and expectations accepted by the society of which the individual is a member" (p. 623). Additionally, according to Cross, Bazron, Dennis, and Isaacs (1989), a culturally skilled therapist is one who values diversity, has a sense of his or her own culture, and uses the "dynamics of difference" (p. 20) to offer sensitive and appropriate systems of care for his or her clients.

So, given that diversity and culture are multidimensional constructs, how do occupational therapy educators teach the skills required for cultural competence? The intent of this chapter is to describe how the faculty of the University of Pittsburgh's master of occupational therapy (MOT) program systematically threaded cultural and diversity awareness through the curriculum.

Planning and Implementing the Pattern_____

Our first step was to agree as a faculty that since every client from every background is a valuable person, cultural and diversity issues address the core question of how clients are treated. With this unified view, it was easy to see that cultural and diversity awareness was not going to be just another of our curriculum threads; it was going to be a strong one. So our next step was to design the pattern for threading it on a course-by-course and term-by-term basis through our MOT curriculum. Through associated readings and related assignments, faculty identified and analyzed how culture and diversity were taught. Because culture and diversity significantly impact all aspects of the occupational therapy process—that is, evaluating, intervening, and targeting intervention outcomes—we decided to begin the thread in the first course of the first term of the curriculum. Lecture content and learning activities were designed to address and support clinical care issues.

Cultural and diversity awareness is a full module in the Foundations of Occupation Science and Occupational Therapy course that our students take in the first term of the MOT program. The module is designed to engage students in the investigative process as a method for achieving the needed self-awareness requisite in attaining cultural awareness. There are three primary learning activities associated with the module. The first learning activity requires self-reflection by focusing on the students' thoughts, experiences, roles, and communication. It is a paper-and-pencil activity completed independently by each student before the start of the module. The intended outcome is for students to recognize their own cultural ties and affiliations, attitudes, biases, and openings to better understand the power that culture has in their lives and other people's lives. The following is sample content from the self-reflection learning activity:

- *First thoughts.* Look at each word and jot down the first two or three words that come to your mind. No censorship of thoughts should occur. Positive or negative, just write your first thoughts. (Examples: Asian, mentally ill, Irish, overweight, women, etc.)

- *First experiences.* Think about your first experience in treating the following conditions. Include who told you about this remedy. You may include all myths and remedies you have heard or tried. (Examples: hiccups, fevers, bee stings, etc.)

- *Identifying your social roles.* Circle the items in each of the following sections that best describe you. Place a check mark by the items you circled that seem to be most important or significant for any reason to you at this time in your life. (Each section focuses on different roles. Examples: conservative, liberal, Hispanic, Anglo-Saxon American, wife, nephew, gay, laborer, professional, etc.)

- *Communication checklist.* Using a scale of 1 (low agreement) to 5 (high agreement), rate how strongly you agree with each statement. (Examples: "I listen as much as I speak." "I avoid jargon or slang." "I do not judge people based on their accents or language fluency." "I make an effort to talk about differences." etc.)

The second learning activity focuses on health-related scenarios. The activity is conducted through small-group discussion. The following are examples:

- You walk into a Brazilian teenager's hospital room to perform an evaluation. She is crying softly. You have not seen her as a client before, but you know that she is new to this country and cannot speak English. What would you do in this situation?

- A male occupational therapist with neatly combed, long sideburns and collar-length hair approaches a male client and introduces himself. The client retorts with an obscenity, stating in a loud voice that he is paying for "real treatment" and is not going to be treated by a "punk." The client's fists are clenched. What should the occupational therapist do in this situation? What cultural or personal biases and past experiences may be contributing to the patient's reaction?

The third learning activity is a diversity presentation and quiz. The activity is completed in small groups of two or three students. Each group selects a culture, researches the cultural norms, and prepares a PowerPoint presentation and quiz. The presentations and quizzes are made available to all students through the course's web site. Students are required to review each presentation and take the associated quiz. The presentations are to include culture descriptors, health care issues, and information sources. The following are issues students should consider:

- Medical issues

- Perception of health

- Perception of illness/disease/disability

- Patient-practitioner relationships

- Methods of dealing with stress

- Past experiences with health care

- Expectations of independence

- Male/female issues

- Age issues

- Perception of mental illness

- Definitions of anatomy and physiology (view of the body)

- Diet and nutrition

- Caring and curing

- Pain

- Pharmacology

- Dealing with loss

- Identification of disease

- Self-treatment issues

In each subsequent term, students have theory and practice courses. Each theory and practice course uses a clinical case format that includes an occupational profile, which describes the client's occupational history (activities having unique meaning and purpose in a person's life) and experiences, patterns of daily living, interests, values, and needs. Clinical cases have been developed to address a range of ages, diagnoses, cultures, and practice settings. Faculty collaborated on the placement of clinical cases for each course to ensure that breadth and depth of issues are systematically increased as students progress through the MOT curriculum.

In addition to the learning activities that specifically target culture and diversity, there are learning activities that have culture and diversity woven into their format. For example, in the Group Theory and Practice course, students complete group development learning activities that include a written protocol. The protocol outlines the group's topic, title, sources/references, description/rationale, goals, selection criteria, structure, environment, materials, format, and variations. Students must also identify possible cultural issues related to their group intervention. Culture is also addressed through the occupation and participation learning activity in the Occupation Across the Life Span course. Students write a paper that addresses the impact of culture on occupational engagement at various life stages. The outcome is to examine and explore how occupations and participation by individuals within an identified culture can be influenced and affected by context or environmental factors. This course also explores cultural trends, potential bias, and ageism as it relates to older adults. Another course, Rehabilitation Theory and Practice, also includes cultural sound bites. Students are required to identify literature and/or to conduct an interview with a person from their target culture. They then relate that information to the content of each session through class discussion, specifically identifying how the content would be altered for diverse populations.

The Benefits of Threading _____

The faculty began the systematic development of culture and diversity threading in the MOT curriculum over three years ago. Although the intent was to enhance the cultural development and competency of the students, it has had a twofold effect. For students, the threading has allowed for a deeper learning process. As students advance through the curriculum learning more complex clinical skills, their awareness and incorporation of culture and diversity become internalized and intuitive, and they demonstrate increased cultural competency. Additionally, the process has assisted the faculty themselves in validating their cultural competency and sharing with the students the experience of cultural discovery.

References

American Council for Occupational Therapy Education. (2006, January). *Standards for an accredited master's-level educational program for the occupational therapist.* Bethesda, MD: Author.

American Occupational Therapy Association. (2002). Occupational therapy practice framework: Domain and process. *American Journal of Occupational Therapy, 56*(6), 609–639.

Cross, T. L., Bazron, B. J., Dennis, K. W., & Isaacs, M. R. (1989). *Towards a culturally competent system of care: Vol. 1.* Washington, DC: Georgetown University Child Development Center.

29

Enhancing Multicultural Education in Rehabilitation Counseling

Michael Pramuka

Enhancing Multicultural Education in Rehabilitation Counseling is an introductory course in counseling practice and theory for the graduate-level program in rehabilitation counseling at the University of Pittsburgh. Although most students have applied experience in community rehabilitation, mental health, or education systems, their educational backgrounds, counseling perspectives, and familiarity with serving individuals from cultural backgrounds different from their own are varied and often based on informal training. There is general consensus in the field on the value and necessity of including multicultural education and diversity training, as well as of specific recommendations on multicultural competencies and skills for professional counselors (Sue, 1991; Sue, Arredondo, & McDavis, 1992), including self-awareness of worldviews, understanding client worldviews, and practice of culturally sensitive strategies. In addition, current counseling textbooks incorporate specific information about cultures and multicultural considerations in applying counseling theories (see Corey, 2004).

The impetus for changes in this course came from three directions: 1) The national accreditation body for the profession of rehabilitation counseling (Council on Rehabilitation Education) disseminated new educational standards specifically directed to multicultural issues in professional identity, in understanding disability, and in the counseling relationship; 2) there is a growing body of literature in the field stressing the importance of prioritizing client choice and client values and recognizing an empowerment approach to counseling (Kosciulek & Wheaton, 2003); and 3) I was invited to participate in a two-week faculty diversity seminar hosted by the provost's office of the University of

Pittsburgh in which modification of a course syllabus to enhance the diversity of the course was the required output.

Implementation

Three modifications were made to the course: 1) a broad orientation to diversity and a definition of culture that emphasized nonethnic identities (to heighten the likelihood that multicultural issues occur); 2) a shift in perspective on power and empowerment that carried through lectures, case studies, and weekly journals; and 3) a culture-specific research project/presentation.

Multicultural Activity 1: Assume Diversity

As part of this course, students' diversity and multicultural issues were infused into its overview, goals, and assignments. A goal was added to "develop an awareness of personal power bases, internalized oppression, and personal bias in gender, race, and ability status as a basis for addressing empowerment and multicultural approaches to counseling and rehabilitation." In addition, students were encouraged to identify cultures and diversity beyond ethnicity, gender, and race, including institutional status (e.g., military status, prisoners), economic disparities, class differences, linguistic differences, educational status, sexual orientation, ability status, or religious affiliation. This highlights the reality that most professional relationships will have at least some multicultural component to them—even if a client appears to share age, ethnicity, and gender status with the student or professional—and further substantiates the necessity of working from a multicultural perspective from the start of the professional relationship. Students were also encouraged in role playing and practice counseling sessions to label themselves as part of a culture unfamiliar to them to explore their personal understanding, knowledge, and comfort with that culture.

Multicultural Activity 2: Find the Power in Empowerment

In response to both Sue's emphasis on counselor awareness and the inclusion of empowerment-based approaches (Kosciulek & Wheaton, 2003), I noted that students tended to globally ascribe "disempowerment" to clients from traditionally underserved backgrounds. Further, when students were asked to comment on the power base of a client that had eroded and by what mechanism or by whom the power had been minimized, it became clear that the essence of personal power was glossed over in discussions of empowerment and diversity, whether those discussions related to personal background or to professional-client relationships. Power was discussed frequently but only as a monolithic, absent-versus-present phenomenon. I therefore added some readings (Croteau, Talbot, Lance, & Evans, 2002; Harley, Jolivette, McCormick, & Tice, 2002; Young,

2000) and lectured to provide a general framework on personal power and oppression, and I subsequently required students to identify in weekly journal responses to course content and classroom activities both their own and client/consumer power bases, both strong and weak. When any group of persons or an individual was described as having been "disempowered," students were required to identify in what ways and by whom/what power had been diminished. From a rehabilitation or a counseling perspective, understanding whether an individual is attempting to return to a previous level of "function" (power) or achieving it for the first time without previous experience is relevant to developing useful strategies. It is also imperative for clinicians to recognize remaining or stable power bases in consumers on which to build. For example, an individual with a disability may be newly disempowered by funding cuts for personal assistance (external and transitional), a young adult may experience stable but modifiable disempowerment due to an inadequate educational background, or an African-American may be disempowered via racial discrimination endemic to current American society. In each there is a differential in what options the individual has for change and to maximize power ("empowerment"). Similarly, each of these persons might hold significant power in other domains that can act as leverage in designing counseling interventions.

Multicultural Activity 3: Multicultural Expressions in Our Community

Although there are numerous and excellent academic resources for students to learn about the general characteristics and values of various cultural groups, clinicians must also provide direct services to a real person, make appropriate referrals locally, and develop a network of multicultural colleagues who might provide peer support and guidance when serving a consumer from an unfamiliar culture. This will be most effective when clinicians understand and know the resources that are part of their multicultural clients' lives. Clinicians need to be aware that a Latina might attend a Spanish-speaking church with many support services, a gay man might form political opinions and actions based on reading a national gay magazine, and a person with epilepsy might daily read a national web site on living with epilepsy as a basis for medical decisions.

Students were therefore assigned to research local and national resources for a specific culture of their choosing that might likely be represented in professional work locally and to provide a short educational lecture/workshop for the rest of the class. Students were not allowed to choose their own cultural affiliations but were instead encouraged to choose one unfamiliar to them and use peers from that culture as a starting point in their research, interviewing at least one member of this culture. Students were encouraged to use, but not limited to, reviews of local and national media (newspapers, magazines, TV shows), web sites, local and national organizations, films, literature, events/holidays, and cultural symbols.

Although the framework for presentation was not prescribed, I requested that students include commentary on the following items in their presentations: estimated size/population of cultural community, history and perceptions of oppression or discrimination, perspectives of culture on mainstream media/politics, subcultures, integration or relationship to mainstream culture, and professional issues in providing services to members of this culture.

Outcomes

This course has been taught twice with these modifications to enhance diversity and multicultural awareness. The first time only the first two components were used; the third assignment on multicultural expressions has just been added and used in conjunction with the first two modifications. Although there has been no formal assessment of these multicultural/diversity aspects to the course, numerous observations can be made. Many students are alternately mystified and irritated with discussions of multicultural issues, frequently taking the stance that cultural issues don't matter in the current, more integrated world. The assignment on multicultural expressions was most easily and successfully completed by all students, and presentations were generally lively and informative. Some students attempted to defer to other students in the class who were either visible or self-identified members of the culture under discussion during the presentation and who were at times in conflict with the presenter. Beginning counseling students are often uncomfortable in role-playing situations and tend to avoid exploration of minority status in their practice sessions without explicit redirection by the instructor, but in general they were able to articulate the value of assuming a multicultural perspective in the initiation of any new professional relationship. The repeated assignment to find the "power" in disempowerment was most challenging for students. Most stopped including this information in their weekly journals within two weeks and had to be reminded and offered numerous examples before continuing to do so, and many chose to explore impersonal aspects of power in a counseling theory or therapeutic approach rather than addressing immediate or personal experience. Overall, it appeared that the students' naiveté regarding their own racial and minority identity status and their discomfort in acknowledging their own relative privilege and power was central to the inconsistent response to this assignment.

Conclusions

There is significant discussion in professional literature on multicultural issues and empowerment in the field of rehabilitation counseling as well as formal incorporation of multicultural and diversity requirements into national accrediting standards for graduate study in the field. It is a challenge, however, to develop instructional approaches that successfully bridge the general concepts and academic literature to applied personal experiences for beginning graduate students. The three course modifications summarized here required students to identify and define diversity, to explore sources of power, and to present detailed information on community life for a specific cultural group.

Overall, the modifications to syllabi, coursework, and assignments described here have introduced a much more integrated and multifaceted approach to diversity than was previously provided in this course. The difficulty and discomfort evident in student participation is interpreted as a sign that more work with multicultural issues is necessary before students can fully integrate these perspectives in their own identify and in their future professional work.

References

Corey, G. (2004). *Theory and practice of counseling and psychotherapy* (7th ed.). Boston, MA: Brooks/Cole.

Croteau, J. M., Talbot, D. M., Lance, T. S., & Evans, N. J. (2002). A qualitative study of the interplay between privilege and oppression. *Journal of Multicultural Counseling and Development, 30,* 239–258.

Harley, D. A., Jolivette, K., McCormick, K., & Tice, K. (2002). Race, class and gender: A constellation of positionalities with implications for counseling. *Journal of Multicultural Counseling and Development, 30,* 216–238.

Kosciulek, J. F., & Wheaton, J. E. (2003). Rehabilitation counseling with individuals with disabilities: An empowerment framework. *Rehabilitation Education, 17*(4), 207–214.

Sue, D. W. (1991). A model for cultural diversity training. *Journal of Counseling and Development, 70,* 99–105.

Sue, D. W., Arredondo, P., & McDavis, R. J. (1992). Multicultural counseling competencies and standards: A call to the profession. *Journal of Multicultural Counseling and Development, 26*(2), 64–84.

Young, I. M. (2000). Five faces of oppression. In M. Adams, W. J. Blumenfeld, R. Castaneda, H. W. Hackman, M. L. Peters, & X. Ziniga (Eds.), *Readings for social diversity and social justice.* New York, NY: Routledge.

30

Enhancing Diversity Appreciation in a Nursing Degree Completion Curriculum

Lisa Marie Bernardo, Susan A. Albrecht

At the University of Pittsburgh, the Introduction to Nursing Science course provides a broad overview and synthesis of the issues and trends most relevant to the practice of professional nursing. Historical, contemporary, and potential influences on professional nursing practice are reviewed. An emphasis on the unique and varied roles of nurses in today's interdisciplinary health care environment is examined within the context of individual, family, community, and global health. Characteristics and major changes in health care delivery systems (federal, state, and local) are discussed. Components of professional nursing values and core practice competencies are presented. The concept of an evidence-based approach to clinical practice is introduced. Critical thinking strategies are introduced in the context of the nursing process.

Upon completion of this course, students are able to:

- Critically examine historical, contemporary, and potential influences related to the practice of professional nursing

- Analyze elements in the U.S. health care delivery system within the context of global health

- Identify the development and expansion of relevant nursing roles to secure and improve the health of individuals, families, communities, and populations in a variety of settings

- Differentiate the roles of other members of the interdisciplinary health care delivery team

- Explain the essential characteristics and the steps to beginning an evidence-based approach to clinical practice

- Relate critical thinking and decision-making skills to the nursing process

- Identify aspects of professional values, accountability, responsibility, and leadership

- Explore their emerging professional values regarding cultural diversity and sensitivity, spirituality, and special populations

This two-credit course introduces registered nurse students returning for baccalaureate or master's degrees to their academic curriculum and builds on the knowledge, skills, and abilities they acquired in their nursing practice and previous education.

Recent data indicate that within the next 50 years, the United States' racial composition will change: European Americans will comprise less than 50% of the total population, and African-American, Hispanic, and Asian populations will increase to 12%, 25%, and 8%, respectively (American Nurses Association, 1998). The registered nurse population, however, currently does not enjoy such diversity, as 88.4% (an estimated 2,380,639) of registered nurses are Caucasian female (U.S. Department of Health and Human Services, 2004). To help registered nurses appreciate diversity among themselves and in the patients, families, communities, and populations in their care, nurses' academic and ongoing education must provide opportunities that speak to diversity and values, beliefs, and preferences.

Registered nurses, regardless of their initial academic preparation, are held accountable by their standards of practice and code of ethics to administer nursing care to individuals, families, communities, and populations with respect to those people's and group's diversity and uniqueness. "The nurse, in all professional relationships, practices with compassion and respect for the inherent dignity, worth, and uniqueness of every individual, unrestricted by consideration of social or economic status, personal attributes or the nature of health problems" (American Nurses Association, 2001, p. 1). As such, registered nurses are held accountable for nursing decisions and actions regardless of their personal preferences, beliefs, and values (Maze, 2005). Schools and colleges of nursing, in compliance with accreditation standards promulgated by the American Association of Colleges of Nursing and the National League for Nursing, are accountable for weaving patient, family, community, and population diversity, beliefs, preferences, and values into nursing curricula. The University of Pittsburgh, for example, has level objectives (defined outcomes for each year of undergraduate nursing education), which include the application of cultural diversity into nursing care. The majority of undergraduate nursing courses have an objective related to diversity and nursing care.

To integrate registered nurse students' moral and ethical responsibilities into their new academic world, we begin with the first course, discussed here. This two-credit course is taught in a workshop and online format, in which registered nurses attend two three-hour workshops and complete readings, assignments, and examinations online. Because these nurses pass through the curriculum as a cohort, the workshops allow them the opportunity to meet one another and to share their experiences as registered nurses and college students. The number of students in the course ranges from 12 to 40.

To facilitate their collegiality and to assist them in integrating concepts into nursing practice, we engage the students in a diversity exercise during the second workshop.

Implementation

Before the second workshop, students complete various online readings and assignments. One set of readings and assignments relate to ethical and legal responsibilities of registered nurses. Students are expected to apply this knowledge during the workshop.

At the workshop, an exercise is conducted. The objective of this exercise is for students to apply knowledge of nursing ethics and legal responsibilities to the care of patients who are of varying backgrounds, including different ages, genders, cultures, and societal statuses. This activity is accomplished through a video titled *Patient Diversity: Beyond the Vital Signs.* This video is a series of vignettes involving patients, families, and health care professionals (played by professional actors) whose underlying themes relate to appreciating diversity in a health care setting. During the video, the health care professionals must make judgments and treatment actions based on the patients' information, the law, and professional moral and ethical standards. We play a vignette and then open the class for discussion. We ask probing questions, such as these:

- What is the underlying diversity theme?

- What is the nurse's legal obligation? What aspect of the state nurse practice act is the nurse upholding?

- What is the nurse's ethical obligation? Which ethical code(s) is the nurse violating or upholding?

- What would *you* do as the nurse? Why?

Outcomes

This exercise requires about an hour to complete. The video evokes discussion of similar situations in which students have found themselves as registered nurses. The group discussion provides peer and professional support for their decisions. Students gain insight into their own values and preferences, placing those values and preferences in context with nursing's professional ethics and legal standards.

Many questions arise, such as what the right and wrong approaches to given situations are. Many times students desire a standard answer, and they have difficulty with ambiguity. However, the ethical and legal framework from which they propose their nursing actions permit a grounded, logical approach to diversity.

This video—or similar videos depicting situations in which nurses find themselves with patients, families, and communities different from themselves— is a useful adjunct to traditional classroom teaching. Because these students are practicing registered nurses, they readily relate to the scenarios. This approach may not be useful to prelicensure nursing students, who may not have a nursing practice context to evaluate the scenarios. Such students may, however, be more likely to appreciate and relate to the patients' situations from their own personal experiences.

Variations on video vignettes and classroom discussions can be integrated into human simulation teaching situations, where diversity issues are raised during the simulated care of a patient. Watching an online video stream may not allow for interactive discourse, even with synchronous discussion threads. Such online discussion may not engage nurses who prefer an oral learning style (Fox, 2005), unless ongoing practice, expectations, and acceptance for online discussion forums are predetermined.

Conclusions

Registered nurses come from a plethora of ages, customs, beliefs, preferences, and values. Although Caucasian females dominate the nursing profession, steps must be taken to improve the gender, cultural, and ethnic diversity within the nursing profession. Teaching strategies to welcome, accept, and educate people of diverse backgrounds entering the nursing profession must be explored, so that students of varying backgrounds have the same opportunity to learn (Flinn, 2004).

Appreciation and integration of diversity into nursing curricula is demanded by cultural and ethnic diversity within the U.S. population. Registered nurses caring for patients, families, communities, and populations must respect others' preferences, values, and diversity. This course allows registered nurses to build on their experiences and previous education and to approach diversity from the context of their legal and ethical obligations.

References

American Nurses Association. (1998). *Discrimination and racism in health care: Position statement.* Retrieved February 22, 2007, from http://nursingworld.org/readroom/position/ethics/etdisrac.htm

American Nurses Association. (2001). *Code of ethics for nurses with interpretive statements.* Washington, DC: Author.

Flinn, J. (2004). Teaching strategies used with success in the multicultural classroom. *Nurse Educator, 29*(1), 10–12.

Fox, L. (2005). Diversity in online teaching: When culture and online education conflict. *Home Health Care Management & Practice, 17*(4), 342–345.

Maze, C. (2005). Registered nurses' personal rights vs. professional responsibility in caring for members of underserved and disenfranchised populations. *Journal of Clinical Nursing, 14,* 546–554.

U.S. Department of Health and Human Services. (2004). *The registered nurse population: National sample survey of registered nurses, March 2004: Preliminary findings.* Washington, DC: Author.

Resources

Agency for Health Care Policy and Research: www.ahrq.gov/research/minorix.htm

American Nurses Association: www.nursingworld.org

American Public Health Association: www.apha.org/public

Journal of Transcultural Nursing: http://tcn.sagepub.com/

U.S. Department of Health and Human Services, Office of Minority Health: www.omhrc.gov/

31

Enhancing Diversity Training and Culturally Responsive Caring in the First Year of the Pharmacy Curriculum

Gary P. Stoehr, Teresa E. Donegan

The mission of the pharmacy profession at the University of Pittsburgh is to provide pharmaceutical care, a patient-centered practice model that seeks to identify, resolve, or prevent drug-related problems. In this model of practice, the pharmacist assumes responsibility for the patient's drug-related needs to achieve positive outcomes that improve the quality of each patient's life (Cipolle, Strand, & Morley, 2004). Implicit in this model is the involvement of the patient, the physician, and the pharmacist in decisions involving drug therapy.

Minority and immigrant populations may have varying perceptions about illness, disease, and their causes that differ from those of Western cultures. Culture influences not only belief systems about health, healing, and care but also ways of seeking help (Goode, 2006). Given the increasing diversity in the U.S. population, pharmacists and other health care providers must be able to understand and work with patients from a variety of cultural backgrounds.

Colleges and schools of pharmacy are responsible for teaching students to effectively care for patients, many of whom may be different by virtue of their culture, ethnicity, disability, or economic circumstances.

Implementation

Courses in the professional curriculum are designed to integrate scientific concepts and clinical practice to ensure that students understand content in a clinical context. The faculty strive to provide continuity and integration of content and skill development within each year and across the curriculum. Although there are other areas in the curriculum that focus on developing cultural sensitivity, we decided, because of space constraints, to concentrate on our current initiatives to enhance diversity training and culturally responsive care in the first year of the curriculum. In the first year, the Profession of Pharmacy course works in tandem with the Experiential Learning course to give students the opportunity to apply theoretical principles to real-life situations. In the Profession of Pharmacy course, there are practicum sessions each week that use active learning methods to engage students in discussion, challenging them to solve patient-based problems (cases) and/or to clarify difficult concepts taught in prior classes.

The Experiential Learning course is conducted primarily at service sites in the community under the supervision of community preceptors. Faculty offer monthly four-hour class sessions throughout the term to debrief students on the lessons learned from their experiences. An important component of the course is students' weekly reflective journal, which relates the material to principles they learn from both the Experiential Learning and Profession of Pharmacy classes. The specific mission of this course is to prepare students to work collaboratively with other health providers to achieve effective use of medicines and to maximize the health and well-being of patients and of society as a whole. Sites are selected to foster an interest in community service and to promote interactions with different populations to enhance students' cultural sensitivity.

The Profession of Pharmacy Course

The Profession of Pharmacy is divided into sections I and II and is part of a six-term sequence of courses intended to introduce students to four themes: professional inquiry, the human dimensions of pharmacy, clinical skills, and management. During the first year, instructors develop learning objectives to raise students' awareness of the impact that culture has on health care, to provide some of the knowledge and skills needed to effectively interact with persons from diverse cultures, and to stimulate students to engage in interactions with persons or populations that may be different from their own culture.

We adapted the Campinha-Bacote model of cultural competency (Campinha-Bacote, 2003) to the delivery of culturally responsive pharmaceutical care. *Culturally responsive* is used purposefully to reflect the never-ending nature of developing the capacity to learn from, and care for, those who are different from us. The basic elements of the model are represented by the acronym ASKED: awareness, skills, knowledge, encounters, and desire.

Awareness involves a willingness to continuously question and acknowledge personal biases and prejudices toward different cultures. Prejudgments and stereotypes are most often the barriers to empathizing with, and taking into account, an individual's unique circumstances.

Skills are essential to determine how an individual's culture might impact the delivery of pharmaceutical care, which includes the capacity to perform a patient assessment in a culturally responsive manner.

Knowledge includes a generalized familiarity with differing patients' worldviews and health care beliefs.

Encounters in face-to-face interactions through active engagement are one of the requisites of culturally responsive care.

A *desire* to become culturally responsive is necessary for the development of this capacity.

To stimulate their awareness of diversity and cultural issues, students participate in an interactive session designed to challenge their preconceived notions about issues of diversity. During the session, students form circles of 12, six sitting in an inner circle facing six students in an outer circle. Students are then given a series of questions about diversity to discuss with their partner. One example is: "Tell your partner something about your racial, ethnic, and class background, as well as something painful or difficult about your background (past or present)." Then students are given a minute to discuss the question with their partner. Once each person has spoken and listened, then students seated in the outer circle move to their left and another diversity question is discussed. After each question, students rotate until all the questions have been answered. Following this session, instructors debrief the class by asking students for the most important learning points of the exercise. The instructor then reinforces the idea that knowledge of other cultures can be a starting point for assessing patients (generalizing) rather than as an end point (stereotyping). Common stereotypes for various cultures and diversity groups are then discussed, and the danger of stereotyping is made clear through case examples related to health care.

In preparation for the next class, students review scenarios posted on web sites that highlight the impact of culture on health beliefs and medication use. They are also required to identify at least four health disparities that exist in U.S. minority populations and to develop questions to ask a panel of faculty and students representing a variety of ethnic and cultural groups. One year panelists included a Muslim student, a Nigerian student, and Latino, Russian, Indian, Serbian, and Chinese faculty members. Invariably, panelists discuss verbal and nonverbal means of address and respect, the importance of family decision-making, and the use of nontraditional remedies. Students are struck by the need to address patients formally and the possibility that even simple directions given by their physician or pharmacist may be misinterpreted or not followed because of misunderstanding or a conflict of health care beliefs.

In the spring term, students travel to senior centers to conduct a medication interview of elderly persons under the supervision of a faculty preceptor. In preparation for this session, students learn about the impact that the aging population has on the U.S. health care system and the struggle that some seniors have in paying for medications and adhering to complex regimens. Students are required to establish a therapeutic relationship with at least one person of a different culture during the term in addition to the seniors they interview at the centers.

Experiential Learning Course

Two weeks after students begin visiting their service-learning site, they are asked to attend breakout sessions to discuss their initial expectations, perceptions, and apprehensions about working with a different population. The discussions are facilitated by community preceptors who represent the major populations students serve, including, but not limited to, mental health, seniors, children, the underserved or homeless, and hospital or oncology patients. Students are asked to be honest and candid in discussing their initial preconceptions and apprehensions. The aim of the sessions is to help students become aware of their biases and more open to exploring others' worldviews. Ideally, students will become more actively cognizant of their biases when working with new and different populations and be more culturally responsive in tailoring the care of those populations. Students are asked to submit a reflection paper on their preconceptions about working with the population they're investigating and to discuss any shifts that occurred through their first few weeks of encounters.

Outcomes

Profession of Pharmacy Course

Lecture was a good method for introducing students to the knowledge needed to practice in a diverse society, and the sessions on diversity and culture were well received. To stimulate more discussion of diversity, students organized a "diversity lunch"; each group of students prepared an ethnic dish to share with classmates. Everyone enjoyed sampling food from other cultures and took pride in their cultural and ethnic heritage through this event.

The faculty and students who participated in the panel enjoyed the interaction with the class and expressed a desire to return the following year. They also wished they had been invited to participate in the diversity lunch.

Almost every student commented on their experience at the senior centers in their final reflection paper. For most students this was a transforming event, the first time that they felt like a professional pharmacist. The reception by seniors at the centers was likewise very positive. One group of seniors gave students a standing ovation when they left the center. Another thanked a student who helped her enroll in a medication assistance program by telling the student, "You saved me over $600 on my medication. Thank you, thank you!" Another said that no one had taken the time to explain the purpose of her medications as well as the student pharmacist at her site had.

To more fully implement the Campinha-Bacote cultural competency model, students will need more encounters with patients of other cultures. Although courses can simulate experiences with persons of other cultures in cases and role-playing exercises, there is no substitute for patient encounters. Because western Pennsylvania, where the University of Pittsburgh is located, is not diverse, the pharmacy program will likely need to send students to distant sites to give them the experience they need to develop and practice skills in communicating with other cultures.

We also plan to incorporate more simulations during class time. We purchased *BaFa' BaFa'*, a cross-cultural simulation game, to use next year along with other simulations and cases.

Experiential Learning Course

The facilitators commented that they appreciated students' candor as well as genuine interest in better understanding and helping the populations they served. The reflection papers showed that although there are some students who have a great deal of experience in working with different cultures, many have not and had several preconceptions. Many students had biases about those in the mental health population. Students feared if they did not know the diagnosis they might say "the wrong thing," which would make a patient volatile or upset. Facilitators helped address their apprehensions and assuage their anxiety. Students commented that they appreciated the opportunity to discuss their initial apprehensions with their peers and facilitator. Their reflections showed that their encounters and the breakout sessions helped dispel initial preconceptions. The most common lesson learned was that students began to recognize that despite differences in circumstances or culture, they and their patients are more alike than they expected. This supports Campinha-Bacote's assertion that one of the best teachers of empathy is face-to-face encounters.

Conclusions

Students welcome discussion of other cultures and view themselves as accepting of others. Hands-on opportunities to interact with persons of other cultures are essential for developing the capacity to be more culturally responsive. Students need numerous opportunities with varying cultures to become more knowledgeable about, and sensitive to, those who are different. They also need guidance from faculty and site preceptors to address apprehensions and biases and to become more skilled in how to deliver culturally responsive care. Our current challenge is to find a way to increase the number of encounters students have not only in the first year but across the curriculum.

References

Campinha-Bacote, J. (2003, January 31). Many faces: Addressing diversity in health care. *Online Journal of Issues in Nursing, 8*(1). Retrieved February 22, 2007, from www.nursingworld.org/ojin/topic20/tpc20_2.htm

Cipolle, R. J., Strand, L. M., & Morley, P. C. (2004). *Pharmaceutical care practice: The clinician's guide* (2nd ed.). New York, NY: McGraw-Hill.

Goode, T. D. (2006). *Promoting cultural diversity and cultural competency.* Retrieved February 22, 2007, from www11.georgetown.edu/research/gucchd/nccc/documents/Checklist BehavioralHealth.pdf

Resources
Web Sites

Interdisciplinary Student Community-Oriented Prevention Enhancement Service at George Washington University: www.gwu.edu/~iscopes/LearningMods_Culture.htm

Program for Multicultural Health at the University of Michigan: www.med.umich.edu/multi cultural/ccp/tools.htm

Ethnomed, University of Washington Harborview Medical Center: http://ethnomed.org/

Texas Health Steps Cultural Competency Web-Based Long Distance Learning Program: www.dshs.state.tx.us/thsteps/cultural/about.shtm

University of South Carolina College of Medicine: http://etl2.library.musc.edu/cultural/competency/competency_9.php

Publications

Assemi, M., Cullander, C., & Hudmon, K. S. (2004). Implementation and evaluation of cultural competency training for pharmacy students. *The Annals of Pharmacotherapy, 38,* 781–786.

Burroughs, V., Maxey, R., Crawley, L. M., & Levy, R. A. (2002). *Cultural and genetic diversity in America: The need for individualized pharmaceutical treatment.* Reston, VA: National Pharmaceutical Council.

Burroughs, V., Maxey, R., Crawley, L. M., & Levy, R. A. (2002). Racial and ethnic differences in response to medicines: Towards individualized pharmaceutical treatment. *Journal of the National Medical Association, 94*(10), 1–26.

Kleinman, A., Eisenberg, L., & Good, B. (1978). Culture, illness, and care: Clinical lessons from anthropologic and cross-cultural research. *Annals of Internal Medicine, 88,* 251–258.

Westberg, S. M., Bumgardner, M. A., & Lind, P. R. (2005). Enhancing cultural competency in a college of pharmacy curriculum. *American Journal of Pharmacy Education, 69*(5), 1–9.

Simulations

Assemi, M., & Cullander, C. (2004). *Cultural competency in pharmaceutical care delivery: A training template for a one-day pharmacy student elective course.* (Available from The Center for the Health Professions, University of California, San Francisco: www.futurehealth .ucsf.edu/cnetwork/resources/curricula/intro.html)

Shirts, R. G. (1977). *BaFa' BaFa': A cross-culture simulation.* (Available from Simulation Training Systems, DelMar, CA: www.stsintl.com)

32

Training Dentists to Meet the Needs of a Multicultural Society

Deborah E. Polk, Richard W. Rubin

In the first two years of their four years of professional training, dental students are immersed in basic science courses. Although our students do not begin to interact with patients until the end of their second year, we believe that training in diversity and multiculturalism is important and must begin early. Thus, diversity and multiculturalism training is incorporated into two courses occurring in the first two years of dental training at the University of Pittsburgh. This early training is both didactic and experiential. The two courses are Professionalism and Social Issues in Dentistry Today, in which didactic training in diversity and multiculturalism is one component of a curriculum that covers many topics, and Student Community Outreach Program and Education (SCOPE), in which community service and reflective journaling are the primary components of the course. The professionalism course and the community outreach course complement one another. The professionalism course provides specific, focused skill-building opportunities, whereas the community outreach course provides direct contact with persons from many different cultures. The two courses should be considered together. Either by itself would not be as strong as the combination of the two together. In this chapter, we describe the implementation of diversity and multiculturalism training in these two courses.

Professionalism and Social Issues in Dentistry Today

Among the goals of Professionalism and Social Issues in Dentistry Today are familiarizing students with social issues that impact the practice of dentistry and introducing students to the responsibilities involved in being a professional. For those students who must acquire new skills and behaviors to be able to practice in a culturally competent manner, we adopted a skill-building approach.

In this skill-building approach, we focus on two domains relevant to working in a multicultural society. First, we focus on the identification of patient and dentist values, including practicing identifying them and determining whether they are shared. We adopted this focus because one of the primary ways that a culture is manifest is through its values. And different cultures have different values, particularly regarding health care interactions. Although it is tempting for dentists to assume that they and their patients share the same values, this is not always the case. To provide respectful and culturally sensitive care, dentists must determine what patients' values are and incorporate them into treatment planning. For example, the dentist may value saving as many teeth as possible regardless of the time or expense, whereas the patient may value having a disease-free mouth as quickly and inexpensively as possible. Unless the dentist and patient realize that they are operating under different values and arrive at a mutually acceptable solution, at least one, if not both, will be dissatisfied with the outcome and interaction.

Second, we focus on the identification of patient and dentist expectations regarding sharing decision-making. Making decisions is an important aspect of delivering and receiving health care. Because expectations regarding how such decisions will be made vary widely, it is important for dentists to be familiar with the different possibilities and be able to determine the approaches favored by their patients. For example, some patients may prefer to have the dentist make all the decisions. Others may prefer to be the sole decision-maker. Still others may seek collaboration with the dentist. To facilitate skill building around values and decision-making models, we use the following multimodal approach:

- Lecture, which provides definitions for culture and values and sources of information that students could turn to, as needed, about specific cultures

- In-class exercise, in which students identify from a list of work values those that are most important to them personally

- Reading, which presents information about four different decision-making models dentists and their patients could adopt

- Facilitated small-group discussions, in which students view videos of dentists and patients interacting, identify the dentists' and patients' values, and discuss whether the values are shared (they also identify the decision-making models the dentist and the patient are adopting and discuss whether the dentist and patient share the same decision-making model)

Ultimately, the goal is for these students to know how to handle situations when their values and decision-making model differ from those of their patients.

But before they can do that, they must learn how to listen for the patient's values and decision-making models. They need to learn what it sounds like when a patient is expressing a value or adopting a decision-making model. They need to learn to compare the patient's value and decision-making model to their own. All this needs to happen before they can negotiate differences between their own values or decision-making model and those of their patients. The objective of this training is to provide opportunities for the students to obtain these preliminary skills.

After conducting a questionnaire-based evaluation of the training, we learned that different students respond to different components. Some students find the lecture or reading most helpful, whereas others find the in-class exercise or facilitated small-group discussion most helpful. Based on the results of this evaluation, we decided not to drop any of the various training components.

Notable in our training approach is what we do not do. We do not discuss specific approaches for specific cultures. We made this choice for several reasons. First, there is no way to anticipate and discuss all the different cultures our students may interact with over their careers. Second, because cultures are always evolving and because any individual patient's behavior may be determined by more than his or her culture alone, we do not believe it is possible to provide definitive approaches that would always be appropriate for persons from any particular culture. We also don't provide opportunities to interact with persons from different cultures. Given the specific foundational skills we are focusing on, we believe that live interactions that involve so much more than the specific skills we are seeking to develop will distract from the development of these skills. Instead, we have decided to emphasize in our training specific treatment-relevant interpersonal skills that a dentist could use with anyone. These skills will enable the dentist to provide respectful and culturally sensitive treatment.

At the same time as the students are obtaining these interpersonal skills, they are also involved in community activities, through SCOPE, that are designed to bring them in contact with persons from diverse backgrounds.

Student Community Outreach Program and Education _____

The three goals of the SCOPE course are as follows:

- To develop the students' cultural competence and communication skills

- To create more empathic, personally committed dentists

- To create a social norm of community-mindedness among dentists

The SCOPE program combines both community service and reflective journaling. Over their first two years at school, students perform 40 hours of nondental public-health-related service in a variety of community settings. At the end of their second year, they submit a written journal reflecting on their community experiences and how their personal and professional attitudes and beliefs were affected.

We believe that the community service experiences create a learning environment in which students can expand their personal and professional insight, gain experience in a variety of cultural environments, and help serve the needs of the community. Examples of non-dental public health-related service include volunteering for groups that address issues related to disaster relief, mental and physical disabilities, and families with sick children, and participating in fundraisers for groups targeting AIDS, diabetes, and breast cancer. We require students to perform service that is both non-dental and public health related so that they obtain the opportunity to place oral health in its larger ecological context. This is particularly important as health care in general moves from viewing health and disease from a single cause-and-effect model, such as a single pathogen causing infection, to viewing it as the result of multiple factors operating on different levels, such as incorporating roles for social relationships, living conditions, neighborhoods, and communities. We also require students to participate in more than one of the different service opportunities over the 40 hours. We have found that the insight they gain from their service experience does not necessarily occur from each of their service interactions. Often, the service must be personally meaningful to the student for it to result in changes in self-knowledge and insight into others. Because it may take exposure to several different service interactions before students are able to identify the kind of interaction that will best facilitate personal growth, we have them participate in many different types of service opportunities. Finally, as mentioned, the service commitment is for 40 hours. This provides a balance between providing enough experience to have a significant impact in the students' lives yet not becoming burdensome.

With respect to the journals, the key to obtaining meaning from students' service experience is reflection. Therefore, we tell them not to provide a day-to-day account of where and for how long they volunteered but instead to address what they got out of the experience, how the experience influenced them, and how it may affect their practice of dentistry. The emphasis is on self-reflection and insight. Both positive and negative experiences are acceptable. Journals are typically three to five pages long. Here are two examples from students' journals.

> I had learned all about [AIDS] over and over throughout my formal schooling but had never known anybody with the deadly disease or even anybody whose life had been affected by it. I knew all the facts, but in the back of my mind, I was still a little uncomfortable with the thought of volunteering at this [fundraiser for AIDS outreach organization]. . . . It was a great

chance for me to meet and chat with the people from the community. . . . have already participated in the [fundraiser] again . . . and hope that more students have as positive an experience as I have had.

Overall, my day at [the festival for disabled children] was a very challenging but extremely fulfilling one. I learned a great deal about how difficult it is to take care of a moderate to severely disabled child. I also learned how amazing each child is through my interactions with the other children at the festival . . . My experience at the festival was a great one and will be an experience that I will hang on to and cherish the rest of my life.

By coding the student journals for self-reported change, we showed that SCOPE activity helps develop virtues consistent with being more culturally competent (Rubin, 2004). When we compared students' attitudes and beliefs regarding cultural competence and social responsibility before and after they underwent the SCOPE experiences, we found that their attitudes and beliefs became more culturally competent and socially responsible through their SCOPE activity (Rubin, Rustveld, & Weyant, under review).

What we don't do in this course is tell students what service projects to engage in or provide examples of other students' journals. We believe that the process of self-discovery is an important component of this course. The students must take responsibility for finding experiences from which they can learn and grow. Furthermore, they must articulate their learning in their own words.

Conclusion

Educators now recognize that two important elements in shaping modern dental practitioners are developing cultural competencies and attitudes of social responsibility. Although students enter dental school with differing degrees of cultural competency, programs such as the professionalism course and SCOPE experience provide frameworks for students to develop perspectives and skills that will benefit them throughout their careers.

References

Rubin, R. W. (2004). Developing cultural competence and social responsibility in preclinical dental students. *Journal of Dental Education, 68*, 460–467.

Rubin, R. W., Rustveld, L., & Weyant, R. J. (under review). Exploring dental students' cultural competence and social responsibility. *Journal of Dental Education.*

33

Guidelines for Disability Diversity

Katherine D. Seelman

The course I have chosen to discuss is the Individual and Social Experience of Disability, taught at the University of Pittsburgh. The goal of this course is to describe and analyze the individual and social experience of people with disabilities viewed through the lens of the disabled individual and using core concepts from disability studies and the social sciences to develop skills in research, practice, and advocacy. Listed here are the course objectives:

- Identify and analyze approaches to the study of disability using the medical and the social/integrative models of disability.

- Identify and analyze the individual experience of disability using disability studies concepts (such as disability identity, advocacy, and empowerment) and sociological concepts (such as social role and social movements).

- Identify and analyze the social context of disability using concepts such as disability culture, technology, social supports and service systems, participation, community integration, and environmental factors.

- Identify and analyze the political and economic context of disability using concepts such as social movement, civil/human rights, and benefits and services policies.

- Apply the medical and social models to compare the orientation and usefulness of rehabilitation and disability literature in areas such as medical condition, personal attendant services, inclusive education, human rights, and voting.

- Develop skills in literature review.

Background and Impetus for Changing the Course _____

The following points illustrate my rationale for modifying this course with respect to disability as a form of diversity:

- Incorporate new approaches to disability and to the educational context for inclusion of students with disabilities in higher education as an important part of the learning experience of disabled and nondisabled students in health sciences.

- Explore the role of the rehabilitation professional when a fellow professional is disabled.

- Explore the role of the rehabilitation professional as a faculty member when a student with a disability requires professional assistance during class.

Implementation_____

The following changes were made:

- Local citizens with disabilities (parents, business people, lawyers) were invited as guest speakers to address the class in areas such as deaf and disability culture, parenting children with disabilities, working with a disability, housing for the disabled, aging with a disability, and disability services.

- Course content on demographics was amended to add disability diversity factors such as disability and condition, ethnicity, gender, and age.

- Added to the course was content on instructional needs and inclusive practices, including instructional tools (e.g., software), online class notes, accessible tools (e.g., captioning for the deaf and hard of hearing and video description for the blind), and links to online supports.

- Instructional modes were varied and included lectures, visual outlines, group activities, demonstrations (e.g., how a person who is blind uses a computer), and external disability culture events (e.g., theater and dance).

- The number of opportunities for student-instructor contact was increased.

Outcomes_____

I observed the following differences in the classroom environment as a result of the changes implemented:

- Students expressed a sense of raised consciousness about how people with and without disabilities share similar goals and objectives, such as employment, and how people with disabilities may pursue those objectives using different methods, such as teleworking (because transportation may be inaccessible or unavailable).

- Students compared disabled persons' history of institutionalization and oppression to that of African-Americans.

- Students were interested in disability dance and deaf storytelling.

- Students were uncomfortable with the attitudinal differences exhibited in the literature that showed that people with severe disabilities placed a higher value on their quality of life than did rehabilitation professionals.

- Instructors and students enjoyed the dialogue with visitors who "walked and rolled" the talk of living with a disability.

Conclusions

Overall, it appears that multiple modes of teaching this type of course are useful, especially dialoguing with people who have disabilities and who share similar life objectives, such as parenting and working, with those who do not have a disability. It should also be pointed out that some tensions may also exist because some people with disabilities perceive nondisabled people, perhaps especially health professionals, as creating barriers to their inclusion in mainstream life. In addition, tensions may exist because universities are not accessible. University administrators, faculty, and staff may be perceived as having an attitude that conveys discomfort or disapproval. Programs, information, and buildings may not be accessible, and assistive technology may not be available.

Resources

Association of Higher Education and Disability: www.ahead.org

Center for Applied Assistive Technology: www.cast.org

DO-IT at the University of Washington: www.washington.edu/doit/

National Center for the Study of Postsecondary Educational Supports: www.ncset.hawaii .edu/contact/default.htm

San Diego Community College District: www.sandiegocet.net/dsps/index.php

Scott, S. S., McGuire, J. M., & Foley, T. E. (2003). Universal design for instruction: A framework for anticipating and responding to disability and other diverse learning needs in the college classroom. *Equity & Excellence in Education, 36*(1), 40–49.

Seelman, K. D. (2006). Trends in rehabilitation and disability: Transition from a medical model to an integrative model. In C. R. Reynolds & E. Fletcher-Janzen (Eds.), *The encyclopedia of special education* (3rd ed.). New York, NY: Wiley.

34

Enhancing Interdisciplinary Communication: Electronic Health Record Technology for Health and Rehabilitation Students

Valerie J. M. Watzlaf, Valire Carr Copeland, Mindy L. Columbus

This chapter provides an opportunity to explore the way in which an electronic health records course can foster interdisciplinary health care training through professional diversity. Interdisciplinary teamwork in a health care setting requires the expertise of a variety of different health care professionals. These professionals bring diversity on two fronts. The first and most obvious is their professional training and expertise—a diverse background of expert knowledge from each of their disciplines. The second is the diversity of their own social identity, including gender, race, class, religion, sexual orientation, and immigration status. The lens through which such professionals carry out their professional training is communicated through their individual and unique sociocultural background.

The course facilitated the opportunity for students to begin to value an interdisciplinary perspective by having the reciprocal process of appreciating others' expertise and having others appreciate theirs. To gain this training perspective during the undergraduate and graduate matriculation process is very unique. Often, learning to work in an interdisciplinary environment commences with actual employment. And traditional coursework makes it almost impossible to create real-life simulations in the classroom. This course filled that gap. Diversity is much broader than race, class, gender, and religion. We took into consideration the conceptual meaning of *diversity*—which means "difference"— because difference is evident on many levels in professional health care training.

For example, social workers bring the psychosocial aspects as well as the social determinants of illness whereas the audiologist, physical therapist, and others bring in the biological aspect of health and illness.

Therefore, with support from the Center for Instructional Development and Distance Education at the University of Pittsburgh, we developed an online innovative, interdisciplinary course to teach students about electronic health record (EHR) technologies. The EHR course gave students from many different disciplines—such as rehabilitation science, physical therapy, occupational therapy, emergency medicine, communication science and disorders, and social work—the opportunity to become involved in an educational experience that requires sharing the unique qualities of their various fields. Evaluating EHR technologies and other discipline-specific health information systems that could be used by similar health care organizations was a major part of the course.

This course was officially titled HRS-1490/2490: Electronic Health Record Technology. (It was offered to both undergraduate and graduate students in the School of Health and Rehabilitation Sciences and the School of Social Work.)

The course description was as follows: This course provided the health and rehabilitation professional with principles of, and approaches to, EHR technology. Theoretical and pragmatic issues related to EHR technology—such as design and development, standards and clinical terminologies, privacy and security issues, model EHR systems, evaluation of EHR software systems, and outcomes research using the EHR—were addressed. The responsibilities of the health and rehabilitation professional (physical therapist, occupational therapist, speech-language pathologist, health information professional, social worker, emergency medicine professional, etc.) in the development and use of the EHR were examined. Requirements of accrediting and licensing agencies of EHR technology as well as the strategic initiatives of the Office of the National Center for Health Information Technology (ONCHIT) were also presented and discussed. The responsibilities and involvement of the health and rehabilitation professional in the development, use, evaluation, and dissemination of EHR technology was emphasized.

The course objectives were as follows:

- Explain the difference between a paper health record and an EHR, and discuss the advantages and disadvantages of each.

- Describe and discuss how the EHR can be used by the health and rehabilitation professional for analyzing patient care—from planning a study, to developing quality indicators, to performing statistical analysis, to developing methods of improvement.

- Explain the requirements of accrediting and/or licensing agencies concerned with assessing the quality of EHR systems.

- Develop data elements and standards that are necessary components of an EHR system, paying special attention to ones related to health and rehabilitation science.

- Discuss the use, importance, and need for standards and clinical terminologies in a health care setting and the role that the health and rehabilitation professional plays.

- Distinguish the components of an EHR system that have a direct impact on reimbursement.

- Discuss the impact of the Joint Commission on Accreditation of Healthcare Organizations, state regulations, and federal regulations (such as initiatives from the Health Insurance Portability and Accountability Act [HIPAA] and ONCHIT) on the EHR technology development process.

- Describe different EHR technology software and systems and determine which may be most successful in health and rehabilitation.

- Demonstrate a knowledge base in the standards, clinical terminologies, and data elements necessary to develop an effective EHR system within any health care facility.

- Demonstrate the need for adopting an EHR system through case studies, research, and evaluating existing systems.

- Assess the risk that could result from improper use, access, disruption, modification, or destruction of health care information in an EHR system.

- Recognize the use of current technology (reminder systems, computerized physician order entry, barcodes, speech recognition, and so forth, and the effectiveness of these systems in disease prevention and health promotion.

- Determine how an EHR system can be used to prevent infectious disease outbreaks and bioterrorism events.

- Evaluate different EHR systems, paying special attention to their capacity to incorporate data elements, standards, and systems related to health and rehabilitation.

- Develop a mock EHR system, incorporating all the necessary data elements and components that are especially useful for health and rehabilitation professionals.

- Describe and discuss the advantages and disadvantages of using the EHR for outcomes research, evidence-based practice, and epidemiological studies.

- Design a brief outcomes research proposal using the EHR.

Implementation

The EHR technology course included 13 interactive multimedia modules. The title of each module and a brief description are listed here.

- *Overview of EHR technology.* Definitions of various terms for all aspects of an EHR system were provided, along with advantages and disadvantages of paper versus electronic medical records.

- *ONCHIT strategic initiatives.* Goals and strategic initiatives of the ONCHIT were discussed, and discussion board assignments centered on how each of the strategic initiatives could be accomplished by using the EHR.

- *Design and development of the EHR.* A description of different EHR designs and development of such systems was explored. Links to appropriate web sites that house these systems was provided so that students could actually see the different designs available. For example, the Veterans Health Care Administration provided an excellent demonstration of its system, called VistA.

- *Implementation and management of EHR systems.* The development, implementation, and management of an EHR system was discussed in this module. Several health care professionals find themselves managing an EHR system within their facility with very little training in health care technology systems. Therefore, the focus of this part of the module discussed how best to manage and administer the EHR system that is currently used by a facility as well how best to get one started. The 100 most wired health care facilities according to the American Hospital Association (Hospitals and Health Care Networks, 2004) was targeted to see how those facilities effectively implemented an EHR system. Discussion board assignments centered on factors that students believed are most valuable in health information technology in relation to their specific discipline and on why they would want to work for a particular facility.

- *Standards, data elements, structure, and content of an EHR system.* This module focused on a description of the major standards organizations, such as Health Level 7; American Society for Testing and Materials (ASTM); National Council for Prescription Drug Programs; Digital Imaging and Communications in Medicine; and Logical Observation Identifiers, Names and Codes. And it further focused on how those organizations relate to an EHR system. A major emphasis of this module included the need for standards in an EHR system and the content standards of the ASTM.

- *ASTM standards for the content of an EHR study.* A study by Watzlaf, Zeng, Jarymowycz, and Firouzan (2004) was discussed. This national study, "Standards for the Content of the Electronic Health Record," examined the awareness, use, and usefulness of the ASTM standards by users in health care facilities of all environments, vendors, and consultants.

- *Clinical terminologies of an EHR system.* Clinical terminologies that would most likely be used in an EHR today and in the future, based on an evaluation for EHR applicability, were overviewed in this module.

- *Patient safety and the EHR.* This module described both active errors and latent errors and their impact on the safety of patient care. It also described how the use of the EHR can improve the incidence of medical errors and how all health care professionals should strive toward using the EHR when providing patient care. Examples describing latent and active errors were provided with recommendations on how to decrease their incidence while using the EHR.

- *Outcomes research.* This module centered on how the EHR, once established in a health care setting, can be used effectively when conducting outcomes research.

- *Development of outcomes research proposal.* This module provided an overview of developing an outcomes research proposal with specific steps to include when generating the actual proposal. Students were required to design a brief outcomes research proposal in which the EHR was used.

- *The legal EHR.* The legal EHR and the four basic principles of authentication for legal admissibility for health records were discussed with a focus on the admissibility requirements for the EHR. Data integrity, access control, network security, and audit trail criteria in an EHR system was also discussed. Case studies related to misuse of confidential patient information were provided and discussed over the discussion board.

- *The personal health record.* The personal health record (PHR) was defined, and the attributes of a PHR were discussed. Lastly, we discussed, analyzed, and evaluated various PHR tools currently available to consumers, and students developed fictitious PHRs.

- *Privacy, security, ethical issues, and HIPAA safeguards for the EHR.* This module discussed the privacy, security, and ethical issues that surround the use of the EHR from the viewpoint of the health and rehabilitation professional. It also discussed the HIPAA regulations that fully cover these issues and the ones that are less clear.

All of the modules focused on how health professionals benefit from using the EHR. Online teaching and course evaluations were administered with assistance from the Office of Measurement and Evaluation of Teaching at the University of

Pittsburgh. Student interviews were also conducted. Changes will be made to the course based on the feedback received. The course will continue to be provided to allied health students at the university. In the future, we hope that it can serve as a model to other allied health colleges and universities across the country.

Outcomes

Students were satisfied with the content of the course and felt that it was a good course and a good overview to EHR technology. Students especially appreciated the audio presentation that accompanied each module with lecture notes and PowerPoint slides. Some students did prefer to have more in-class meetings, especially at the beginning of the course. Just about all the students stated that they would have preferred more hands-on use of the EHR. We did have one in-class meeting in which students used the VistA system as well as assignments in which students accessed EHRs online, but students stated that they wanted more demonstrations of, and time with, other EHR systems. Therefore, at this time, we are contacting other vendors to access their EHR software. We would also like students to develop an EHR system that is specific to their discipline; this will be an ongoing interdisciplinary assignment that will be added to the course.

Conclusion

Overall, the EHR technology course provided to students of diversified health care backgrounds was a true success. It gave students the opportunity to meet and discuss issues related to EHR technology, including privacy and security issues. It also provided students the opportunity to learn about the EHR and its importance across varied health care backgrounds.

References

Hospitals and Health Care Networks. (2004). *The 100 most wired vroom.* Retrieved February 28, 2007, from www.hhnmag.com/hhnmag_app/jsp/articledisplay.jsp?dcrpath=AHA/PubsNewsArticle/data/0407HHN_FEA_Most_Wired&domain=HHNMAG

Watzlaf, V., Zeng, X., Jarymowycz, C., & Firouzan, P. (2004). Standards for the content of the electronic health record. *Perspectives in Health Information Management, 1*(1).

Part V

Natural and Social Sciences

35

Diversity Across the Curriculum: Teaching the Business Case for Diversity

Audrey J. Murrell, Raymond Jones

Our course, Organizational Behavior, is the core introductory course within our business school curriculum (both graduate and undergraduate) that helps students understand how to effectively manage people within an organization. As such, it is a building block, or a foundation, within the business school curriculum. This course also offers an important opportunity to understand and develop the knowledge and skills necessary to be an effective manager. Students must examine behavior in organizations across three levels: individual (e.g., social perception, work attitudes, motivation), group (e.g., group dynamics, team effectiveness, conflict resolution), and organization (e.g., leadership, power, change). A key objective is to increase students' ability to facilitate organizational effectiveness within a changing, diverse, and global work environment. This chapter describes some of the steps we undertook to transform the approach to teaching diversity within this core management course and to helping students understand the business case for diversity.

Background

Although the core organizational behavior class requires students to understand and apply the key theories and management practices discussed throughout the term, it also requires the development of analytic skills that help identify and solve organizational dilemmas. We also seek to develop students' appreciation for the importance that the human factor plays in driving organizational effectiveness. Often, students with a particular major or concentration tend to focus exclusively on the importance of that discipline (e.g., accounting, finance, marketing, information systems). We stress three important principles to students that are important for effectiveness in the course and for their careers:

- People power organizational performance.

- Human capital serves to help an organization be effective.

- Organizational behavior must be viewed from a strategic, or long-term, organization-wide lens.

This core management course is important because of the accreditation standards put forth by the Association to Advance Collegiate Schools of Business (AACSB). According to the AACSB's web site, accreditation is a process of voluntary, nongovernmental review of educational institutions and programs. Institutional accreditation reviews entire colleges and universities. Institutions that earn accreditation confirm their commitment to quality and continuous improvement through a rigorous and comprehensive peer review. In 2003, AACSB members approved a revised set of standards that are relevant and applicable to all business programs globally and that support and encourage excellence in management education worldwide. These revised standards for business schools include a minimum exposure to a traditional curriculum that focuses on behavioral science and to some new important topics, but interestingly, the AACSB does not provide guidelines for including diversity within the curriculum for business schools. It does, however, stress the importance of understanding the global dimensions of organizations. So, although the organizational behavior course is required for accreditation, the role of diversity within that curriculum, its content, and the extent of coverage vary across institutions and instructors.

Setting the Broader Context

Although accreditation standards may not dictate the importance of including diversity as a core aspect of the curriculum, the changing nature of the workplace provides an even stronger mandate for this transformation. The fact that the workforce is becoming increasingly diverse has been well documented (Bell, 2006; Cox & Blake, 1991; Thomas & Ely, 1996). The nonwhite population is growing more rapidly than the total population, according to the most recent census figures. From 1990 to 2008, the black population will grow by 31%, compared with 11% for the white population and 25% for the total population. The white population will grow by only 3.2% between 2005 and 2010, according to recent census data and projections (U.S. Census Bureau, 2005). Adding to this diversity, the Latino population will grow at a rate of 14.4% and Asian Americans/Pacific

Islanders will grow at a rate of 15.4%, while the growth rate for the overall population during that timeframe will be about 4.2%. Nearly 67 million people of Latino origin are expected to be added to the nation's population between 2000 and 2050. Their numbers are projected to grow from 35.6 million to 102.6 million, an increase of 188%. Their share of the nation's population should nearly double, from 12.6% to 24.4% (U.S. Census Bureau, 2005).

One consequence of these demographic projections for the business school curriculum is that students must be taught how to support and enable relationships among people who come from diverse cultures, backgrounds, and perspectives. A key objective of curriculum transformation is that teachers must grapple with how to engage this diverse population in a common enterprise among disparate groups who "do not share a common history or culture" (Caproni, 2005, p. 269). However, this transformation is done with students who often do not share the same experience, culture, knowledge, or history on the importance of diversity within a business school curriculum. Therefore, teachers must help them prepare for their future experience, which will most certainly involve more cross-racial (and cross-cultural) interactions within organizations (Murrell & Hayes-James, 2001). The business school curriculum must also help them understand that diversity is part of a broader issue of how to balance the needs of multiple diverse stakeholders and yet enable business to operate in a productive and socially responsible manner (Jones & Murrell, 2001).

Implementation Strategy

With the challenge and the importance of our task clear, we began the process of curriculum transformation. However, we did not begin with a completely blank slate. Most textbooks in this area include a chapter on diversity that is typically discussed in one lecture, not throughout the term. If assigned, this topic is usually relegated to one day, which is often referred to as "diversity day," and does not really help students understand the broad complexity or communicate to them the importance of this issue for today's organization. Thus, we didn't want diversity to be just a single topic that is discussed for one lecture within the course but an issue that is embedded throughout the curriculum.

Many of the changes to the curriculum occurred outside of the lecture materials, within the examples, case studies, exercises, and projects that were used to support the core teaching. For example, in discussing an important topic such as communication in organizations, we selected a case study that describes a woman manager having problems with a male subordinate. This accomplishes the dual purpose of presenting material on communication while also addressing diversity in communication style as a function of gender. The result of this approach was to both broaden and deepen the material presented within the course and to help students understand that the business case for diversity was more than just a side topic; it is embedded in all that businesspeople do and manage within their organizations.

An added impact of this implementation strategy is that we were able to disrupt the traditional view of roles, leadership, and power in organizational settings by using diverse examples, exercises, and cases throughout the course. Instead of assuming the traditional model of a male leader and a female subordinate, our more careful attention to the examples and illustrations provided an opportunity for us to address the subtle cues that are often communicated to students within the classroom. Our changes to the organizational behavior curriculum were geared toward putting different models, examples of leaders, and ways of thinking in front of students. Although the chapter on diversity was still part of the source syllabus, we included diversity in many different ways as part of our implementation strategy.

Lessons Learned

Our work in this transformation process is an ongoing effort, but there are two important lessons that we have learned to this point. First, and not surprisingly, both learning and transformation are a process, not an outcome. Although we focused our efforts on key learning objectives and outcome measures, we are constantly reminded that each student arrives at a certain place in his or her understanding and ability to analyze issues dealing with diversity in organizations. We began with some end point in mind but quickly learned that the most important outcome is the change we create in students' knowledge and thinking, regardless of the specific letter grade they receive in the course.

Our second most important lesson learned concerns the limitations of our current metrics for curriculum transformation and student learning. A great deal of attention is currently focused on how to measure the objectives of instruction and student learning. We set forth to transform the way we approached teaching the business case for diversity and to better equip our students to do the same with their future organizations. We quickly discovered, however, the limited arsenal of tools at our disposal to document both the process we used to transform our coursework and the change that students experienced from the beginning of our course to the end. This suggests a great need within our discipline (and we suspect others as well) to develop more rigorous tools for understanding and documenting key aspects of the *learning process,* not just the outcomes. We are currently trying to create our own tools for showing to the students, and to ourselves, that we have accomplished our goals in terms of increasing students' knowledge on important issues concerning diversity in organizations.

References

Bell, M. P. (2006). *Diversity in organizations.* Mason, OH: Thomson South-Western.

Caproni, P. J. (2005). *Management skills for everyday life: The practical coach* (2nd ed.). Upper Saddle River, NJ: Prentice Hall.

Cox, T. H., & Blake, S. (1991). Managing cultural diversity: Implications for organizational competitiveness. *Academy of Management Executive, 5*(3), 45–56.

Jones, R., & Murrell, A. J. (2001). Signaling positive corporate social performance. *Business and Society, 40*(1), 59–78.

Murrell, A. J., & Hayes-James, E. (2001). Gender and diversity within organizations. *Sex Roles, 45*(5/6), 243–257.

Thomas, D. A., & Ely, R. J. (1996). Making differences matter: A new paradigm for managing diversity. *Harvard Business Review, 74,* 79–90.

U.S. Census Bureau. (2005). *Fact sheet for race, ethnic, ancestry group.* Retrieved February 23, 2007, from http://factfinder.census.gov

36

Introducing Students to Islam and *The Qur'an*

Jack Meacham

Why introduce our students to the religion of Islam and to the holy book of Muslims, *The Qur'an?* Islam is, along with Judaism and Christianity, one of the world's great monotheistic religions and, after Christianity, the second most popular religion in the world. The number of adherents to Islam is increasing more rapidly than for other world religions in Asia, Africa, Europe, Canada, and the United States. The integration of Muslims is currently a major issue for the countries of the European Union, with controversies over religious dress in France and over the admission of Turkey, a Muslim and secular republic, into the EU. It's of global significance that the countries with the greatest oil reserves are Muslim. The United States has invaded and occupies two countries, Afghanistan and Iraq, most of whose citizens are Muslim. For any particular course (e.g., comparative literature, history, political science, art history, religious studies, philosophy, or economics), one or more of these reasons might be important as a rationale for integrating Islam and *The Qur'an* into the coursework.

My suggestions for teaching about Islam and *The Qur'an* stem from my own experience in introducing these topics into World Civilizations, a two-semester general education course for first-year students. I have expanded on the material provided in the typical history-survey textbook with, each semester, three to four lectures focused on Islam, *The Qur'an,* and the history of Islamic civilizations; and I devote two of the weekly recitation classes to reading and discussing selections from *The Qur'an.* I have lived and traveled in Muslim countries, as a Peace Corps volunteer in Turkey and as a Fulbright scholar in Bosnia and Herzegovina. However, aside from a few personal stories, there is little that I bring to my teaching that isn't readily available to others who would like to give more attention to Islam and Islamic history, science, art, politics, and societies. The one

213

advantage that I have had is the opportunity to recognize how much I didn't know and to become comfortable confessing my ignorance and asking questions.

Teaching About Islam and *The Qur'an*
Introducing the Religion of Islam

What is the general learning goal in introducing students to Islam and *The Qur'an?* It is not to encourage students to agree with the tenets of Islam or to convince students to convert from their own religious beliefs to those of Islam. Rather, the learning goal is for students to become more knowledgeable about Islam, to become familiar with what Muslims believe and do, and to recognize and reject common stereotypes and misunderstandings. This may be unclear to some students, who might be concerned about potential challenges to their own religious beliefs and identity, or to the teacher's colleagues, who might fear that the line between merely teaching about religion to teaching religion has been crossed. Thus, the student learning goal should be made explicit, either on the course syllabus or for the students in class—or, best, both.

In addressing common stereotypes and misunderstandings, I begin with some easy and nonthreatening questions, such as where Muslims live and what they believe and do. I ask my students to test their knowledge by raising their hands in response to simple multiple choice questions (transparencies laid on an overhead projector or PowerPoint slides), after which I provide the answers, elaborate, and solicit student questions and comments. For example, my students should know which countries have the largest Muslim populations. Many are surprised to learn that this list begins with Indonesia, Pakistan, and India and that the Arab countries account for only a small proportion of Muslims (about a sixth). A map of the world, showing the countries with substantial Muslim populations from Morocco to Indonesia and from Kazakhstan to Nigeria, can be illuminating for many students.

I hope that my students know that Muslims do not worship Muhammad. In some semesters, most appear to know this; in other semesters, many miss this question, and so I retain it in my set. Students can be surprised to learn that Muslims worship the same god as do Jews and Christians. For Muslims, Judaism, Christianity, and Islam are merely three forms of the same religion, the religion of Abraham. One way to elucidate the essence of a religion is to ask what is required for nonbelievers to convert. Raising this question provides an opportunity for non-Muslim students to consider their own core religious beliefs and perhaps to broaden the class discussion beyond Islam. In the case of Islam, those who wish to convert must affirm their faith publicly and with sincerity by declaring that "there is no god but God and Muhammad is His prophet." Conversion to Islam throughout history has not been primarily through conquest, or "by the sword."

The Qur'an imposes a strict prohibition against forcible conversion in Chapter 2 (The Cow), verse 256: "There shall be no compulsion in religion."

Teaching With *The Qur'an*

One of the best translations of *The Qur'an* is one of the least expensive for students, a Penguin Classic, *The Koran,* translated by Dawood (2004). Translations that, like Dawood's, show chapter and verse numbers on page margins make it easy for students to find reading assignments and verses that we are discussing in class. I appreciate Dawood's translation of the Arabic word *Allah* as *God,* which helps students see commonalities among Judaism, Christianity, and Islam. I remind students that we are reading *The Qur'an* in translation and that different translations can sometimes imply different meanings. For many Muslims and in particular for Arabic speakers, the language of the Qur'an is extraordinarily powerful and beautiful. For this reason, I play at least one recitation from the CD that accompanies *Approaching the Qur'an* (Sells, 1999)— usually chapter, or *sura,* 82 (The Cataclysm) or 99 (The Earthquake)—because these are also chapters that I ask students to read.

To reinforce the students' understanding that Judaism, Christianity, and Islam are three forms of the same religion, I ask them to read and discuss selections such as the following: Chapter 2 (The Cow), verses 136–139 affirm belief in God and what was revealed by Abraham, Moses, Jesus, and other prophets. Chapter 3 (The 'Imrans), verses 42–59 describe the virgin birth of Jesus. Chapter 7 (The Heights), verses 137–153 recount the story of Moses, the crossing of the sea, and the tablets and commandments. At chapter 57 (Iron), verse 27, students read, "We gave Jesus the Gospel, and put compassion and mercy in the hearts of his followers." Additional selections that support the same learning goal include chapter 19 (Mary), verses 16–36 and chapter 28 (The Story), verses 29–43. I leave it to my students, the majority of whom are Christian and Jewish, to discover similarities between their own faith and Islam.

A second learning objective is for students to know what *The Qur'an* asks Muslims to believe and do. I introduce this topic with a summary based on my own reading. In doing so, I hope to forestall the unthinking response of some students, which is to cite the Five Pillars of Islam that they are familiar with from high school and Internet sites, and instead to challenge them to construct a deeper understanding of Islam based on their own reading, discussing, and reflecting on *The Qur'an.* Second, I'm attempting to model for students how to be a naive learner seeking a fuller understanding without merely relying on an authoritative or "correct" answer. My summary, which changes from semester to semester, can read like this: Avoid being self-centered, lacking compassion for those in need, pursuing possessions and wealth, hoarding possessions, and engaging in self-delusion; and instead strive to be generous, to have concern for social justice, to give to those who are less fortunate, to share your wealth, and to combat idols such as materialism.

Chapter 17 (The Night Journey), verses 22–39 list commandments similar to the ten that are familiar to Jewish and Christian students. I ask students to consider which commandments are the same and which appear in only one holy text. (Don't count on students to be able to recall the commandments of their own faith; instead, be prepared to write these on the blackboard.) Additional selections that provide guidance for Muslims on how to live as God wants them to include chapter 2 (The Cow), verse 177; chapter 82 (The Cataclysm); and chapter 103 (The Declining Day). All of these emphasize the evaluation of individuals' souls on the Last Day of Judgment. Other short selections that expand on what Muslims should believe and do include chapter 92 (Night), chapter 99 (The Earthquake), and chapter 107 (Alms). The chapters of *The Qur'an* are in order by length, with the shortest at the end; chapters 60 onward are short enough to be assigned in their entirety.

A third learning objective is to know what *The Qur'an* says about relations between Muslims and people of other faiths. The teachings of both the Torah and the Gospel of Jesus are affirmed in chapter 5 (The Table), verses 44–48. Verse 40 in chapter 22 (The Pilgrimage) notes God's role in the defense of "monasteries and churches, synagogues and mosques in which His praise is daily celebrated." Chapter 60 (She Who Is Tested), verse 8 provides one of many openings for tolerance: "God does not forbid you to be kind and equitable to those who have neither made war on your religion nor driven you from your homes." The prohibition against forcible conversion in chapter 2 (The Cow), verse 256 has already been noted; this is reinforced in chapter 109 (The Unbelievers): "You have your own religion, and I have mine."

A fourth learning objective is to know the conditions under which Muslims may fight and kill. Muslims are enjoined in chapter 2 (The Cow), verse 190 not to attack first. They may fight those who attack them, although this response must be proportional to the initial attack (verse 194). Standing between those two verses is verse 191, "Slay them wherever you find them," which is sometimes quoted out of this context. Chapter 8 (The Spoils), verse 61 reads, "If they incline to peace, make peace with them." Another verse that's too often quoted out of context is chapter 9 (Repentence), verse 5. Interpreting this verse—"slay the idolators"—in the context of verses 1–7 makes clear that the reference is to those who fail to honor agreements. Haleem (2001, p. 65) is helpful in understanding these verses. Many students are surprised that there is no obvious reference in the Qur'an to the notion of holy war. *Jihad* in *The Qur'an* refers to the struggle of individual Muslims with themselves as they strive to live their lives as God asks them to do.

A fifth learning objective is to understand what *The Qur'an* says about the place of women and their rights in Muslim society. Chapter 4 (Women), verse 124 and chapter 33 (The Confederate Tribes), verse 35 make clear that women are equal to men in God's sight. Chapter 2 (The Cow), verses 228–232 and chapter 4 (Women), verses 7–22 set forth regulations on divorce and inheritance that were, in the 7th century, quite forward looking. The rights held by women in medieval Christian Europe and even in 19th-century America were far more limited. Chapter 4 (Women), verses 34–35 is open to gross misinterpretation. I strongly recommend reading "Difficulties in Marriage" in Haleem (2001, pp. 46–55) before engaging students with these two verses.

I encourage students to construct their own understanding of these verses from *The Qur'an* rather than rely on what I might say. So that students are prepared for discussion, I ask them to read several of the verses ahead of class and to write a few sentences summarizing or reacting to those verses. In class, I arrange students in groups to share and discuss what they have written. In some classes, I give groups of students who have been assigned different sets of verses a few minutes to prepare before presenting their verses and interpretations to each other. Some students do struggle to find meaning in these verses, but other students can be tremendously insightful and eloquent in their interpretations, and from these students we learn much. It would, of course, be a mistake to call on Muslim students to provide "the Muslim interpretation" of particular verses, just as we would not expect other students to speak for or to defend members of their own faiths. In general, the Muslim students in my courses have contributed to the same extent as non-Muslim students, although they sometimes stop by after class to express approval at how our discussion proceeded or to provide an elaboration of our interpretation of particular verses.

Conclusion

Most students accept that the goal of a liberal education is to prepare them to live in a changing world and that becoming free from ignorance requires that they recognize the importance of historical and cultural contexts (Association of American Colleges and Universities, 1998). Once they begin to listen, read, and discuss, they find learning about the religion of Islam and *The Qur'an* to be worthwhile, for they are discovering much that they had not known before. My impression is that many of today's students—even those who confidently identify themselves as members of a particular faith—are in fact not deeply familiar with their own religious texts and with what they are expected to believe as members of that faith. Learning about Islam and *The Qur'an* can provide an important opportunity for all students to inquire into their own religious beliefs and heritage and to question and reaffirm what they believe. Even Muslim students have told me that they learned about Islam by our focus in class on particular verses and by their reflecting on our discussion. I hope that my non-Muslim students have learned to view Islam not as something strange and fearful but instead as something that is now familiar and that they can in the future be comfortable learning more about.

References

Association of American Colleges and Universities. (1998). *Statement on liberal learning.* Retrieved February 23, 2007, from www.aacu.org/About/statements/liberal_learning.cfm

Dawood, N. J. (Trans.). (2004). *The Koran* (Rev. ed.). New York, NY: Penguin Books.

Haleem, M. A. (2001). *Understanding the Qur'an: Themes and style.* New York, NY: I. B. Tauris.

Sells, M. (Trans.). (1999). *Approaching the Qur'an: The early revelations.* Ashland, OR: White Cloud Press.

37

On Diversity and the Teaching of Religions in India

Fred W. Clothey

A sequence of courses I have been teaching for a number of years is a two-semester study of religion in India. The first semester has generally focused on the classical period; the second semester has focused on the premodern and contemporary. I have been tinkering with these courses, especially in recent years, so that they better reflect my commitment to issues of diversity.

For virtually my entire career, I have been committed to the belief that North Americans need to include in their horizons of understanding the people of Asia. The need for such understanding has become even more urgent in the past two decades for a variety of reasons. One is that such countries as China and India are emerging as major centers of economic, technological, and military power to the point that the 21st century is projected to be a century of Asian hegemony. In addition, more and more of our neighbors are people of Asian descent. In fact, since 1965 when immigration laws were changed, Asia and Latin America have become the main source of immigrants to the United States. From 1931 to 1960, only 5% of all legal immigrants came from Asia and 15% from Latin America, whereas 58% came from Europe and 21% from Canada (Daniels, 1986, p. 41). In the 1970s three quarters of all immigrants came from Latin America (41%) and Asia (34%; Daniels, 1986, p. 41). Because my special interest has been South Asia, I have been intrigued to watch the explosion of the Asian Indian population in the United States. At first, the influx of Asian Indians into the United States was relatively modest; as of 1970, they numbered only 75,000 (Daniels, 1986, p. 42). Today, however, according to the 2000 census, the Asian Indian population has reached nearly 2 million, an increase of 106% over the 1990 census. It is the fastest growing Asian American population and the third largest in the United States after that of the Chinese and of Filipinos. Further, religious institutions

219

built by people of South Asian descent are mushrooming all across North America, five of them in the Pittsburgh area alone.

In addition to the need to pay attention to Asia and its people is the evident need to understand the world's (and North America's) *religious* diversity. I have long believed that one of the best ways to understand the human experience is to understand its religious expressions. Again, today, that need has become more evident, as many of the world's headlines attest. Few questions are more compelling than whether—with our diverse ethnic, linguistic, and religious orientations—we can all share the same planet. We have only begun to come to terms with the various forms of sexism and racism. We are even less self-conscious of our religionism—the propensity to measure, judge, and even dismiss people of other traditions by the standards we claim for our own. To think of people of alternative religions or traditions as "heathen" or "noble savages" or "terrorists" is hardly conducive to peaceful coexistence. To treat them with benign neglect is to ignore them and treat them as if they did not exist. Living and thinking in religious enclaves make us victims of any demagogue or press release that claims religion X is such and such. It also robs us of perspective on ourselves and condemns us to perpetual parochialism.

So I taught the religions of South Asia for years with the conviction that the subject was ipso facto good for students' self-understanding and sensitivity to the larger world. Yet, as I have thought increasingly about the issues of diversity and the world's pluralism, I found myself looking more deeply into the ways these concerns are expressed on the South Asian landscape itself. My courses on India have come to reflect these concerns. Two dimensions in particular will illustrate these changes.

The first is that in looking at South Asia (and its diaspora), it's not enough to look at its majority stream (usually called Hinduism) as though it were some pure tradition that developed in isolation. Rather, the subcontinent has been enriched by scores of diverse indigenous groups as well as by migrants from outside— saints, warriors, scholars, merchants—who have in various ways influenced, and been influenced by, it. Some of these groups reflect minority religious traditions that now are included in my courses. In fact, a significant portion of my courses includes discussion of Islam because well over half a billion of the world's Muslims live in South Asia, far more than live in the Middle East. South Asian Islam is itself diverse and multifaceted, and its accommodations to the South Asian landscape are fascinating. Similarly, discussion of such minority groups as Jews and Parsis (Zoroastrians) find their way into my syllabus.

In addition to examining the minority groups in and of themselves, their interactions (along with those of other migrants and indigenous peoples) with the majority are significant and fascinating. That is, Hinduism cannot be understood adequately without recognizing how it has been impacted by Buddhists and Jains, Muslims and Christians. We learn much from the history of these interactions between majority and minority communities; the responses have ranged from orthopraxy, fundamentalism, even violence in the name of religion, on the one hand—to accommodations, hybridizations, and syncretisms, on the other. In sum, my courses on Indian religions now routinely include both a consideration of the transnational character of developments in India (i.e., the impact of people and ideas coming in and going out) as well as the history of minority communities and their interactions in the majority culture. It is clear that globalization and multiculturalism have been a part of the South Asian scene for generations.

Another significant shift in my focus has been in my increased interest in the role of subaltern peoples, both in the history of India's religions and in its contemporary character. Historically, the study of Indian religions was confined to its texts, especially those written in Sanskrit. But these texts were written by, and were available only to, elites. However, by the 1990s my own research was largely focused on the religious expressions of subaltern people. In the summers of 1990 and 1994, for example, I spent considerable time in the slums of Mumbai, seeking to understand the ways in which lower class Hindus, Muslims, and Christians were expressing their identities through their rituals and shrines. In 1991 my research on the Indian diaspora in Malaysia focused on folks who descended from indentured servants to Southeast Asia. Later, between 1998 and 2002, as I accompanied students in the Pitt-in-India program to the city of Hyderabad each summer, I spent time exploring the ways village shrines and folk deities were being urbanized and classicized. Such observations led to the inevitable conclusion that a similar process of classicization had been going on for centuries. The high gods of the Hindu pantheon, for example, had their roots in hunting or agricultural communities. Elaborate court rituals had co-opted elements of village religion; classical texts had been refined and were disseminated by village dramas, oral stories, and songs; and so on. The classical and the folk had been interacting for generations, each affecting the other.

Now when I teach the religions of India, I include sections on the nature and contributions of subaltern communities. Documentary films, photographs, anecdotes, and role playing (some such exercises based on my own research) help students envision the religious expressions of subalterns. In teaching classical religion, I make it a point to demonstrate the role of folk culture where possible and to explore the interactions between *classical* and *folk*, terms that themselves are too simplistic to be altogether helpful. Among other things, this form of study moves students beyond books and texts, which cannot capture the richness of India's religious expressions, and opens them up to the visual and the performed as well as to the diversity apparent on the subcontinent.

I have come to think of these creative interactions as occurring on boundaries—that is, in times of transition and of religious, ethnic, and cultural pluralism. These boundaries have often been times when such questions as "What does it mean to be religious?" and "Who am I, after all?" come to be asked more explicitly. Because our own era is fraught with boundaries, these sorts of questions are with us in abundance. Many of us who teach courses on Asia, irrespective of our ethnic backgrounds, insofar as we spend time in the cultures about which we teach and are trying to understand them, find ourselves living, thinking, and working on the boundaries between religions, cultures, and academic disciplines. The borders between cultures and academic disciplines become fuzzy, and we find ourselves forging newer expressions of self and academic identities. Some of our students, themselves of diverse background, become aware of their own boundaries and of ways to rethink their own identities in light of what they have been learning. We invite other students to join us on our boundaries so that together we can grope toward a more sensitive and inclusive understanding of our place on the planet.

References

Daniels, R. (1986). *History of Indian immigration to the United States.* New Delhi, India: Asia Society.

38

Teaching Diversity for Social Change

Kathryn Russell

I felt at times I became angry at other people's views and beliefs. However, by the last month or so of class I began to accept people's answers. I began to think more and try and see where that person was coming from. After the "incident" in class when we got all of our feelings out, I had told you how I was angry at first, but the more I listened, the more I understood. I must say one positive thing I have learned here is to try and listen carefully first and show respect. I feel the class has opened my eyes quite a bit, and I hope to curb any prejudices I may still carry with me. The way you handled situations in class was excellent. We were dealing with some hot topics, but you let the conversations heat up a little bit and ended them when they were approaching hostility and anger. It was indeed an interesting semester and a class I can honestly say I will pay attention to after I graduate in May.

I am proud of these comments, which came from a young white male student who took my general education class in prejudice and discrimination at the State University of New York College–Cortland (SUNY–Cortland) in 2003. He speaks to a number of issues that make the class rewarding though difficult to teach. In this chapter I will not only speak from my own experience but also include my students' own voices to give the reader a sense of what diversity classes mean to them.

Background

In the fall of 1988, SUNY–Cortland instituted a requirement in prejudice and discrimination (P&D) as part of its general education (GE) program, one of the first of such undergraduate requirements in the country (Magner, 1990; Francis & Russell, 1993). Not satisfied with curricular reform that merely looked at cultural differences, we wanted our courses to acknowledge the stratification of social power, and we aimed at playing a role in dismantling these institutions. Arts and Sciences Dean John Stockwell enthusiastically supported the initiative, arguing that higher education is uniquely positioned to be a social change agent because of our capacity to analyze forms of racism and sexism and to debate strategies for overcoming them (see Francis & Russell, 1993). Courses from a number of disciplines were listed under one GE category, and students could select from that menu. A description of Cortland's P&D category can be found in the college catalog (SUNY–Cortland, 2005, p. 37).

SUNY–Cortland students do indeed have transformative experiences in P&D courses. They typically report comments like these:

> This class has shown me about topics and issues that I wasn't really aware of or wasn't aware of how serious they were. It made me think about who I am and what I do.

> Some of the issues that we dealt with in here were so very explosive and new to me and my upbringing that I found myself wanting and expecting more from my family, when before I just hid those things. This was good for me and a very real challenge in facing the issues of today that my children and I need to be constantly aware of.

> I have been making a conscious effort to change the way I think and act. I no longer sit back and allow others to be outright racist in my company. I make sure I tell them I think they are wrong and try to justify my reasons why.

Implementation

The Cortland philosophy department's P&D offering is called Prejudice, Discrimination, and Morality. My own course description reads as follows:

> This course will examine prejudice, discrimination, and oppression due to race, ethnicity, disability, sexual orientation, gender, and class. Ideas about social change will be evaluated as ways to enhance freedom, justice, and equality. We will be particularly interested in how power is distributed according to social group and how institutionalized patterns of behavior allow inequality to persist.

In my experience, classes about oppression cannot be approached as though they were like any other class just with a different content. The material is sometimes volatile, often causes anxiety, and calls forth the need to change the world radically. Some of my students reported:

> This class has really changed my attitudes and views toward a lot of major issues. I have made myself think more about my actions toward others and the way I might oppress others. I hope that through my actions, I'm able to change others' attitudes.

> I hope some day we can all be brothers and sisters—a world where equality exists in reality and not just on paper. Maybe we won't get to see it, but we can take part in steps to rid our world of discrimination.

Coming to grips with this material is neither quick nor easy. As one student put it, "At times in class I was extremely emotional; it took time for me to realize what really is going on in life."

Diversity classes require a transformative pedagogy like that recommended by Paolo Freire in *Pedagogy of the Oppressed* (2000), a process he labeled "education for critical consciousness." As educators, we need to be as concerned with "uncovering" the canon as we are with "covering" the traditional syllabus. Revealing the presuppositions behind what has traditionally counted as knowledge can unlock a critical awareness in students that makes them want to learn more. If some students are to become agents of social change, we cannot use the content and technique we have all become comfortable with. The shift in consciousness we need calls for arranging students' desks in a circle, talking in small groups, processing difficult topics through writing and using videos and other media, and taking risks. Throughout the semester, I try to guide students in unlearning what they think they know, and I try to inspire them to have the courage to be uncertain in the face of ambiguity, to be socially engaged, and to speak and act on the basis of their own principles.

I spend the great bulk of the semester teaching students about what institutions are and how they work, helping them understand key analytical concepts, and talking about social policies and ethical analysis. Students have said that one of the most positive aspects of the class is developing analytical reading and writing skills. However, given the nature of the course, I have found that it is particularly important for the class to be student centered. This approach resonates with students, as one in particular commented:

> I liked this class because it wasn't an ordinary sit-down-and-feed-me class. I felt like I was part of a group that dealt with issues in depth. This way of learning is much better than the basic wind-up-teacher method.

The First Day: Breaking the Ice

Using an identity exercise for pairs of students that I learned at a diversity conference, I ask students to team up with someone they do not know. I explain that the exercise is not only for talking but also for active listening. First, one person in the pair talks as the other listens; then they switch roles. After a couple of minutes, I ask them to find a new partner. I go through five or six different sets of pairings, asking these sorts of questions:

- Describe your ethnic group and why you are proud of it.
  (1 minute each person)

- Are there prejudices about your ethnic group that bother you? Why do they bother you? What sort of attitudes would you rather people have?
  (2–3 minutes each)

- When did you first realize that people could be treated differently based on your gender? What did you learn? What values were conveyed to you by the experience? (3 minutes each)

For the next series of pairings, I move to variations of the last question and address skin color, income levels, sexuality, language spoken, and disabilities. This exercise broaches the sensitive topics of the class in a fun way, encourages students to examine their own behaviors and beliefs, and leads to a focus on socialization as we notice the patterns of similarities among students' experiences.

Creating a Safe Space

During the first week, I ask students to write about what happens in classrooms where students are afraid to speak up and about what they need from other students and from me to feel free to voice their opinions. The class and I then brainstorm a list on the board. I collect the students' writings, and at the beginning of the next session, I read anonymously from some of them. This always gets the class's attention, and the students seem to be especially sensitive to the presence of other vulnerable beings in their midst. We summarize what we need from each other and make a conscious commitment—once again, in writing—to conform to these guidelines. Later in the semester, if a student violates one of these agreed-upon rules, we can hark back to these earlier agreements.

Who's Here?

This exercise is useful for illuminating the diversity of students in the classroom and encouraging an awareness that we cannot always tell "what" people are by looking at them. We sit in a circle. I ask people to stand up if a characteristic applies to them and note how they feel about standing up. I start with relatively comfortable subjects like "Who is left-handed?" Then I move to questions like "Who has Native American ancestors?" "Who has people in their family who came from Africa?" and so on for other ethnic groups. I also ask about topics like "Who has gays or lesbians among their family or friends?" and about socioeconomic issues. We talk about what questions had the most or least people standing and why, and about what sorts of identities felt the most safe or most dangerous and why.

Collaborative Group Project on Sexism in the Media

Working in a group early in the semester allows students to discover allies in the class, and they enjoy finding examples of media sexism they might otherwise have not noticed. As one student commented, "This class has made me look at things I would normally pass by and not think twice about." A danger in discussing sexism is that some male students can feel targeted. When asked to write a note to future students, one man said:

> Well, pal, in this class it sucks to be a guy, but it will open your eyes to common, everyday things. You'll start to see how women really are sexually objectified. If you're smart, you'll change the way you look at things and/or the way you treat women.

It seems he found the material a double-edged sword but ultimately worthwhile. I encourage the class to look for female *and* male gender constructs, but the women in the class (and the fact that sexism subordinates women, not men) tend to focus us on issues facing women.

I direct my students to my Stereotypes in Context web site (Russell, 1999), where I present stereotypes as part of a culture's ideology, reflecting its power relations. I had been assigning projects on identifying stereotypes for years, but I wanted students to move beyond pointing to examples and be able to offer a cultural critique and concentrate on issues of power. The site explains what makes something a stereotype, gives examples from mass media, and offers exercises demonstrating how to put issues in a context. I also draw on the tools of media literacy to encourage recognition that media messages have embedded values and points of view stemming from the culture at large and that such messages are carefully constructed by businesses whose primary motive is profit. Other pages incorporate material from British aesthetician John Berger's *Ways of Seeing* (1990) to illustrate how ads function as forms of communication that appeal to the fantasy life of consumers. I have several quotations from Berger and ask students to paraphrase them; I assign the class to bring in examples of ads that appeal to fantasies that call into play constructions of race, gender, class, or sexuality. Since advertising is ultimately about money, the site also includes pages on the political economy of ads in a consumerist society.

Managing Classroom Tension

Diversity classes are not inevitably volatile, but some faculty members avoid teaching them out of fear of potential conflict. One student said, "I find myself often very uncomfortable in this class. I do enjoy the class very much (it's probably one of the best I've taken in the past four years), but I don't enjoy feeling uncomfortable." As a teacher, I have had to learn that conflict and discomfort are not "bad," and that they are not necessarily "my fault." As one of my students said, "It is important for the instructor not to take the tension personally." Nor is it helpful to ignore conflict—in doing so, I might lose a teachable moment. The class and I are, after all, involved in the tricky, dangerous business of learning to communicate across differences so that we can build a society that is more humane. Conflict can be a creative turning point that enables the class to move to a deeper level of trust and understanding. I have gleaned many lessons about how to handle conflict when it does occur.

Admit that I cannot do it alone. When the discussion gets so heated that it's scary or when I have a boring session during which students are not willing to talk, I cry on the shoulder of a friend—literally or figuratively—and together we figure out how to make the next session better.

I have been fortunate to be able to pair several of my diversity classes with a class in academic writing—two professors teaching two different, but linked, classes to the same cohort of students. These synergistic combinations increase the meaningfulness of each class because we subvert our disciplinary boundaries, and we both teach conceptual content and rhetorical strategies. We can also act as allies of each other. But even when my class is not paired, I find colleagues to process things with.

Rely on other students to respond when a student says something inappropriate; I am not there to do ideological battle with the students. For example, in my spring 2005 class when we were talking about how clothing is socially coded, one man said he would never wear a pink shirt because that would be "too faggy." I explained I was not comfortable with that word, and then I posed the problem to the class for discussion. The president of the Rainbow Alliance was in the class, so she addressed the issue in a helpful way, given her experience doing panels on homosexuality in other classes. Actually, these two students became friends during a group project, and at the end of the semester during a discussion about language, the young man, who was always quite vocal, referred back to his earlier remark and recounted how he had learned that words carry a lot of social baggage and that people have to be conscious of what they might convey to others through their words.

Have students write about incidents so that they can dump their feelings on paper and tell an authority figure what they think. At the next session, read some of the remarks anonymously, remind them about the guidelines for safe space they agreed to, and get students in a circle for a discussion so that issues can come to some sort of resolution. I used this technique when discussion became heated after a black female student in my class recounted having had a water balloon thrown at her from a dorm window. Of course, she was upset, and when she described this event as racially biased, a conflict among the students erupted. One black woman said in an angry way that she thought the white students in the class were all "fakes": they just say things in class to impress the teacher, but they don't do anything against racism. Several white students felt this was unfair and defended themselves vigorously. The next lesson was relevant here.

When conflict does occur, I have to exert leadership as a professional—it's a balancing act, to be sure, but I need to acknowledge the fear and anger that students have while not blaming or discounting anyone's feelings. It took a couple of sessions to process what happened, but the class ended up being one of my most successful.

Angry White Men

Though I emphasize that we are trying to understand institutions and their history and that students should not personalize the issues—indeed overpersonalizing the material can be a form of resistance—the class can be a difficult one for a student who feels lumped into a group that is causing all the problems. Here is an example of that sort of response:

> I feel that, throughout the year, as a white male I was the bad guy. Many of the articles read pointed a lot of fingers and neg-lected to mention that white males are helping change things. I think some more sensitivity is needed in this area. Rather than being called a racist, sexist, and class oppressor all semester long, I think there needs to be some positive input toward the role of white males in society.

Perhaps this male student was overly sensitive, but I think he had a point; and he also recognizes the necessity of change. Over the years I have incorporated more and more material on working-class issues and on poverty. I tend to emphasize how capitalist power relations leave most men at an unearned disadvantage. I have also tried to include more material on what positive changes are being made by white working-class and poor men, women from all racial and ethnic groups, and men of color. I also emphasize the role of being an ally, always holding out the possibility of helping change things.

Conclusion

Although some progress has been made in accomplishing the goals of diversity studies, much remains to be done. Students of color can still legitimately complain that college catalogs sporting images of black and Latino students on their covers are opportunistic. The courses listed inside are usually taught by white faculty from a Eurocentric point of view to an overwhelmingly white student body. Feminist students still fight against a masculinist culture that pervades the campus atmosphere, making date rape and other forms of violence against women all too common. Instead of becoming discouraged, however, educators can recognize the need to take transformative pedagogy to a deeper, more systematic level, using such efforts to build far-reaching social change.

References

Berger, J. (1990). *Ways of seeing.* London, UK: Penguin Books.

Francis, P. L., & Russell, K. (1993, Fall). Transforming the core curriculum: A requirement in prejudice and discrimination. *Transformations, 4*(2), 46–57.

Freire, P. (2000). *Pedagogy of the oppressed.* New York, NY: Continuum.

Magner, D. K. (1990, March 28). Difficult questions face colleges that require students to take courses that explore issues relating to race. *The Chronicle of Higher Education,* pp. A20–A21.

Russell, K. (1999). *Stereotypes in context.* Retrieved February 23, 2007, from http://web.cortland .edu/russellk/courses/prjdis/html/scbase.htm

State University of New York College–Cortland. (2005). *Degree requirements.* Retrieved February 23, 2007, from www.cortland.edu/catalog/undergrad200506/urequirements.pdf

39

Diversifying a Political Science Core Class: American Political Process

Reinhard Heinisch

American Political Process (APP) is one of those courses that appears to be easy but in reality is quite challenging to adapt to the agenda of diversity and inclusiveness. Unlike classes in geology or physics, this introductory course on American government seems to be a natural fit for the major themes of the diversity agenda. Where else if not in such a class would students be exposed to the struggle for equal rights or the history of slavery and segregation? Which other course would naturally cover important Supreme Court rulings on civil rights? In fact, standard textbooks routinely devote at least one chapter to diversity-related themes that can be readily incorporated into such a course.

The Challenges When Adapting APP

The primary challenge of teaching APP is precisely that it may be overwhelmed by the expectation of what this course can do to incorporate issues of diversity. In short, APP may be expected to accomplish that which most other courses cannot: to serve as a principal means of diversifying the curriculum. At the University of Pittsburgh–Johnstown, APP faces a series of additional challenges. Limited resources dictate that it must be a large course, drawing regularly several sections of more than 80 students. In addition, the class is a popular elective that allows students to satisfy a general education requirement. APP is also intended as the introduction to the political science major and, as such, a prerequisite for most other courses in the department. A further complicating factor lies in the varied academic backgrounds of our student population. More selective or less discerning institutions may instead decide to benchmark higher or lower when setting learning objectives and assessing course outcomes. A final difficulty is the somewhat homogeneous and culturally conservative student body and insular nature of the school's setting. As a comprehensive institution in rural western Pennsylvania that places an emphasis on the professions, the University of Pittsburgh–Johnstown tends to draw more utilitarian-minded students than those of the typical liberal arts college, who may be more receptive to a diversity agenda.

The Original Course Outline

The course is traditionally taught to provide an overview of the most important features of American politics. It is extremely wide ranging in scope, stretching from 17th-century English philosophy to Social Security, from the Federalist Papers to the American presidency and Watergate, from campaigns and elections to the court system and foreign policy. A special emphasis is placed on the constitutional process and the institutions of government. The course must also review familiar events and dates from American history because students often lack any knowledge of even the most basic facts and concepts. Naturally, there also used to be a segment on civil rights, but it was merely one of many topics, all of which stood in relative isolation from each other. This section appeared generally about halfway into the course at an appropriate juncture between covering the institutions and societal aspects of American politics. Yet such a treatment of the subject matter was deeply dissatisfying from the standpoint of raising awareness about a history of discrimination as well as the growing complexity of contemporary American society.

As an alternative, it would have been possible to rely on radical textbooks and emphasize more of a history-from-below approach. In such versions, however, the founding fathers often become cartoon figures, presented as little more than self-righteous elitists and slaveholders driven primarily by economic self-interest. Such accounts frequently gloss over both the historical context and the fact that the system created by the framers of the U.S. Constitution, however elitist and flawed, contained the means of redressing the injustices contained therein. Radical perspectives and even polemics can certainly be stimulating and, thus, excellent teaching tools, but they require students that already be more familiar with the traditional view than is the case here. In fact, an all too radical approach would probably result in a backlash by alienating students socialized in a culturally more conservative environment.

The Revised Course

Extensive discussions in the context of a university-sponsored diversity seminar were invaluable in devising solutions to the challenges just described. The task was to maintain the course as a complex introduction to the varied aspects of American government that would satisfy both the beginner and the student in the major but that would nonetheless provide a meaningful and substantive exposure to questions of cultural, ethnic, and gender diversity. The key was to weave this agenda into the very fabric of the course without succumbing to simplistic revisionism.

Ordinary Lives—Political Lives

In its new format the course begins with the distribution of a representative sample of some 80 biographies. These are brief one-page sketches containing the demographic and personal information of individuals who vary in terms of age, gender, education level, ethnic origin, religion, sexual orientation, occupation, and nationality of birth. Viewing the world from these other identities, students are allowed to imagine what expectations these people would have from politics and what political interests they would pursue. For many students it is a stretch to imagine a reality beyond their own. It is important to remember, however, that the point here is not to achieve a nuanced reality but to raise the students' consciousness and start the learning process. This has proved a valuable pedagogical tool used in many modern museums and simulation competitions (e.g., Model United Nations). Taking the Rawlsian notion of justice as the point of departure, the class debates the foundations of government and requires students to consider what lives they would lead with their new identities and what kinds of ambitions and realistic opportunities they would have given their biographical backgrounds.

Once we establish certain connections between distinct demographic features and political interests, we approach the question pondered by framers of the Constitution and their philosophical forebears, particularly Thomas Hobbes and John Locke: What kind of government would be the right one for people that fit the Hobbesian or Lockean view of human nature—"man" seen as a rational, self-interested maximizer of wealth whose life without government and, thus, order would be nasty, brutish, and short. This exercise is not intended to expose the flawed nature of the constitutional process but to show that the founders of the American model were bound by their time and horizon of experiences, which invariably shaped their thinking and the documents they created. It becomes thus an even more astounding tribute whenever the foundational documents transcend their historicism and aim for a true universalism. In this manner, the students can understand how different experiences can result in different goal formation and, thus, different political interests.

The course shows how the constitutional framework filters and eliminates certain political ambitions while it strengthens and focuses others, thus boosting (intentionally or unintentionally) the welfare and well-being of some groups over, or at the expense of, others. We learn how certain values and concepts (e.g., individualism, self-reliance, and autonomy) are given greater preference in the American narrative than others. The discussion of the institutions of government—where they come from, who set them up, and by what mechanism they decide whether an interest is legitimate—leads students to realize that, at its inception, the Constitution reflected the intentions and interests of a property-owning elite of Protestant Anglo-Saxon origin. Its genius, however, lay in the flexibility and potential that had yet to be realized in a protracted struggle by different groups for equal rights and equal protection.

A substantial segment is devoted to civil rights. Here we examine in detail the situation of women and African-Americans and both groups' struggle for greater equality. Students are also encouraged to investigate the history of other groups, such as gays and lesbians, Latinos, Chicanos, Asian Americans, or people with disabilities—for this purpose extra credit options are made available. Students also complete assignments in which they research advocacy groups and their agenda and investigate specific questions of the history of civil rights (the Underground Railroad, the Jim Crow laws, the Comstock laws and reproductive information, landmark civil rights cases, etc.). Invited speakers and videos augment the class materials (e.g., segments from the PBS series *Eyes on the Prize* or from *Malcolm X*). Whenever possible, students are encouraged to attend relevant lectures (e.g., one by Bill Means, a Lakota Indian leader).

The subsequent segment on civil liberties and the courts serves as an introduction to the American legal system. Issues of diversity can be easily incorporated by discussing the courts' historical role in addressing and remedying discrimination when political institutions proved unable or intransigent. To emphasize diversity in a context other than the specific issue of civil rights, I invite professionals of minority backgrounds to speak to the class about their work for the government—I frequently rely, for example, on an African-American friend who is a U.S. assistant district attorney to help discuss the criminal justice system.

Politics and the People

Given the course's expanded emphasis on diversity, there are, by necessity, topics that require trimming and tweaking without being omitted entirely. Issues such as campaigns and elections, political parties, the media, and lobbying and interest groups were thus fused together into a larger bloc titled "Politics and the People." The unifying feature of these different issue areas is that they all are positioned at the intersection of government institutions and the public at large. Thus, it is not difficult to address issues of diversity by returning again to the concept of political filtering or mainstreaming discussed earlier. It provides an understanding of why the interests of certain groups are more readily taken up more and acted on than those of others.

Interest articulation and aggregation also play an important role when discussing public policy, the final part of the course. Here the aforementioned biographies help address the common misperception that "the people" represent a unified whole and that divisions among them are not genuine. Showing the PBS documentary *Class* is designed to highlight the importance of how class stratification in American society translates into politics and subsequently influences public policy. The course covers public policy by emphasizing social and economic policy, "other" domestic policy, and foreign and security policy. In each area, the following questions are raised and discussed: What are the goals and means of the policy? Whose interests are served? Who has input? Which ideas and values influence the selection of objectives, mechanisms, and perceived solutions?

In economic policy the students learn, for example, about trade-offs between economic policy choices. This segment also allows for an extensive discussion of both social programs (e.g., Social Security, Medicare, Medicaid) and the varying conceptions of poverty and welfare. Particularly in policy areas such as health care, crime and law enforcement, education, and social protection, the issues of diversity and equal access can be easily made a focus of class discussion. Foreign and security policy, by contrast, tends to have less direct connection to diversity. Nonetheless, the disproportional contribution by minorities, immigrants, and lower income Americans to national security through military service presents itself as an important topic for discussion. Particularly, in light of the United States' Middle East policy and the pervasive media coverage of terrorism and radical Islam, it may be useful to discuss such issues in a broader global political context. It is also helpful to get students to consider the situation of Muslims in the United States. To gain a better understanding, we invite members of the local Muslim community for an unscripted forum of exchange with our students. This affords both students and community members a chance to interact and address mutual misconceptions.

Conclusion

The revised course set out with an ambitious set of goals. As any instructor will know, the extent to which all objectives can be achieved depends on the students and on a variety of factors that change from semester to semester. Sometimes, there are dominant political issues that can strengthen the focus on diversity or detract from it. Generally, I have found that students respond positively to the course revision. Most gratifying is that there has been no indication that the students feel they have some political agenda thrust on them. By contrast, they see these questions as a natural extension of what a course in American politics ought to be about. It is undoubtedly helpful if those instructors who incorporate diversity issues into their classes cooperate and coordinate with each other, thus reinforcing the students' experience and rendering the effect more powerful. Most crucially, any discussion of diversity must be substantive, pertinent, and interesting enough to stand on its own. Today's media-savvy and jaded student audiences will quickly detect ideological zeal or self-righteous high-mindedness and thus tune out. This, however, would ultimately do more harm than good despite the instructor's most Herculean efforts to expose students to this rich and important topic.

40

Designing an Advanced Course in Cross-Cultural Psychology

Dereece Smither

The advanced seminar course at the University of Pittsburgh–Johnstown is a small discussion-driven course for psychology majors. It is characterized as an intensive course that requires students to read and discuss current pursuits in the field of psychology. Students, therefore, must have completed several required classes, including Introductory Statistics and Research Methods, before taking the course; most of them are juniors and seniors. The topics offered each semester depend on the expertise and interest of the professor or professors assigned to teach it. I had been interested in teaching a course in multicultural/cross-cultural aspects of psychology since I had a cross-cultural developmental psychology course as a graduate student. The class was one of only two graduate psychology courses offered that had a multicultural/cross-cultural focus (the other was a course in multicultural counseling). I found my own experience with the course to be extremely enlightening, informative, and relevant, bringing a new perspective to all the canons of developmental psychology. So when given a choice to design an upper level course, I decided to teach a cross-cultural course that was broader in scope with the hope of providing the students an experience similar to my own.

Implementation

The purpose of the seminar was to introduce students to important issues related to diversity in the field of psychology. I believe there is great value in studying various cultures from both practical *and* theoretical perspectives. Because they are living in a world whose intercultural connectedness is growing exponentially, psychology students need to be aware of the differences and the similarities between various populations to ensure the generalizability of psychological theories and research findings. It was assumed that all the students in the class had had previous classes in psychology; therefore, the focus of this class was on examining traditional themes in psychology through a cross-cultural lens.

Course Goals and Objectives

I had several goals and objectives I hoped to address throughout the course. Morey and Kitano (1997) suggest several ways of generating and organizing goals and objectives for a diversity course. From these suggestions I derived my primary goal: exposing students to the field of psychology's current move toward globalization. Two additional goals, which I considered no less important, were expanding the students' competence in communicating ideas and improving their critical thinking skills. These three main aims led to the following specific goals and objectives that I wanted to focus on in the course:

1. Reexamining traditional psychological theories

    - To expose students to knowledge and understanding regarding the impact of culture on various topical areas in psychology

    - To discuss the history and contributions of various cultural groups and the effect of the absence of multicultural perspectives on the historical development of psychological theory

2. Encouraging understanding of the value of diversity and equity

    - To examine the social construction of identities and world knowledge by race, gender, ethnicity, class, sexual orientation, physical ability, nation of origin, and so forth

    - To demonstrate sensitivity to cultural differences by recognizing the students' own and others' biases and to understand how such biases impact social interactions

    - To differentiate between personal discomfort and intellectual disagreement in social and cultural conflict situations

3. Enhance the written expression of ideas

    - To develop the students' ability to write on a topic, their general writing skills, and their use of APA style

4. Encourage oral expression of ideas

    - To expect students to prepare ahead of class and to play an active role in classroom activities

    - To insist on mutual respect among students and between the students and the instructor

5. Develop critical thinking skills

- To ask students to generate their own personal outlook that allows them to appraise information and make better judgments about information with which they are confronted

- To engage students in activities and discussion that require analysis and problem solving regarding psychological phenomena

To put these goals into practice, I used various in-class and out-of-class activities and assignments. To focus on the reexamination of psychological theories, I asked students to read chapters and articles that challenged the universality of those theories (e.g., Segall, Dasen, Berry, & Poortinga, 1999) and provided an updated description of the major areas of psychological research. The main areas of reexamination were research and assessment, and perceptual and cognitive processes. Topics traditionally thought to pertain more directly to multiculturalism and diversity—such as gender and sexual orientation, intercultural relations and conflict—were also covered extensively in this course. To meet the goal of enhancing communication, I asked that the students come prepared for each class by making sure that they had read, and generated discussion questions on, the assignment. Though there were no tests in this course, students were very frequently assessed on their ability to speak and write about the weekly topics. They were also evaluated on their ability to apply their knowledge of cross-cultural psychological themes to papers on popular literature and films and to carry out a major literature review on a diversity-related topic. These evaluations were also useful in gauging the improvement of the students' critical thinking skills.

Outcomes

I believe my cross-cultural psychology class was successful at achieving many of the previously stated goals and objectives in a relatively short time. This was evidenced in the students' responses to their final topic paper titled, "What, If Anything, Did I Learn?" In this paper students gave a personal evaluation of whether they believed that course goals and objectives had been achieved. The following is a sample of the statements that the students assessed (by describing their level of agreement with each on a 5-point scale where 1= *strongly disagree* and 5 = *strongly agree*). These questions were derived from a seminar on evaluating learning objectives in the classroom (Anderson, 2000).

- This course introduced ideas I had not previously encountered.

- This course has helped me to ask questions, analyze arguments, connect ideas, and think systematically about problems and issues.

- This course has helped me to become more self-assured in expressing my understanding of a topic orally.

- In this class I have learned to move away from use of dichotomous thinking.

- In this class I have come to understand it is acceptable to experience cognitive ambiguity and/or conflict about a topic, especially new ideas which conflict with ideas I already hold.

- I find myself talking with other students outside of class about material covered in this course.

- This course has made me consider similar courses in psychology and related fields.

Most of the students agreed or strongly agreed with these and other statements, especially those having to do with critical thinking. Many of the students' comments reminded me of my own after my first cross-culture-based class. Though students were especially enthusiastic about the value of in-class discussions, that enthusiasm waned significantly when they discussed the value of the writing component of the course. Even so, they too acknowledged a change in their ability to demonstrate their knowledge in written form.

In my own evaluation, I found that as the course progressed, students demonstrated better writing skills, better skill at expressing their opinions, and better skill at merging others' ideas with their own. It also became apparent that reexamination of psychological theories helped them to understand these theories more clearly overall and to be able to communicate problems with those theories based on cross-cultural analysis. So far, I have taught this course twice, and I have had similar reviews from students about what they had learned.

Conclusions

The students were not the only ones who learned some new things about the field. I was constantly reminded of how far psychology has come and how far the field has to go in using the principles of psychology to explain and predict the behavior and mental processes of *all* people. Further, teaching this class has enriched my research activities by adding a compelling complexity to them. Since I have taught the class, many of the themes have carried over into my other classes. I have recently reorganized my Introduction to Psychology course so that diversity and critical thinking are themes that persist throughout the course. Also, I have taught a second advanced seminar, Gender and Psychology, which had a very similar structure and similar outcomes. In summary, I have had a lot of success in setting up a class focusing on multiculturalism, implementing my goals, and measuring student learning outcomes.

References

Anderson, J. A. (2000, October). *Turning lectures into collaborative learning environments to pro-mote active student learning.* Paper presented at the Seventh Annual Institute on Teaching and Mentoring, Orlando, FL.

Morey, A. I., & Kitano, M. K. (1997). *Multicultural course transformation in higher education: A broader truth.* Needham Heights, MA: Allyn & Bacon.

Segall, M. H., Dasen, P. R., Berry, J. W., & Poortinga, Y. H. (1999). *Human behavior in global perspective: An introduction to cross-cultural psychology* (2nd ed.). Needham Heights, MA: Allyn & Bacon.

41

Incorporating Diversity Into a History of Psychology Course

John W. Mullennix

The History and Systems of Psychology course at the University of Pittsburgh–Johnstown is an upper level undergraduate class that fulfills a curriculum requirement for psychology majors. Nonmajors may take the class as well, with permission of the instructor. When I began teaching this course 10 years ago, I designed it specifically to be interdisciplinary in nature. I wished students to examine the evolution of the field of psychology through this course, which I viewed as part psychology, part history, and part philosophy. In the first portion of the course, I spent a good deal of time discussing the philosophical underpinnings of the discipline of psychology. I began with the early Greek philosophers (i.e., Socrates, Plato, Aristotle), progressed to the early and medieval Christian philosophers (St. Augustine, Thomas Aquinas) and the Renaissance (Descartes, da Vinci, etc.), and finished with the Mental Passivity movement (Hobbes, Locke, Hume) and the German rationalists (Kant, Hegel, Schopenhauer). In this part of the course, I stressed the duality of rationalist and empiricist thought that began in ancient Greece and persisted over time to influence early schools of psychology in the mid 1800s to the early 1900s.

For the rest of the course, I turned my attention to examining the early emerging discipline of psychology. Traditionally, I've accomplished this by examining some of the advancements in scientific methodology and human anatomy/physiology that have impacted psychology, followed by an in-depth look at each school of thought (e.g., structuralism, behaviorism, gestaltism, etc.) in roughly chronological order. When I discuss each school of thought, I focus on the primary theoretical features of the paradigm, the classic studies of interest, and the people and personalities involved. The following list of course objectives summarized what I expected students to learn:

- To compare and contrast various historical schools of thought in psychology

- To analyze how various schools of thought have led to the state of the field today

- To critique original works from major historical figures in the field with regard to their impact on the current field

- To become conversant in the language of those historical figures who helped shape the field

- To have a general working knowledge of the philosophers and historical figures in the field in terms of who they were and why they were important

In terms of class assignments, students were required to read, analyze, and critique three original works from major historical figures in psychology (e.g., Pavlov, Watson, James, Skinner, etc.). They also performed a group assignment in which they assembled a multimedia presentation on what they believed the field of psychology would look like 50 years from the present day.

Impetus for Change

After teaching this course for many years, I realized that, with respect to multiculturalism and whether a course is exclusive, inclusive, or transformed (Kitano, 1997), the way I taught the course probably fell in between the categories of exclusion and inclusion. An exclusive course, as defined by Kitano:

> presents and maintains traditional, mainstream experiences and perspectives on the discipline. . . . The instructor conveys information in a didactic manner, and students demonstrate their acquisition of knowledge through objective or subjective written examinations. . . . In the exclusive classroom, class time is not given to discussion of social issues not directly related to the discipline. (p. 23)

On the other hand:

> an inclusive course presents traditional views but adds alternative perspectives. Content integration in an inclusive course can range from simple addition of new viewpoints without elaboration to efforts at analyzing and understanding reasons for historical exclusion. The instructor uses a wide array of teaching methods to support students' active learning of course content. . . . The instructor monitors student participation and employs learning activities that support participation by all students. (p. 23)

And, finally:

> A transformed course challenges traditional views and assumptions; encourages new ways of thinking; and re-conceptualizes the field in light of new knowledge, scholarship, and new ways of knowing. . . . Methods capitalize on the experience and knowledge that students bring and encourage personal as well as academic growth. (p. 23)

In essence, my goal for modifying this course, with respect to issues of diversity and multiculturalism, was to move it from the exclusive-inclusive level to the inclusive-transformed level. One reason for this change lies with the characteristics of the student population at the university I teach. The students are overwhelmingly Caucasian, Protestant/Catholic individuals drawn from the rural area of western and central Pennsylvania. Many of these students are the first people in their families to attend college, and many have not traveled outside the immediate geographic area. In terms of their future careers in psychology, many of the majors take jobs in urban settings or other areas of the United States, where they encounter diverse populations they have little experience with. I feel strongly that students need to develop a sensibility and sensitivity about other cultures and populations that will serve them well in the future, particularly when working with people in a clinical or social services capacity. I view a high level of social consciousness and knowledge about diversity and multiculturalism as essential for these students.

Another reason for change was the more global goal of fostering critical thinking. In the history of psychology, many contributors to the field were ignored for years because of their status as women, ethnic minorities, or non-Western researchers. I felt that I needed to emphasize more strongly an analysis of the societal conditions that led to these situations and have students work through the logic of how these types of situations occur and how to understand them.

Implementation

In general, when overhauling existing courses, I am loath to change numerous aspects of the course simultaneously. As a result, I decided to make incremental changes to the course and see how they worked before making more extensive changes. First of all, I incorporated three additional course objectives:

- To recognize the historical contribution of American minorities and women to the field

- To recognize the effect that sociocultural factors have had on the development of psychology

- To synthesize a sophisticated view of the historical development of psychology that encompasses various issues related to the social context of the time periods involved

To begin the transition to a course that emphasizes diversity and multiculturalism, I made several changes. The first change was in the assigned readings. Ultimately, I will choose a new text for the course that emphasizes the history of psychology within a larger social context, which will help in terms of how I frame the discussion of the historical figures and schools of thought in psychology. But for the time being, I inserted a number of new readings into the course that focus on women, African-Americans, and Asians who have impacted psychology over time. These readings were woven throughout the course. By having students read these articles, I hoped to create an atmosphere whereby the readings suggested a number of issues that could be discussed at various points throughout the semester.

I also introduced two new writing assignments. The first was a biographical exercise. For this assignment, students selected a historical figure from the history of psychology who was a member of a nondominant culture from the late 1800s or early 1900s (my definition of *nondominant* refers to people from cultures or countries outside Western Europe and the United States, to women, or to ethnic minorities within the United States). They either chose someone from a list I provided or found a person on their own. Some examples of historical figures the students wrote about included Mary Whiton Calkins, Kenneth Clark, Edna Heidbreder, Francis Cecil Sumner, Chen Li, and Zing-Yang Kuo. The second new assignment was to read and critique an article about a female psychologist named Ethel Puffer who, in the early 1900s, faced many obstacles in her work. I felt that students would gain a greater appreciation for the problems American women had gaining status in the field in the early 1900s.

Overall, these initial changes were modest. When I offer the course again, I will make further changes that are more substantial. The first change will be to explicitly incorporate into class content and discussion the neglected role of women and minorities in American psychology. The second change will be to the critical analysis papers for the course. In the modified assignments, students will have to explicitly address how the sociocultural zeitgeist of the historical times affected the author's work. The third change will be to insert a two-week examination of a psychological disorder—namely, hysteria—and how this disorder was handled with respect to the schools of thought in psychology. This will provide an opportunity to explore how gender, race, and class factors related to the treatment of this disorder over time and will provide an opportunity to examine how non-Western cultures handled this disorder. I believe that these changes will open a window to class discussion on how these diversity-related issues affected psychology in the past and how they affect psychology today.

Outcomes

The student feedback I received in terms of the initial changes I had made was illuminating. Many students expressed surprise at the idea that there were historical figures in psychology whose work had been ignored and/or suppressed because of their status as women, ethnic minorities, or non-Westernized cultures. For example, in class I discussed the story of Mary Whiton Calkins. In 1890, Calkins took graduate courses in psychology at Harvard with William James, one of the most famous figures in the history of psychology. Although James later wrote that her doctoral examination was the most brilliant examination for the Ph.D. that they had had observed at Harvard (Furumoto, 1980), Harvard refused to grant her a doctoral degree because of her gender. Despite this, she obtained a position at Wellesley College and later became the first woman elected president of the American Psychological Association. When I talked about this story, students were generally astonished. This lecture segued into a general discussion about the reasons why these types of events occurred at those times. Students also seemed to appreciate the writing assignments, and some of them remarked that the biographical exercise forced them to think about people in the history of psychology in a completely different light. But in terms of more tangible demonstrations of changes in students' attitudes and/or thinking, I will have to wait until I receive feedback from students who have graduated and moved on to graduate programs or jobs to see how this course may have impacted them in the long run.

Conclusion

I believe that the incorporation of the new readings and assignments lent themselves to opening up class discussions of how gender, race, and class issues have impacted the development of psychology as a field. In addition, I believe such changes sparked discussions of whether these issues still affect the field today, and I hope they raised students' consciousness about diversity. I did not receive any negative feedback on the changes. The initial incremental changes I made took well, so I am ready to move forth with further changes. As I continue to teach this course, I do believe that it will move closer to the inclusive-transformed level.

Another point to mention is that, although the student population is fairly homogenous at the University of Pittsburgh–Johnstown, there are increasing numbers of women, members of ethnic minorities, people of differing sexual orientations, and foreign students in the student body. Positioned as I am— namely, as an American, Caucasian, middle-class, heterosexual male—I have tried to understand to a greater degree how my status affects my interactions with students from different backgrounds. I want to ensure a safe atmosphere where all students feel comfortable in expressing their opinions. Related to this issue, I inserted updated guidelines into the course syllabus emphasizing rules for class discussion that specify appropriate conduct for interacting with others in the class.

Finally, although I have put a considerable amount of thought and work into transforming this course, it is an experiment. As an experiment, certain aspects of change will succeed; others will fail. But overall, for the reasons that I cited at the beginning of this chapter, not only do I believe that it is desirable to prepare my students for a future diverse and multicultural world; I believe that it is necessary. I hope that in some small way what they experience in this particular course generalizes to their thought processes and the manner in which they later approach the postdegree world and their personal interactions with others.

References

Furumoto, L. (1980). Mary Whiton Calkins (1863–1930). *Psychology of Women Quarterly, 5,* 55–68.

Kitano, M. K. (1997). What a course will look like after multicultural change. In A. I. Morey & M. K. Kitano (Eds.), *Multicultural course transformation in higher education: A broader truth* (pp. 18–34). Needham Heights, MA: Allyn & Bacon.

42

Cultural Diversity and the Public Speaking Course

John W. Gareis, Ellen R. Cohn

Of all the communication courses that can be tailored to emphasize cultural diversity, one of the most adaptable but often overlooked is public speaking. Whether taught as a standalone subject or as part of an introductory hybrid course including interpersonal and small-group communication, the public speaking course is typically designed to enhance students' skills in researching, organizing, and delivering speeches. With a few minor but important changes, however, this basic skills course can also provide an opportunity for students to learn to communicate with and speak to a culturally diverse audience.

To make a public speaking course more culturally diverse it is necessary to incorporate three separate but related ingredients. These elements are syllabus based, instructor based, and student based.

Syllabus-Based Ingredients

Because the syllabus serves as both a guide for the course and as a working contract between the instructor and students, it must detail both the assignments and the instructor's expectations for the students. This means, then, that if cultural diversity is going to be an integral part of the course, it must be highlighted initially on the syllabus through the statement of purpose, course goals, and assignments. The following is an example of incorporating a diversity statement into the course goals of a syllabus.

Course Goals for Public Speaking

There are several major goals for this course. It is our hope that by the end of the semester you will have increased your competence in each of the following areas:

- *Attitude and confidence.* You will welcome, rather than avoid, public speaking opportunities, and you will prepare for and execute them with confidence.

- *Self-evaluation skills.* You will apply appropriate criteria to assess your public speaking efforts and recognize that with continued practice these skills can improve over your lifetime.

- *Cultural competency goals and audience analysis/adaptation skills.* You will be able to assess the unique needs of each audience and adapt both the content and delivery of your speech accordingly. Ethical and effective communication requires that speakers are able to understand and adapt to the needs of people of different backgrounds and cultures (including different races; genders; ethnicities; religions; economic, social, and family circumstances; geographic regions; languages; ages; health disparities; disabilities, etc.), as well as to the rhetorical expectations of diverse contexts and occasions. You will think about complex issues from different cultural perspectives. You will demonstrate empathy (verbally and nonverbally) in your speeches concerning an audience's feelings and circumstances. As the semester progresses, you will also demonstrate in your speeches (verbally and nonverbally) increased comfort talking about cultures or subcultures different from your own and differentiate between personal discomfort and intellectual discomfort in cultural conflict situations.

- *Organizational skills.* You will be able to select among organizational patterns to present your thoughts in the most logical, efficient, and effective manner.

- *Stylistic skills.* You will be able to select language that is vivid, grammatically correct, precise, succinct, and appropriate for the speaking occasion. The language will be compatible with that of your individual communicative style. You will be able to prepare a cohesive speech with smooth transitions between ideas.

- *Research skills.* You will be able to efficiently use the resources of the university library system to obtain research material for your speeches. In doing so, you should be able to identify sources of information that are both credible and appropriate for your selected topic and to seek information that is inclusive of diverse viewpoints. You will select speech topics that are current and relevant and strive to educate your audience about issues reflective of a multicultural society that exists within a larger global community.

- *Delivery skills.* You will be able to express your ideas by demonstrating competency in verbal and nonverbal communication skills.

- *Critical listening skills.* You will be able to engage in active, critical listening and apply the concepts learned in this course to analyze both the ideas and the delivery skills of other speakers.

Notice that to this otherwise standard list of outcomes, the instructor has added "cultural competency goals." By relating the issue of diversity to audience analysis, another given in public speaking courses, the instructor has legitimated it as a standard goal of public speaking.

There is also an addition to the syllabus designated as "research skills." Here students are informed that they are required to choose topics that are "current and relevant and to strive to educate [the] audience about issues reflective of a multicultural society."

Both of these syllabus-based changes are significant because they open the door for assignments that highlight diversity without making such assignments seem like add-ons. This is important because both students and instructors seem to do better with assignments grounded in life than with those that appear to have no relationship to reality beyond the classroom.

Feedback and assessment are also important elements of the process and are typically addressed in the course syllabus. An example of a rubric used to assess students' comfort and skill while speaking about persons from a culture different from their own is provided in Table 42.1.

Instructor-Based Ingredients

Once cultural diversity is established as part of the course via the syllabus, it is time to get things rolling. Here the instructor has to remember that words in a syllabus alone do not make the course culturally diverse. Instead, the instructor must become a living example of the behaviors he or she wants the students to demonstrate. Instructor-based ingredients, then, include modeling the expected behavior and offering a variety of examples related to the expected outcome.

Modeling Behavior

We have discovered that one of the most important things an instructor can do by way of modeling behavior related to cultural diversity is to use gender neutral language. A speaker is not inherently a "he" and audiences are not always men. An instructor must intentionally expand his or her vocabulary and find new ways to generalize audiences. He or she must also explain the practice to students and then, good-naturedly, remind them when they lapse. We always remind our students that culturally sensitive speech, like grammatical and clear speech, is not

Table 42.1

Rubric for Speaking About Persons of a Different Culture

This rubric assesses students' comfort and skill while speaking about persons from a culture different from their own.			
Levels of Achievement			
Criteria	High	Medium	Low
Language	Language is inclusive and sensitive. It demonstrates a high degree of awareness and adaptation to the preferences of members of the underserved group.	Language is awkward and sometimes not optimal, but it is not likely to be perceived as offensive.	Language violates community standards and the spirit of university policy, and it is offensive to members of the other culture.
Source references	References are included that are authored by individuals of the group (and/or their families and advocates) or that are written in authentic "voices."	References are authored by individuals who are outside the culture but who are directly familiar with it.	References are authored by individuals outside the culture who have limited or no direct familiarity with it.
Nonverbal communication	The speaker appears confident and/or relaxed, with an open posture.	The speaker evidences elements of both comfort and tension.	The speaker has a closed posture (crossed arms, etc.) and a tense appearance.
Paralanguage	Vocal quality and relative fluency suggest high levels of speaker comfort.	Vocalics and relative fluency suggest varying levels of comfort.	Vocalics and relative fluency suggest low levels of comfort.
Relevance of topic and content	Speech topic is highly relevant and significant to members of the culture.	Speech topic has only fair relevance to members of the culture.	Speech topic is marginally relevant or not relevant at all.
Empathy	Language and content suggest an *I/thou** relationship to the content as it applies to a culture.	Language and content suggest an *I/you* relationship to the content as it applies to a culture.	Language and content suggest an *I/you* relationship to the content as it applies to a culture.
Student rating (self-perception of comfort in speaking about persons of a different culture)	High	Medium	Low
* *According to Buber (1923/1996), communication with others typically occurs in one of two ways. In an* I/Thou *relationship, I and the Other are seen as a whole persons who have achieved perfect understanding. In an* I/you *relationship, the other is still a whole person, but we have not reached perfect understanding.*			

something you turn on only when doing a formal presentation. Unless it is practiced constantly, it becomes just one more thing to concentrate on when one is faced with other stressors associated with public speaking. Indeed, this practice might seem awkward at first, but soon it becomes second nature and noninclusive speech begins to sound peculiar.

Culturally Diverse Examples

What is a public speaking class without examples of good speeches? Likewise, what is a public speaking course with an emphasis on cultural diversity without examples of good speeches from diverse voices? In all fairness to public speaking classes and texts, there have historically been a smattering of diverse voices represented by way of reprinted speeches like Bette Ann Stead's (1982) "Why Does the Secretary Hate Me?" and Martin Luther King's incomparable "I Have a Dream" (1963). Although these are good examples, we are advocating a more extensive and inclusive pool of examples. Public speaking instructors should consider the inclusion of such diverse voices as John Jay Chapman, Cesar Chavez, Lynne Cheney, Bill Clinton, Louis Farrakhan, Teresa Heinz, Barack Obama, Ronald Reagan, Adrienne Rich, Alice Walker, and Oprah Winfrey.

The point of this partial list is not to provide speakers or speeches with which everyone in class will agree but to emphasize the need to give all speakers a fair hearing and to examine the strengths and shortcomings of many different speeches. Not only do sample speeches provide students an opportunity to learn by modeling; they also provide insight into opposing opinions in a nonthreatening way.

Student-Based Ingredients

The final aspect of a diversity-centered public speaking class to consider is student assignments. Again, it is standard fare to have students write and deliver at least one informative and one persuasive speech. Either (or both) of these speaking assignments provides an opportunity for a directed assignment related to culture and diversity. For example, the informative assignment might include the traditional introduction speech, in which classmates interview each other and then introduce the interviewees to the class, with a twist. Instead of asking the typical demographic questions, have students ask questions related to culture or heritage.

The informative assignment is a great opportunity for students to share information about their own or a researched culture. Several semesters ago, a visiting student from Qatar presented an informative speech on the history and government of his country. It met all the requirements of the informative speech in that it provided new information to students in a creative manner. Students seem to enjoy opportunities to talk about something that is important to them.

The persuasive assignment, like the informative speech, can be used to highlight issues related to culture and diversity. The main difference, however, is that, although the informative speech is designed to instruct or provide information, the persuasive speaking assignment requires students to advocate acceptance of a policy or course of action. With such current issues as immigration, a required national language, and the debates over gay rights, the possibilities here are endless.

Conclusions

Although it focuses primarily on the basic skills associated with oral communication, the public speaking course can be natural context in which to emphasize and experience cultural diversity. By attending to some specific syllabus-based, instructor-based, and student-based ingredients, such a course can help create articulate participants in a culturally diverse society.

References

Buber, M. (1996). *I and thou.* New York, NY: Touchstone. (Original work published 1923)

King, M. L., Jr. (1963, August 28). *I have a dream.* Speech delivered in Washington, DC.

Stead, B. A. (1982, March 21). *Why does the secretary hate me?* Speech delivered to the Society of Women Engineers, Houston, TX.

43

"But That's Not How My Family Does It!" Reducing the "Weird!" of Cultural Difference in Family Communication

Lorin Basden Arnold

M y goal in the Family Communication course is to facilitate an in-depth discussion of theories, research, and experience in family communication. In this course, the class and I address research that has been done in the field of family communication and measure it against the appropriate scholarly standards. We also examine its utility in helping us understand and analyze empirical phenomena in our own family lives and the lives of others, across a variety of cultures.

Impetus for Changes

When I first started teaching Family Communication, I thought I had it all figured out. I had been teaching Interpersonal Communication classes for years, and it seemed as if the two were similar. But I found that, though students' experiences with romance and friendship are naturalized for them, their experiences with family are so naturalized that they often have a very difficult time accepting ways to "do family" other than their own (or the one they have learned as the cultural ideal). This has led me to make some changes in how I teach family communication, how I help students consider the sticky issues of right and wrong in family behavior and the impact of culture on those moral and ethical evaluations. In this article, I consider only one of the changes I made: the use of film as a tool for opening a discussion of culture.

Implementation_____

In my Family Communication class, we view two films over the course of the semester. Because my goal for these examples is to have students think through issues of culture and diversity in terms of real families, the films chosen are both documentaries.

The first film that students are asked to view is titled *Martha and Ethel* (Johnstone & Ettinger, 1993). This film considers the lives of two women who became nannies to upper class families in the mid-1900s. Martha was born and raised in Oberkirch, Germany. Ethel was born and raised in a small town in South Carolina. Martha is white; Ethel is black. The documentary includes extensive interviews with both women, as well as with members of the families.

The nannies shown in *Martha and Ethel* are very different from one another in behavior and in background. Ethel is expressively loving to "her children"; she showers them with kisses and affection, while still expecting good behavior. Ethel takes a strong role in parenting the children, deciding on her own when they need to be punished and refusing to punish when the parents command it. The children view her as their second mother. Ethel's relationship in the family is such that, when the children leave home and the parents divorce, she remains in the company of the mother, less as an employee and almost more as a roommate (though some of the power differences remain). Martha, on the other hand, is extremely firm with the children and does not provide explicit expressions of affection. She believes that children should be seen and not heard and that her primary job is to teach them that life is hard and that if they wish to succeed in life they must learn to be hard and obey the rules. Although she maintains strong control over what goes on in the nursery, she sees herself as an employee, and the family members see her in that way as well. Despite the lack of outward affection in their relationship, the children assume responsibility for Martha as she gets older. They watch over her, visit her, and even take her on a trip to her hometown, to which she had never been able to return. Though the family's children all indicate that Martha showed little explicit affection when they were children, the affection that they have for one another is more expressed in their adult relationships.

Martha and Ethel is a touching and effective film to use in the classroom setting. Following the film, students gather in groups to analyze it and then discuss it as a class. Groups are asked to consider issues such as the nature of family, family culture, intimacy, and affection, and how various cultures impact those issues.

Students feel an immediate sense of connection to Ethel. Her way of interacting with "her" children is what my students generally expect to see from parental figures (even when they say that they did not experience it in their own families), because it is part of our mainstream cultural expectation of parent-child relationships. However, for most of my students, Ethel's existence is still very different from theirs. She is black; they are mostly white. She was raised in a poor family in the South and works for a wealthy family; they are mostly middle-class students from New Jersey and surrounding areas. Additionally, they are surprised that Ethel parents these children and that, from their perspective, the "real" parents hand over caring for the children to the nanny.

Students are always more conflicted about Martha. During the film, I frequently hear exclamations of surprise or even disgust over Martha's apparent lack of concern or love for her charges. As the film proceeds and students are able to see how the children in Martha's family reach their own understandings about her behavior, they too begin to see how culture has impacted Martha's response to the children. By the end of the film and the group project, students are less bothered by Martha's behavior; however, they often still view her actions as "strange."

The second film that students are asked to view is another documentary, entitled *Daughter from Danang* (Dolgin & Franco, 2002). The film is about a woman, Heidi, who was born to a Vietnamese woman during the war and was fathered by an American soldier. Due to the rumored murders of Vietnamese American babies, Heidi's mother allowed her to be taken out of Vietnam, at the age of 7, during Operation Babylift. She believed that her daughter would be returned to her after the danger had passed, but the daughter was instead adopted by a woman from Pulaski, Tennessee, where she was raised in a very unpleasant family atmosphere. Growing up, Heidi was forced to deny her Amerasian identity; only as an adult was she able to consider what it might mean to her to have a family and history in Vietnam. In the film, we travel with Heidi, who, having never felt truly loved by her adoptive mother, returns to Vietnam in the hopes of reuniting with a family that would really love her.

As the class and I see Heidi arrive in Vietnam and interact with her family, culture becomes a primary factor in the communication process. The cultural barrier proves difficult for everyone, and both verbal and nonverbal communication are strained and unclear. We see the family members struggling with how to respond to one another. Heidi's mother, overjoyed with seeing her daughter after so many years, is anxious to be both physically and psychologically close to her and desires to spend each waking moment with her. There is also much discussion of the past, both the family's immediate past and more distant past, with visits to the family shrine and interactions related to the family ancestors. The family members all live close to one another in small, often one- or two-room, houses without plumbing or full electricity. The family members provide support to each other, in both day-to-day (providing child care, etc.) and financial matters. The family interactions are strange to Heidi, who doesn't understand why there is no personal space, why dinners last so long, and why everything is so "awful" and who longs for her middle-class ranch home in

Tennessee. The climax of the documentary is a series of misunderstandings and miscommunications about the nature of family and family responsibilities that result in Heidi's cutting her visit short and indicating to the filmmakers that she doesn't know whether she will ever contact her Vietnamese relatives again.

These films and the group projects students complete about them provide an excellent opportunity for discussion of culture and how people's own cultural expectations about family become so naturalized that anything else seems strange. *Martha and Ethel* encourages students to question the very nature of affection, intimacy, and love—things on which family life seems to be founded. Although students know, from their own experiences with friends and other families, that the way that love is expressed varies from one family setting to another, the film brings the point home in a way that is less threatening than a more direct discussion of their own family practices (though it opens up the door for such a discussion).

Students usually condemn the fact that the parents in *Martha and Ethel* allow other people to raise their children. They often point out that the "rich people" didn't seem to care about their offspring, whereas the "poor family" in which Ethel was raised was characterized by loving interaction. This opens the door for considering the role of socioeconomics in our understandings and enactments of family. I encourage students to question both their positive and negative stereotypes of wealth and poverty.

A second issue that quickly comes to light in the film is the differences in how Martha and Ethel expressed their affection for their charges. Students, upon first viewing the film, are offended by Martha's stern attitude and her cold demeanor. They find Ethel's style of interaction much more appealing. Again, this opens a space for a discussion of the nature of affection and the different ways in which affection can be shown. Using the film as an example, we are able to consider the way that the cultures in which Martha and Ethel were raised impacted their understandings of what it means to care for a child and the fact that each woman, in her own way, attempts to do her best for the children in her care. We discuss the benefits of Martha's and Ethel's caretaking styles and address our own biases with regard to the issue of affection and intimacy in the family.

Similarly, *Daughter from Danang* spotlights how family expectations, including how affection and intimacy are revealed, and how socioeconomic and political forces affect the family. In addition, this film stresses the issue of family obligation and produces some particularly vibrant discussions in the classroom. As I listen to students complete the group project about the film, I can often hear them making negative statements about Heidi's Vietnamese family, particularly with regard to the culminating scene in the film, in which Heidi's Vietnamese half brothers ask her to help support the parents financially. Students are often appalled that such a request should be made of her, particularly since she has been away from the family for all of these years and has few memories of them from before her departure. The students also believe that, because the mother "gave Heidi away," she has little right to ask anything in return.

The group project, and the discussion that follows, provide a wonderful opportunity to discuss these issues. In addition to considering how culture has impacted these individuals' ways of showing affection and intimacy, the role of socioeconomic status on lifestyle, and the force of political and historical events on the family, this film allows us to delve into the nature of familial responsibility and how that responsibility is culturally constructed. In mainstream U.S. culture, my students have primarily been taught that adults are financially responsible for themselves and that, if any monetary help is provided in the family, it will generally flow from parent to child, not in the reverse. This is part of why they are so shocked at the request made of Heidi. I use this as a chance to consider how our lifestyles impact our perceptions of others. Students immediately assume that Heidi's family is asking for a substantial sum of money; yet the reality is that if Heidi could send her parents $400 a year, it would double their annual income. Once students realize this difference, we can then discuss how unsurprising it is that they would think otherwise, given the culture in which they have been socialized, and how their understandings of culture impact their perceptions of responsibility and rights in their own family settings and the family settings of others.

Outcomes and Conclusions

The discussion I have provided here is but a partial representation of how much these films provide for the class in terms of revealing the cultural dimensions of family. To accurately and fully discuss them would take far more space than is available. The use of these films for the class has been almost entirely positive. Of course, some students don't like the films or feel that they already knew about the impact of culture. However, the feedback is generally positive. Because the films are examples of someone else, a discussion of family differences—particularly with regard to issues such as race, ethnicity, and socioeconomic status—is seen as less dangerous than talking about the families of the students in the classroom. Although students initially seem to view watching the films as a pleasant diversion, by the end of the semester, they often list the films and the group projects and discussions related to the films as some of the most revealing moments of the semester.

Using films to reveal culture may work better in some classes than others, due to time constraints or other classroom demands. However, on the whole, I believe that the use of films as a gateway to the discussion of culture can be an extremely effective tool in the undergraduate classroom. In watching a well-made film, whether fiction or documentary, we identify with the characters on the screen. This provides a means of entering into a world that might be largely different from our own in a way that does not seem to immediately threaten or challenge the views that have become naturalized by our own experiences. Though I expect to change the specific films used in this class over time as new examples become available, I plan to continue to use film as a way of stimulating our ongoing consideration of the intersection of culture and family in our understandings and enactments.

References

Dolgin, C., & Franco, V. (Producers & Directors). (2002). *Daughter from Danang* [Motion picture]. Berkeley, CA: Interfaze Educational Productions.

Johnstone, J., & Ettinger, B. (Producers & Directors). (1993). *Martha and Ethel* [Motion picture]. Culver City, CA: Columbia Tristar.

44

Infusing Diversity Into an Introductory Communication Course

John W. Gareis, Ellen R. Cohn, Janet Skupien

Human communication has been defined in many different ways, depending on the author's theoretical perspective. There are, therefore, quite possibly as many different definitions of communication as there are communication textbooks.

Tubbs and Moss (2006), the authors of now classic introductory textbooks on communication, define *communication* as "the process of creating a meaning between two or more people" (p. 10). They emphasize the transactional nature of communication, such that "communication can be defined only in relation to some other or others" (p. 10). Ruben and Lea (2006) take a context-specific approach to defining human communication: "Human communication is the process through which individuals in relationships, groups, organizations and societies create, transmit and use information to organize the environment and one another" (p. 17). Leeds-Hurwitz (1989) views human communication as a social phenomenon, wherein society transmits the key aspects of culture from one generation to the next.

After reflecting on these three disparate definitions, it is not surprising that instructors approach introductory communication process courses from a variety of perspectives. Perhaps the most common pedagogical approach is to introduce communication principles and functions (axioms of communication, perception, verbal messages, nonverbal messages, listening) and then present how characteristics of communication function in specific contexts (intrapersonal communication, interpersonal communication, small-group communication, organizational communication, public speaking, mass communication, and intercultural communication; Adler & Rodman, 2003; DeVito 2004; Tubbs & Moss, 2006; Verderber & Verderber, 2004).

In contrast, model- or theory-driven pedagogical approaches (Cragan & Shields, 1998; Griffin, 2006; Infante, Rancer, & Womack, 1990; Miller, 2001; West & Turner, 2000) teach students how theories and models of communication, beginning with Aristotle's model, have evolved over time.

These two approaches are not mutually exclusive. Wood (2004), for example, combines the context-driven and theory-driven approaches by presenting clusters of theories, beginning with theories of symbols and the self, through interpersonal and relational theories, to theories about mass contexts and culture. What these approaches share, however, is a focus on theory and a tendency to view communication from an additive perspective, beginning with the units of communication and ending with cultural- or social-level theories.

In this article, we describe a third approach that attempts to focus, within a theoretical framework, on communication in action, rather than on theories of communication, to explore how symbols and the self—in fact, all levels of communicating—are already infused with cultural significance. This approach was developed over the years at the University of Pittsburgh by a number of instructors—including the three of us and Nina Gregg—with further contributions by course assistants Sheila McBride and the late Carol Houston. In our introductory communication course, communication is taught as a socially constructed phenomenon, and this orientation logically includes readings about, and by, persons from diverse backgrounds and cultures.

Course Description

Communication is central to being human and to the human condition. As human beings, we seek order, patterns, and meanings to our existence. At the same time, communication shapes our perceptions, our thinking, and how we relate to others. In a hybrid distance-education-based version of Communication 0300: Communication Process, we consider communication from two interrelated social perspectives. First, the class examines how humans use communication to create a world of meanings and ideas—that is, to construct reality. As such, we consider how communication and culture shape our identities and how we communicate these identities to ourselves and others. We focus on the different meanings we make of our worlds and how these realities might clash as a result of differences in gender, race, abilities, class, and sexuality; and we explore some of the causes of miscommunication. Second, we consider communication as behavior: behavior with pattern, behavior we learn, behavior in context, multichannel behavior, and multifunctional behavior, to use the categories from one of the class texts.

The course is launched by considering the relationship between communication and reality, via the work of Watzlawick. According to Watzlawick (1977), the concept of a connection between communication and reality is a relatively new idea. He explains that "reality is what is, and communication is merely a way of expressing or explaining it." Watzlawick's work is particularly thought provoking for students because he calls into question that there is, indeed, such a thing as "a reality":

> Our everyday, traditional ideas of reality are delusions which we spend substantial parts of our daily lives shoring up, even at the considerable risk of trying to force facts to fit our definition of reality instead of vice versa. And the most dangerous delusion of all is that there is only one reality. What there are, in fact, are many different versions of reality, some of which are contradictory, but all of which are the results of communication and not reflections of eternal, objective truths.

Watzlawick further distinguishes between first-order reality and second-order reality. First-order reality is that "which is purely physical, objectively discernible properties of things and is intimately linked with correct sensory perception, with questions of so-called common sense or with objective, repeatable, scientific verification." Second-order reality is "the attribution of meaning and value to these things and is based on communication."

An example of culturally differing second-order realities was described by Watzlawick:

> During the last years of World War II and the early postwar years, hundreds of thousands of U.S. soldiers were stationed in or passed through Great Britain, providing a unique opportunity to study the effects of large-scale penetration of one culture by another. One interesting aspect was a comparison of courtship patterns. Both American soldiers and British girls accused one another of being sexually brash. Investigation of this curious double charge brought to light an interesting punctuation problem. In both cultures, courtship behavior from the first eye contact to the ultimate consummation went through approximately thirty steps, but the sequence of these steps was different. Kissing, for example, comes relatively early in the North American pattern (occupying, let us say, step 5) and relatively late in the English pattern (at step 25, let us assume), where it is considered highly erotic behavior. So when the U.S. soldier somehow felt the time was right for a harmless kiss, not only did the girl feel cheated out of twenty steps of what for her would have been proper behavior on his part, she also felt she had to make a quick decision: break off the relationship and run, or get ready for intercourse. If she chose the latter, the soldier was confronted with behavior that according to his culture rules could only be called shameless at this early stage of the relationship.

In this fascinating example, the second-order reality of "the kiss" is obviously quite different for each culture. The man and the woman have divided up and organized their respective worlds in different ways. This is because they have learned different sequences of behavior and employed different punctuation. *Punctuation* here refers to the way in which we divide communication into chunks to better manage it (Leeds-Hurwitz, 1989, p. 96). As such, each person expects the kiss to occur in a different phase of the relationship. Thus, the meaning of the kiss can be interpreted only if it is viewed where it occurs within the entire context of the relationship as part of a culturally organized sequence of behaviors.

Texts and Recommended Readings _____

Because there are few commercially available communication textbooks that present a social interactionist, culture-driven approach to communication, the successive course directors have supplemented the course with readings from the field of sociology.

Communication in Everyday Life: A Social Interpretation by Leeds-Hurwitz (1989) is one text that addresses the question "What is communication?" from a social perspective and presents an innovative approach to communication studies. Leeds-Hurwitz uses observations she made in her school-based research sites to exemplify communication concepts.

The second assigned text is a collection of readings in sociology. Kollock and O'Brien (Kollock & O'Brien, 1993; O'Brien, 2005; O'Brien & Kollock, 1997) edited informative collections of articles and then bound those collections together with essays they authored themselves. Though the book's title does not include the term *communication* and it is not typically marketed as a communication text, it nonetheless contains provocative and communication-related material written by a diverse group of authors about diverse audiences. Across various editions of the text, readings have been eliminated and new readings introduced, but each edition has offered insight into communication in diverse populations and in minority and marginalized groups. Examples of assigned readings follow:

- "Behavior in Private Places: Sustaining Definitions of Reality in Gynecological Examinations," by Joan P. Emerson

- "Sex and Power in Interaction: Conversational Privileges and Duties," by Peter Kollock, Philip Blumstein, and Pepper Schwartz

- "The Madam as Teacher: The Training of House Prostitutes," by Barbara Sherman Heyl

- "Becoming a Marijuana User," by Howard S. Becker

- "The Development of Feeling Norms Underlying Romantic Love Among Adolescent Females," by Robin W. Simon, Donna Eder, and Cathy Evans

- "Of Maids' Uniforms and Blue Jeans: The Drama, Status, and Ambivalence in Clothes and Fashion," by Fred Davis

- "Black Men and Public Space," by Brent Staples

- "Talking Back," by bell hooks

- "The Man Who Mistook His Wife for a Hat," by Oliver Sacks

- "Body Ritual Among the Nacirema," by Horace Miner

- "On Being Sane in Insane Places," by D. L. Rosenhan

- "Double-Consciousness and the Veil," by W. E. B. Du Bois

- "The Nudist Management of Respectability," by Martin S. Weinberg

The two textbooks are supplemented by an instructor-authored manual (Cohn, 2006) that integrates the communication-as-behavior approach with the key principles, contexts, and models that are typically included in introductory communication classes.

Assignment

The course assignment requires students to analyze and understand the communication patterns of a given cultural scene. Students are encouraged to select a scene that is different from their current experience, subculture, or culture. The assignment thus provides an opportunity for students to explore an alternative cultural perspective and, in the process, to gain insight into how their own world is socially constructed.

The assignment is divided into four sections. The first step is for students to select a cultural scene to study for each of the four sections. The assignment is presented as follows.

Criteria for Scene Selection

- Select a real scene where you are both safe and welcome. Be sure to obtain permission, if needed.

- Select a scene you can visit repeatedly. You will probably need to observe at least one to two hours before you write each of the four sections. (You may be either an observer or an observer and participant.)

- The miniculture should have at least 5 and no more than 30 regular participants. (If you have more than that, narrow your focus within the scene.)

- Select a well-established group to observe. The bulk of the participants should have been interacting together for at least three months. At least half the participants should be present each time you observe.

- You should restrict your observations to a specific physical spot within the context.

- Try to observe the same day and time each week.

- Identify and interview an informant to give you further insight.

- Treat information you receive as confidential.

Section 1: Description of the Scene and Context

In this section, students describe both the scene and the larger context within which it appears. The required subheadings for this section follow:

- *Introduction to the scene.* Provide a general overview of the scene.

- *Scene selection.* Introduce the reader to your scene. Discuss why you selected this particular scene. Specify whether you needed to obtain special permission.

- *Informant.* Describe how you came to select a particular informant. Why is he or she a good informant? What are his or her limitations as an informant? Discuss your informant's credibility. Describe his or her communication style and roles.

- *Group of participants.* Describe characteristics of the other participants in the scene.

- *Physical setting.* Describe the physical setting. Be sure to explain how aspects of the physical setting that you identify might affect communication in the setting.

- *Communication context.* Describe the communication context. Be as detailed and specific as possible. This should be a major part of your paper. Remember that "context is thus everything related to a given behavior, except the behavior itself" (Leeds-Hurwitz, 1989, p. 77). Consider as many different relevant aspects of the context as possible, including aspects of the society. What is the geographic and political context, and how does it affect communication? Are there aspects of the day of the week, time of day, month of the year, or proximity to a holiday that affect communication? Are there religious or political issues that might influence communication or recent current events that affect the mood of the participants? Are there age or gender characteristics that affect communication? If you are studying communication that occurs within a particular organization (e.g., a group within the University of Pittsburgh), how do aspects of the organization affect communication? How might the organization's mission, competitive environment, current financial picture, values, leadership, and history affect communication within your scene? What are the communicative expectations of the scene (e.g., expected behavior in an office, social gathering, or religious service)?

Section 2: Culture-Specific Jargon

Present examples of culture-specific jargon, and specify their meanings. You will be developing a glossary of words and phrases specific to the scene. Categorize the jargon whenever possible (e.g., jargon used by employees in the absence of the boss; jargon used by all employees; jargon used by kitchen staff; jargon used by service staff; jargon used by students; jargon used by faculty; etc.) The jargon you select must be specific to the group's particular purpose. Some jargon may be typical of most other groups of its type (such as jargon used in a hospital operating room), or they may be so specific to two or more members of the group that others outside the group would not be able to discern their meaning. You may also include instances of "Pittsburghese" if it has a specific meaning to the group's activities. For example, if a group that watches football games together each week refers to "the terrible towel," it would be appropriate to include this phrase. However, the term *gum band* would not be relevant to the assignment (unless you were studying an office scene, for example).

Section 3: Communication Rules

List seven implicit and seven explicit communication rules that are followed by participants in this setting. For example:

- Explicit rule: Always address the customer as Mr./Miss/Ms. [last name].

- Explicit rule: Never negotiate alone with a client.

- Implicit rule: Treat the staff with kindness and consideration.

- Implicit rule: The supervisor always sits down first.

Select a rule to "conjugate," using Ford's family of rules (Leeds-Hurwitz, 1989, pp. 31–32).

- The rule: Never pass a note to your supervisor when he or she is making a presentation.

- The counterrule: Pass a note to your supervisor when he or she is making a presentation.

- Rule about qualifications and exceptions: Pass a note to your supervisor when he or she is making a presentation if he or she has made an egregious error.

- Consequence of breaking a rule: You may be reprimanded.

- The rule that tells how the rule should be implemented: Exercise restraint, and do not attract attention to yourself, nonverbally or verbally.

Section 4: Nonverbal Communication

- Provide an example in your setting of nonverbal communication that demonstrates that one cannot *not* communicate.

- Provide an example of how nonverbal communication is used to contradict verbal communication in your setting.

- Provide an example of how nonverbal communication is used to demonstrate status or power in your setting.

- Provide an example of how each of the following is used to communicate in your setting, and consider how multiple modalities work together in communication sequences:
  - Chronemics (the use of time)
  - Cosmetics (applicative or reconstructive)
  - Costuming (the use of dress)
  - Haptics (the use of touch)
  - Objectics (the use of objects)
  - Oculesics (the use of the eyes)
  - Olfactics (the use of smell)
  - Organismics (unalterable body characteristics)
  - Kinesics (body movement)
  - Proxemics (use of space)
  - Vocalics (voice and silence)

Conclusion

Human communication can be defined in many different ways. This vignette described how diversity was infused into an introductory undergraduate communication course that primarily approached communication as a socially constructed phenomenon. This theoretical perspective easily enabled the inclusion of readings about, and by, persons from diverse backgrounds and cultures, as well as a term assignment that required students to observe the communication behaviors of persons in cultural scenes.

References

Adler, R. B., & Rodman, G. (2003). *Understanding human communication* (8th ed.). Oxford, UK: Oxford University Press.

Cohn, E. R. (2006). *Communication 0300: Communication process. Study guide for Communication 0300 (7300).* Pittsburgh, PA: University External Studies Program, Center of Instructional Development and Distance Education.

Cragan, J., & Shields, D. (1998). *Understanding communication theory: The communicative forces for human action.* Needham Heights, MA: Allyn & Bacon.

DeVito, J. (2004). *Essentials of human communication.* Needham Heights, MA: Allyn & Bacon.

Griffin, E. (2006). *First look at communication theory with conversations.* Boston, MA: McGraw-Hill.

Infante, D., Rancer, A., & Womack, D. (1990). *Building communication theory.* Prospect Heights, IL: Waveland Press.

Kollock, P., & O'Brien, J. (1993). *The production of reality: Essays and readings in social psychology.* Thousand Oaks, CA: Sage.

Leeds-Hurwitz, W. (1989). *Communication in everyday life.* Westport, CT: Ablex Press.

Miller, K. (2001). *Communication theories: Perspectives, processes, and contexts.* Boston, MA: McGraw-Hill.

O'Brien, J. (2005). *The production of reality: Essays and readings on social interaction.* Thousand Oaks, CA: Pine Forge Press.

O'Brien, J., & Kollock, P. (1997). *The production of reality: Essays and readings on social interaction.* Thousand Oaks, CA: Pine Forge Press.

Ruben, B., & Lea, S. (2006). *Communication and human behavior* (5th ed.). Boston, MA: Pearson.

Tubbs, S. L., & Moss, S. (2006). *Human communication: Principles and contexts* (10th ed.). New York, NY: McGraw-Hill.

Verderber, R. F., & Verderber, K. S. (2004). *Communicate!* Belmont, CA: Wadsworth.

Watzlawick, P. (1977). *How real is real: Confusion, disinformation, and communication.* New York: Vintage Books.

West, R., & Turner, L. (2000). *Introducing communication theory: Analysis and application.* Mountain View, CA: Mayfield.

Wood, J. T. (2004). *Communication theories in action: an introduction* (3rd ed.). Belmont, CA: Thomson Learning.

45

Teaching "Experiential" Intercultural Communication at an Ethnically and Culturally Homogeneous University

Ako Inuzuka

The course I decided to modify, as a result of attending the 2005 provost's faculty diversity seminar at the University of Pittsburgh, is Intercultural Communication. It may seem to be an easy course to incorporate diversity-related issues. It became a challenge, however, when I tried to incorporate practice as well as theory in my intercultural communication class at the University of Pittsburgh–Johnstown, an ethnically and culturally homogeneous university. Here I describe the challenges I encountered and the changes I implemented in this course.

The class is a requirement for communication majors and is a lower division course. I teach two sections of the course every semester. The 2005 fall semester was my first time teaching it at this university. Topic areas covered include history and intercultural communication, identity and privilege, nonverbal communication, verbal communication, folk culture, and popular culture. The course stresses both theoretical and practical application. The specific course objectives are as follows:

- To relate students' understanding of the theories and principles of intercultural communication to their own lives

- To examine the relationship between culture and communication

- To become more critical of how students' cultural identities and positionality influence communication

- To explore how history, discrimination, colonization, and exploitation impact intercultural communication

Because this course is designed to incorporate both theory and practice, I was challenged. How could students in a culturally and ethnically homogeneous area experience culture? When I taught the same course at another university, this was not a problem because the university had a large population of international students. At that university, in addition to three exams, I assigned four assignments: 1) participating in the Cross-Cultural Conversation Connection program; 2) writing reflection papers after participating in that program; 3) serving as the case study discussion leader; and 4) completing an intercultural communication research paper. The first assignment had students participate in a program that paired up American students and international students. They were supposed to meet once a week throughout the semester. For the second assignment, students had to write two reflection papers. The third assignment required students to lead a class discussion on one of the chapters from *Among Us* (Lustig & Koester, 2006), a collection of essays on personal intercultural experiences written mostly by cultural "others." The last assignment was a research paper.

Although my previous university was also located in an ethnically homogeneous area, the large population of international students allowed for an assignment that paired up international students with American students. However, the problem of incorporating the practical part of intercultural communication became salient when I started to prepare this course for students at the University of Pittsburgh–Johnstown, a university with few international students. I had to come up with alternatives to the first two assignments.

As a result of participating in the provost's seminar, I decided to incorporate mainly two changes: 1) to raise the awareness of students' own cultures as "cultures"; and 2) to include topics other than national cultures, such as race/ethnicity, sexual orientation, gender, and socioeconomic class. To allow students to experience other cultures, I included an assignment titled "Self-Reflexivity Paper" that encouraged them to reflect on themselves as members of cultural groups. Because "other" cultures are often the focus of studies in intercultural communication, students' own identities remain unexplored. For this assignment, I used two films: *Ethnic Notions* (Riggs, 1986), a documentary film on the media representation of African-Americans, and *The Celluloid Closet* (Epstein & Friedman, 1995), a documentary film on homosexuality in the media. In addition to those two films, I included an article: "White Privilege and Male Privilege: A Personal Account of Coming to See Correspondences Through Work in Women's Studies," by Peggy McIntosh (1988).

We had class discussions on the movies and the article. Reflecting on the experiences of watching the movies and reading the article, students were supposed to critically analyze their privileges and position in society. Through this assignment, I also attempted to incorporate the second change, to include other types of cultures than national cultures. Intercultural communication was traditionally international communication. Originally used to train diplomats before sending them abroad after World War II (Martin & Nakayama, 2004), intercultural communication still has a strong emphasis on international communication today. Although its focus has shifted toward a more critical approach, incorporating such issues as identity politics and race relations in recent years, the main focus of intercultural communication in classrooms is still international communication. Because of my international background, I have to admit that I tended to do the same in the classroom. International communication remains very important, especially in today's globalized world, but overlooking other types of cultures may be detrimental in fostering truly inclusive understandings of cultures. For this reason, this assignment was designed to have students think critically about their identities in terms of race/ethnicity, sexual orientation, socioeconomic class, gender, and nationality.

The discussed changes were implemented in my class during the fall semester of 2005. Upon watching *Ethnic Notions,* students reacted in various ways. Some students thought that the ways in which African-Americans were depicted in the media were terrible. They had noticed that the media representation of African-Americans was negative but had never imagined that it was *this* negative. On the other hand, some students thought that the media representations of African-Americans, albeit negative, had become more positive in recent years. We talked about the fact that we still predominantly see African-Americans as criminals and drug dealers in today's media. Another issue discussed was whether such depictions are admissible as long as they are "better" than before. After showing *The Celluloid Closet,* I encountered silence in class. After some attempts to facilitate discussion, a few students hesitantly volunteered to present their opinions on the movie. Their main responses to the movie were that they did not know the extent to which homosexuality was concealed in the media and that they never had noticed that gay people were depicted in negative ways in the media. Feeling uneasy about the silence, I informally asked a few students after class about the movie. Their response was that they did not know what to say because the content of the movie was "heavy" and it was not something merely "interesting" or "good." Nevertheless, they found the movie to be eye opening.

In retrospect, the reason why students were more willing to speak up about *Ethnic Notions* despite the fact that the film was merely "interesting" or "good" may be that students, in general, have more experience with race and racism than sexual orientation and heterosexism. Although race and racism may not yet be an issue that is frequently discussed in elementary through higher education, it is likely that most students have had some opportunity to learn about racism in their lives. In this sense, they may have been prepared to discuss racism.

Compared to racism, heterosexism is still largely excluded from the discussion of diversity and multiculturalism. When we talked about McIntosh's article in class, there was a group of students who argued that the situation today is better than 30 years ago when the article was written. We discussed, however, that people today who are not white and heterosexual still essentially lack most of the privileges listed in the article. The overall reaction of my students to McIntosh's article was that it was an eye-opener and that it had never occurred to most of them that they had these privileges because of their race and sexual orientation. A few weeks after these discussions, students had to submit their papers on self-reflexivity. Most students effectively used the movies and the lists of white privileges and heterosexual privileges from McIntosh's article to examine their privileges in society. Many of them also included discussions of their ethnic background and identities based on gender, socioeconomic class, nationality, and region of origin. Some female students commented on their gender-based disadvantages despite privileges due to their race, sexual orientation, and socioeconomic class; whereas other female students wrote that gender oppression is no longer an issue in the U.S. society of today. Reading my students' papers and reflecting on the course, I have noticed that some aspects of identities, such as gender and socioeconomic class, are still underrepresented. Because these topics are intertwined with race, sexual orientation, and nationality, I aim to further incorporate them in the class the following semester.

Through the implementation of the discussed changes, I attempted to achieve two goals: 1) to incorporate practice in the class; and 2) to present topics other than international communication. When I attended the seminar in May 2005, useful suggestions were brought up on how I could tackle that first goal. One suggestion, for instance, was to have online conferences with a group of students from another country. Another was to assign students to interview people who are from another country and live near Johnstown. In addition, in the process of writing this chapter, I encountered a conference paper that discusses the benefits of having students participate in a study abroad program for a few weeks (Penington & Wildermuth, 2005). Although all of these ideas appear to facilitate incorporating practice in intercultural communication classrooms, I believe that the changes I implemented were also effective to achieving the second goal—that is, including topics other than international communication. I also believe that incorporating these changes helped raise awareness that other cultures are not the only cultures but that students' own cultures are also worth investigating. I hope that the experience of examining their own identities as members of cultural groups has helped students question hierarchical ideas of cultures.

References

Epstein, R., & Friedman, J. (Directors). (1995). *The celluloid closet* [Motion picture]. United States: Home Box Office.

Lustig, M. W., & Koester, J. (2006). *Among us: Essays on identity, belonging, and intercultural competence.* Boston, MA: Pearson.

Martin, J. N., & Nakayama, T. K. (2004). *Intercultural communication in contexts.* Boston, MA: McGraw-Hill.

McIntosh, P. (1988). *White privilege and male privilege: A personal account of coming to see correspondences through work in women's studies* (Paper No. 189). Wellesley, MA: Wellesley College, Center for Research on Women.

Penington, B., & Wildermuth, S. (2005, November). *Three weeks there and back again: A qualitative investigation of the impact of short-term travel/study on development of intercultural competency.* Paper presented at the National Communication Association's annual convention, Boston, MA.

Riggs, M. T. (Producer/Writer/Director). (1986). *Ethnic notions* [Motion picture]. United States: California Newsreel.

46

Diversity-Focused Service-Learning in General Studies and Cultural Studies Classes

Meredith Guthrie

Introduction to Women's Studies

The purpose of Introduction to Women's Studies is to introduce the basic concepts and topics of women's studies and feminist thought and action through the interdisciplinary exploration of the diverse experiences of women in the United States. This course focuses on the institutions, social practices, and cultural representations that shape women's lives in American society and how women have, through individual and collective effort, resisted these very structures.

Objectives of the course include:

- Introducing students to the field of women's studies in both theory and practice

- Recognizing gender, race, and class as social constructions

- Identifying contributions women have made to society and history

- Learning about the history of women in the United States and around the world and the various forms of feminism

- Encouraging and reinforcing a strong positive image of women in the classroom and society

Cultural Pluralism in America _____

The purpose of Cultural Pluralism in America is to offer an interdisciplinary exploration of race, ethnicity, class, gender, and sexual orientation in the United States, emphasizing imaginative expressive forms, such as fiction, poetry, film, and the visual arts.

Objectives of the course include:

- More fully appreciating the incredible diversity of culture and cultural expressions in the United States

- Working toward more complete understanding of students' own cultural identities

- Working toward understanding cultural and subcultural groups from which the students do not come

- Experiencing the relationship between culture and lived experiences

- Further developing students' critical reading and critical thinking skills as they are asked to read and analyze information from a variety of perspectives

Background Information _____

A midsized university in Ohio, Bowling Green State University (BGSU) attracts a variety of students from both urban (Cleveland, Detroit, Toledo) and rural areas. Although some of the student body has a great deal of experience living in racially and ethnically diverse communities, others come from predominantly—or completely—white communities. (In fact, I have had students tell me that they had never seen a person of color "in real life" until they came to BGSU.) To serve the needs of this student body, the university requires that each student take at least one cultural diversity class as part of the core curriculum. The learning outcomes of the cultural diversity classes are quite specific, stating that students will learn to:

- Use modes of inquiry into the ways ethnic cultures have shaped American life.

- Identify issues and problems in cultural diversity from the perspectives of diverse cultures and locate themselves in their own culture.

- Engage in critical inquiry into the problems, challenges, and possibilities inherent in a multicultural democracy.

- Develop skills of communication, analysis, and problem solving in a format requiring active participation.

At the introductory level, students may take one of three classes to satisfy their diversity requirement: Cultural Pluralism in America, Introduction to Women's Studies, or Introduction to Ethnic Studies. Although each of these courses has its own curriculum, all three focus on issues presented by the intersections of race, class, gender, and sexuality.

One major problem that the cultural diversity curriculum faced at BGSU was that students often stated in their end-of-term evaluations that the class made them feel "depressed" or "upset." Before taking these classes, many students had never been asked to examine the ways racism, classism, sexism, and homophobia worked in their lives. What could they, individually and together, do to help? Although the classes were effectively teaching students about the challenges of diversity in contemporary life, they weren't doing enough to give students the tools to face those challenges and left students feeling overwhelmed and disempowered. In the fall of 2000, I worked with a group of graduate students and one lecturer to develop a service-learning project, which we named the Community Action Project (CAP), to address these issues in the university's cultural diversity classes. (I worked with Dr. Jeannie Ludlow, Jill-Anne Fowler, Wendy Fournier, Jason Kuscma, Laurie Jordan, and Taeyon Kim. We came from several different disciplines, including American culture studies [the department that taught Cultural Plurality in America], women's studies, and ethnic studies.)

We chose to use a model of service-learning for several reasons. First and foremost, service-learning can be particularly effective in making valuable connections between classroom and real-world knowledge. Service-learning also works to both build and reinforce bridges between universities and the communities around them while developing in students a sense of social responsibility. These projects can be particularly useful in classes that stress diversity because they can demonstrate to students the challenges of living in a diverse society and they can help students learn the tools necessary to address those challenges through grassroots activism. Perhaps most important, service-learning projects can help students feel less cynical, and more optimistic, about their role in making diversity work in the United States.

Implementation

My colleagues and I designed the CAP to be a semester-long group project that was flexible enough to fit within many different types of curricula while still fulfilling the needs of a diversity-focused class. Because we wanted the students to empower themselves through the CAP, the project is as student driven as possible. Although the project provides guidelines and the class instructor facilitates the project, students must both create their own groups and design their own projects. For the same reason, the project forbids student groups from simply volunteering with established organizations. Why? Because we wanted students to learn how to design and carry out their own solutions to social issues. The CAP begins, then, with students forming groups of four to six and working together to design a project that will address a diversity-related problem they have identified in their local community. Instructors can ask students to focus on one area of diversity, as the course curriculum demands. For example, when I used this project in women's studies, I asked students to focus on how to address sexism in their communities; the instructor of an ethnic studies class could ask students to focus on racism. Since racism, sexism, classism, and homophobia intersect, student projects can work on more than one issue at a time. However, in the beginning stages of planning a project, students often find it useful for instructors to narrow the field in this way.

Once each group has designed a project, students work together to write a proposal that states the following:

- The specific issue they are addressing and why they're addressing it

- The research they have conducted to determine what, if anything, is being done locally to address this issue and what background information they need to understand this issue more completely

- How this issue relates to what is being discussed in class

- The specific action they have planned to address their issue

- A schedule of how they will enact their action

- A list of any problems or challenges they may face during the course of their action

As facilitators, instructors examine the proposals to ensure that they fulfill the assignment, connect to the class's curriculum, and propose a feasible action. I usually warn students that most proposals will need to be revised and resubmitted so that they do not feel discouraged.

For example, one group from my class decided that they wanted to focus on issues of disability on campus by determining whether all the university's buildings were handicap accessible. Part of this group's research included reading and understanding the Americans with Disabilities Act (ADA) to see how buildings were legally declared "accessible" and "inaccessible." They proposed that they would divide up the campus into sections and that each student would check the entrances, bathrooms, and elevators (if necessary) in each building in his or her section to make sure that the structures conformed to the ADA. The group would then get together to compile a list of all the buildings that did not conform to the act and present that list to BGSU's facilities administrators. As the instructor of the class, I checked to make sure that their proposed schedule gave the administration enough time to respond to their list of inaccessible buildings before the end of the semester. I also suggested that they write a story for the campus newspaper to raise student awareness. Finally, I urged them to make connections with Disabilities Services, an on-campus resource, to determine whether there was a procedure in place for reporting inaccessible structures. The group made the necessary changes to their proposal and resubmitted it to me.

Another group, composed of education majors, wanted to go into a local high school to warn seniors about the dangers of binge drinking in college. They reasoned that if students were forewarned as high school students, they would avoid many mistakes that college freshmen can make while learning to deal with alcohol. Because some group members were already student teachers at a local school, they had contacts who had already agreed to allow them (pending approval of the script of their talk) to talk to classes. The group provided a detailed schedule of when they would research and write their talk, as well as proposed dates on which they would give their talk at the high school. Because this was for a women's studies course, I suggested that the group retain their focus on binge drinking but focus on gender-related issues associated with alcohol. After some additional research, the group decided to focus on the connections between binge drinking, date rape, and other assaults on women. Their talk would take a two-pronged approach to the issue, both defining date rape and active consent for men and women and giving women useful advice for going out to bars and parties.

Once a group's proposal has been accepted, they are ready to begin their action. As the semester progresses, the instructor facilitates the groups' actions by asking them to connect what they are doing to the class's reading and discussion and by requiring groups to formally check in, via meetings and/or email, to relate their progress. During this time, student groups are learning how to work together to coordinate both schedules and working styles, which can lead to some conflict. Requiring regular updates from groups can help instructors stay on top of these issues before they derail a group from completing the project successfully.

During this time, many groups modify their plan to take advantage of new opportunities or in recognition that they proposed to do too much. For example, the group studying on-campus buildings decided to ask a few people of varying levels of ability to describe their own experiences getting around on campus. The group members defined themselves as 100% able bodied and decided to use themselves as a sort of control group and to see whether they encountered difficulties. They enlisted a group member's elderly grandmother to enter some buildings on campus and also interviewed a blind professor about her experiences. One particularly petite group member discovered that, to her surprise, she had trouble with some buildings' heavy doors, and the grandmother often had difficulty maneuvering over broken sidewalks.

Near the end of the semester, when the groups are finished—or nearly finished—with their projects, students write a short reflection paper that states the following:

- How their group's action progressed

- Their specific part of the group's project (this is the part where I ask students to "justify their grade" by telling me exactly what they did all semester)

- How well their group's project succeeded

- How things could have gone better

- How the group's project relates to the subjects discussed in class

- An evaluation of the other group members' work on the project

The reflection paper sums up the project by connecting the project to the class and evaluating the effectiveness of the groups' proposed actions. Some groups have an easier time than others in determining how effective their actions were. The group that studied access to student buildings got a promise from campus administrators to fix some of the identified problems—a good, tangible result— whereas the group that visited the high school was only able to report on the fact that students seemed interested. Because they could not track the drinking habits of those students once they entered college, the group was left to speculate as to the ultimate effectiveness of their action. Group members also evaluate their fellow group members as part of their reflection paper to help the instructor recognize how much each member contributed to the project. This both helps the instructor in the grading process and gives group members an extra incentive to make sure they are contributing to the project. Finally, the reflection paper gives students the space to recognize how much they have learned and often includes the students' sense of feeling empowered to enact change in their lives.

At the very end of the semester, the project also asks students to present their projects to the class and prepare a poster presentation that is displayed publicly on campus. Both of these presentations give students an opportunity to relate to each other what they have done and to provide the campus community with positive examples.

Because the project takes up so much time and effort, it also comprises a large percentage of students' final grade. In the end, groups are never graded on how well their action succeeds because as much can be learned through failure as through success. Instead, grades are based on how much effort each group—and each student within the group—puts forth and how well they have integrated their project into the class's learning objectives.

Outcomes

At the beginning of the semester, students are often wary of the amount of work the CAP represents. They complain that they do not like group projects, either because of their busy schedules or because they worry they will end up doing all the work, and they worry that the student-driven nature of the project is asking too much of them. At midterm, before they have begun to see the effects of their work, students often feel discouraged because they can see only the difficulties of the project and have yet to feel its rewards. During both of these times, instructors can help facilitate the groups' work by becoming something of a cheerleader, assuring students that soon they will feel the fruits of their labor if only they stay focused. By the end of the semester, however, the majority of students have realized the value of the project, are surprised at the amount of active work in the community they have been able to produce, and are proud of their group's project. Although the changes effected by students in the CAP are small, they help students feel a real sense of agency.

Since its inception, the CAP has become a successful part of BGSU's diversity education curriculum. The CAP is currently part of a pilot project that includes the assignment in the curriculum of selected cultural diversity classes. If the pilot project proves successful, the CAP could be expanded into all the introductory-level diversity classes on campus. Although I am no longer affiliated with BGSU, I feel proud that my former colleagues have continued to support the project.

For more examples of past projects, as well as detailed descriptions of each part of the project, please see the CAP web site (www.bgsu.edu/departments/ wmst/faculty/ljordan/cap.htm). Although the web site is no longer updated (a paper-based instruction manual has been designed for instructors of the course), the site contains valuable information for people who are thinking of designing a similar assignment of their own.

47

Recognizing Student Diversity in Political Communication Classes: A Simple, Effective Approach

Gerald R. Shuster

An instructor who does not have some level of sophistication in determining critical information about the diverse nature of the classroom audience is somewhat analogous to an architect who attempts to begin a project design without the benefit of any knowledge of the client's needs, tastes, or expectations. On the other hand, an instructor who wants to establish some core knowledge about the diverse nature of the classroom audience for a given course need not assume that the process is one that requires an abstract study with statistical data. Just as important is the understanding that the precise knowledge the instructor needs to draw some conclusions about the audience includes diversities of a more subtle nature. Of course, basic elements of diversity—such as ethnicity, skin color, gender, and language—cannot be overlooked. But it is essential to note that other elements are just as critical as the instructor develops the audience analysis.

Rationale

The objective of an instructor, then, is to make a reasonable attempt to target every segment of the student audience when a course syllabus is developed, written, and subsequently integrated into the classroom. Unfortunately, at times what looks good on paper and what seems to focus on every possible type of student who registers for a course results in a situation best explained by the great semanticist S. I. Hayakawa. He concluded that too often the real is not the ideal and the "map is not the territory." Thus, for experienced and conscientious instructors, reviewing and revising course syllabi is necessitated, and adjustments are made as a result of suggestions from students through evaluations, experiences in the classroom, and changes in the content area.

The academic world of the 21st century brings additional objectives to the forefront, suggesting the necessity for adjusting not only the content and requirements identified in course syllabi but also the pedagogical style of the instructor to new concerns and additional criteria for the course. Although not the exclusive reason for change, the concept of achieving diversity in the content of a course ranks among educators' highest areas of concern. In short, many educators are wondering whether their current method of teaching and the content of their courses, as well as assignments and outside experiences, lend themselves to dealing with a more diverse classroom audience.

One could argue that to answer such a question, one would need to have a clear definition of what *diversity* really means. Initially, one might consider referring to a strictly sociological definition to provide guidance for determining the strategy and blueprint for revising and adapting course content and other relevant areas. The objective of this process is to meet the needs of the now defined diverse audience. In some cases and in some classes, using the strictly sociological definition might be just the panacea for the instructor.

In most cases, however, a much more eclectic or less strict definition of diversity might provide the instructor with a better overview of the class and audience and allow the instructor to be more focused on the specific demographics and psychographics of audiences in the classes he or she teaches. In fact, the instructor may wish to actually do an overview of the typical class in any given term and then do a fairly comprehensive but not necessarily sociologically sophisticated audience analysis—in short, perform an audience analysis in much the same way one would do if preparing a lengthy presentation for a new audience.

If the generally accepted formula is followed, before one word is drafted for the presentation, the speaker needs to do a fairly sophisticated and comprehensive audience analysis. This analysis needs to focus on criteria that, for the most part, are relatively easily determined and that encompass elements from fairly obvious demographic areas and details from the more difficult area of psychographics, which can be determined without violating anyone's privacy.

Methodology

An instructor whose objective is to make his or her classes more relevant in terms of meeting the needs of the class's diverse audience needs first to recognize, and then to define, what the nature of the diversity is. Once that objective is achieved, then he or she can determine how the course content, instructional style, and student requirements can be revised and adjusted to meet the needs of the now defined diverse audience. An instructor whose objective is to adapt the course to achieve the objectives just discussed should not perceive the task as a sociological or anthropological exercise but rather a task intended to provide the best possible experience for every person in the class.

There are likely some persons who believe that any changes should be based on more erudite and theoretical formulas to achieve success and meet the needs of 21st-century students. In reality, a more practical plan can achieve the desired objective without requiring time-consuming studies, and, moreover, such a plan can allow the instructor to reevaluate the course more often. Critical to this process, however, is the recognition that one cannot presume that diversity represents differences limited to such areas as skin color, language, political boundaries, gender, religion, sexual orientation, and other factors. To do so is to grossly oversimplify the process. If the process goes further beyond the obvious, the real winners are the students because courses are revised more often on the basis of meeting their needs and recognizing other critical elements of diversity among them.

The test and validation of any theory, however, is in the success of its application. To best describe how the simplified system works and whether its impact on students is positive, a class in political communication is used as a model. On average, there are about 40 students in any given term registered for courses in political communication, a course with a focus on how communication theory and concepts are integrated into a political campaign. For students, a good background in communication theory and concepts, but not in politics and political campaigns, is expected.

As the class begins, it becomes immediately apparent to the instructor that as many as 10 to 12 students are political science majors with a solid base in political science theory and a very limited background in communication theory. In addition, there are 5 to 7 nontraditional students—all over 22 years old and likely working full-time—and nearly as many older students (i.e., at least 65 years old) auditing but actively participating in the class. Typically, most of the other students are traditional students and communication majors. The majority have limited knowledge of, and a limited interest in, politics and political campaigns.

If the instructor defined diversity simply by students' ethnicity, race, or gender, there would be many critical areas of diversity not acknowledged that likely impact the manner in which information from the class is assimilated by the students. Assuming too much prior knowledge of communication theory or general politics from the students could put many of them in a negative mode from the outset. Moreover, in a university environment, attempting to address issues related to political campaign communication strategy by using local elections (in this case, western Pennsylvania) or even statewide elections (in this case, Pennsylvania) to illustrate certain points is likely to create issues of relevance.

Further, to assume that everyone in the class has familiarity with Pennsylvania or western Pennsylvania politics would reinforce a lack of knowledge or concern for an area of diversity as basic as geographic location. Even states contiguous to Pennsylvania—such as New York, Ohio, and New Jersey—have different forms of local governments. Just as important, election procedures as well as issues differ widely between each of them.

The resulting problem for students could be compounded further by the instructor's failure to recognize any international students and their country's form of government, as well as generational differences between students that often preclude references to historical events that may be far more familiar to someone from one generation than to another. Thus, without significant background information being explained and discussed, the value of an example or analogy could be nullified.

There are other elements of diversity that are a bit more subtle but just as critical in terms of potentially negatively impacting students if the course instructor fails to recognize them. These diverse elements run the gamut from political affiliation, level of interest, and political views—whether students are liberal, moderate, or conservative on the political spectrum. An awareness of the level of students' participation in political activities and events is also critical.

Generating the needed background for the class with regard to the areas just described is not as difficult as one might suspect, and, in fact, the method used accomplishes a number of objectives beyond the scope of assessing the diverse nature of the class. Within the first few sessions, the instructor should request that students introduce themselves. But unlike other classes where students just provide some superficial background, in this situation they are urged to respond to a list of suggested questions on an informal basis. The questions range from the standard name, year in the university, major, hometown, and future goals to more focused opinion-oriented questions like level of interest in politics, reason for taking the class, level of knowledge of issues, opinion of politics and politicians, and biggest complaint about government or elected officials.

In addition, a follow-up questionnaire is given to each student to complete anonymously. Information generated from the anonymous questionnaires is more detailed and offers a better perspective in the areas dealing with the class's political diversity. When these two methods are used in tandem to obtain the needed information, two conclusions are apparent. First, most students are not reluctant to discuss their political beliefs either in their oral presentations or in the anonymous questionnaires. In fact, many students voluntarily offer more information than is requested. In addition, students seem to be more embarrassed about their lack of knowledge and/or interest than in divulging their political affiliation or beliefs. Finally, for students who have an expressed interest in politics and current affairs, their interest is high and their views strong.

Outcomes and Conclusion _____

Using these methods, the instructor can generate the depth of information needed at the outset of a class to begin to focus the course on a more well-defined audience. Just as important, the instructor is able to structure information about critical components, theory, and concepts in a way that makes them more relevant to the majority of the class. Additionally, the instructor is in a better position to recognize in advance content areas where students, because of the diverse nature of the class, may encounter the most difficulty understanding and/or appreciating essential concepts.

In conclusion, although few knowledgeable instructors would argue the value and necessity of generating precise information and details involving the diverse nature of the students in their classes, there is likely a wide variation of opinions and suggestions concerning the methodology used to generate the needed information. In addition, where the formulas or recommended methods to obtain the information are too time consuming or sophisticated, avoidance and/or procrastination are often the roads taken. In this case, the result is a lack of enhanced knowledge about the diversity of the classroom audience. But when using the simpler instructor-tested, effective methods detailed earlier, in classes with similar characteristics and objectives like political communication, the simpler and more expeditious methods can achieve the stated objectives successfully—the result in such cases is a win-win situation for both students and instructor.

48

Learning by Teaching: African-American Students Teaching Black Studies

Monica Frölander-Ulf

When I started my first (and only) full-time teaching position—at the University of Pittsburgh–Johnstown (UPJ)—I offered a course called African-American Culture and Society for a number of years. By the early 1980s, interest in the course had waned, and I was feeling increasingly dissatisfied with teaching this course in a racially homogeneous environment, one with practically no African-American faculty on campus. I also was prompted to reflect on my place as a teacher of this course. What was I, a European academic with my particular kind of intellectual and experiential background, capable of offering students in such a course?

In my view, the most crucial contribution that a college education can make is the development of a critical consciousness. In this task, high schools tend to fail miserably. Most of my students have had little, if any, opportunity to seriously study other ways of life. Many have little or no awareness of the degree to which a particular social system and one's objective location within it affect the way one thinks, feels, and behaves. Developing critical consciousness requires that we understand the social and ideological contexts that shape our own attitudes as well as those of others. Ward Churchill, bell hooks, and many others helped me immensely in their insistence that one's own subjective vantage point must be made explicit to ensure intellectual honesty and integrity. None of us are objective. To pretend otherwise is to obscure rather than to enlighten. Only with a clear grasp of my own perspective can I, in turn, ask students to examine the conditions that inform their point of view.

As a Finnish citizen who came to the United States in 1968, I entered this country through the back door, so to speak. My first experiences at Florida State University were shaped by the civil rights and antiwar movements going on around me and by my membership in a very active international students group. In my subsequent anthropology studies at the University of Pittsburgh, I learned most of my U.S. history through the perspectives of Native Americans and African-Americans. Having been introduced to the incredibly rich cultural traditions of the peoples of the African diaspora, I chose to focus my studies on the Caribbean region. My marriage to an African-American man with Native American ancestry and our more than ten years of residence in an all-black neighborhood allowed me to experience these cultures as part of my everyday life. I was also privileged to gain insights into the complexities, hardships, and joys of peoples who have been marginalized by hundreds of years of colonial domination but who have survived and are constantly reaffirming their right to exist, defining who they are, and, in the process, transforming mainstream culture as well.

Although I had not been subjected to the distorted and openly racist versions of U.S. history taught in the K–12 system before the civil rights, black power, and red power movements made these versions unacceptable, I had, instead, learned practically nothing about the world outside Europe. Nor was my generation taught to view colonialism as what it was, an extraordinarily brutal and racist system through which wealth was extracted from the colonies, at great material and human cost to the colonized, to help fuel industrial development in the then major centers of trade and commerce. Finland was a colony of first Sweden for some 600 years and then Russia for another 100 years and did not become independent until 1917. (As part of a small Swedish-speaking Finnish population with a working-class mother and middle-class father, and growing up in a Finnish-speaking community, I occupied a relatively privileged social position. However, apart from speaking Swedish at home, I have always identified myself as a Finn and feel no emotional connection with Sweden or with those who still insist on special privileges as Swedish speakers.)

In spite of the colonial experience, Finnish culture contained a good dose of chauvinism toward the Roma and the Sami, who were not considered "real" Finns by the majority. When I grew up, the country was ethnically and racially very homogeneous, and the voices of the Sami and the Roma had not yet publicly challenged the dominant culture to any great extent.

Thus, my main training ground for understanding the systemic aspects of colonization and its worldwide consequences for recent times was the United States. My main teachers were African-American neighbors, relatives, and friends; students from Kenya, Zimbabwe, Pakistan, Malawi, Hong Kong, and Taiwan; and later many Native American as well as white friends, most of whom had engaged themselves in the antiracist, antisexist, and antiwar movements of the 1960s and 1970s. In the academic world my teachers were social scientists and writers, including Derrick Bell; bell hooks; Ward Churchill; Patricia Hill Collins; Frank Fools Crow; Angela Davis; Vine Deloria, Jr.; Franz Fanon; Audre Lorde; and Ngugi wa Thiong'o.

To share the insights I have received, I ask white students to place themselves, to the extent that it is possible, in the shoes of historically marginalized populations. Experiencing even temporarily a world where "the other's" history and culture are the norm and where we are no longer at the center of the inquiry is a powerful way to learn about who we really are and a starting point for understanding perhaps a little bit more about why the others behave, think, and feel the way they do. Such critical scrutiny is often painful. It may mean relinquishing deeply held beliefs about one's past and present circumstances. It may evoke feelings of guilt, betrayal, fear, or anger.

In contrast, for students who do not readily identify themselves with the dominant culture and whose experiences are rarely, if at all, discussed in their classes, courses that offer them an opportunity to be at the center of the inquiry can be an exhilarating experience. When some years ago, a group of black students approached me with a request that African-American Culture and Society be revived and offered again, I acknowledged the need to provide more courses with African-American perspectives. At the time, there were only 57 black students enrolled at UPJ of a student population totaling a little over 3,000; of some 130 faculty members, only 2 were African-American. Just one course on African-American issues, called Afro-American Literature, taught by a white Euro-American woman, was offered.

However, I had to think long and hard about how to teach the course under more satisfactory circumstances than had previously been the case. Although I knew that my particular training and personal circumstances made me quite capable of offering a course about African-American culture and society, I also recognized the importance of a teacher's ability to speak from his or her own personal experience. Furthermore, the vast majority of the students at UPJ had never had the opportunity to be taught by a teacher of color. As there was still little hope that the social science division would hire a black faculty member to teach this or other African-American or African studies courses—due to a lack of commitment to diversifying the faculty and unwillingness to pay sufficiently high salaries to make such positions attractive—and the small, relatively culturally homogenous and isolated nature of the community—I decided to develop a team-taught course with two undergraduate African-American students as my coteachers. The experience turned out to be successful enough that I believe it can be a model for other faculty who are grappling with similar circumstances. I want to emphasize that it is not a substitute for genuine efforts to make small, rural, or small-town and racially and ethnically homogeneous campuses reflect the diversity of the larger society, but it is a temporary solution with a great many positive aspects. It can also serve as a general model that allows for the involvement of undergraduate students in college-level teaching that's similar to the role of graduate student teaching assistants.

The two coteachers were hired by a committee on a competitive basis, giving preference to students with good communication skills, some knowledge and demonstrated interest in African-American history and cultural expression, and a competitive grade point average. They were each paid a stipend amounting to the minimum wage for the hours dedicated to the course, which I initially raised through a variety of funding sources (work study funds could not be used for this purpose because the job was open only to African-American students). The selection of coteachers began in the semester preceding the one in which the course was to be taught to make it possible for all three of us to meet and to decide on the initial course design, topics and course material selection, and evaluation procedures. As part of their teaching duties, the student teachers were expected to deliver some lectures, organize and lead class discussions, help produce and evaluate exams and other course assignments, and create an audio and/or visual presentation. They also helped the other students with course assignments. My own primary function in the course was to serve as a teacher, resource repository, facilitator, guide, and mentor. In our preparatory discussions I provided my coteachers with a wide range of academic resources (database search routines, journal articles, books, Internet sources, and audiovisual materials) and various models of how African-American Culture and Society could be taught. They were also given samples of exams and other types of assignments and were encouraged to develop some of their own. We then collectively decided on which particular ones to incorporate into the course. In this manner both coteachers had ample opportunity to bring their own preferences and perspectives to the class while I offered guidance to ensure an appropriate level of difficulty and substantive academic content for an upper level undergraduate course. In the classroom we took turns presenting a topic and then commented on each other's presentations before opening up the discussion to the whole class. This helped create a relaxed atmosphere that, I believe, resulted in much more lively class discussions than would have otherwise been the case.

The team-teaching experience also helped strengthen my mentoring skills. I got to know my coteacher students much better than is usually the case at an undergraduate college. I was therefore able to write very detailed and strong recommendations for these students in their subsequent efforts to find jobs or seek graduate school admissions.

Team-teaching this course was an important learning experience for me. A particularly rewarding aspect of it was the insight I gained into black youth culture (in fact, one of the more memorable occasions was the wonderful class demonstration of a step show led by my coteachers). The opportunity to teach was clearly a valuable experience, as well, for the seven assistants who worked with me in four separate courses. (It's worthwhile to note that the seventh student worked with me for no pay because I was unable to ensure continuous funding for the position. She was struggling to stay in college because of severe financial hardship, further strengthening my belief that the coteachers should have been paid for the hours of work they put into this project.) My coteachers expressed pride and contentment in not only learning more about the field of black studies but also in being able to interpret African-American history and contemporary concerns to other students, as one of them put it, "correctly." When asked to evaluate the positive and negative aspects of their teaching experience, four of these coteachers made the following comments:

> Overall, the experience has been a good one. I really enjoyed the teaching, course structure, making exams, and just having a positive role to play. After having done this TA [teaching assistant] job, I have seriously considered becoming a teacher. I realize that teachers have one of the greatest impacts on young people. With this in mind, I think I would like having such a positive role in society. I've had the opportunity to sit "on the other side of the table"! This has definitely given me pleasure and allowed me to appreciate my teachers more (both past and present). This position has helped me become a stronger person because I've had to uphold a professional position at a time when I really wanted to conform to my student role. The only negative aspect of this position is that it caused me some anxiety at various points because I have a fear of speaking in front of people. But since every coin has two sides, this may have been one step in a direction that might help me become less afraid of speaking in front of people.

> I think that being a TA has enhanced my communication skills. Speaking in front of your peers is always hard, but after taking this position, speaking in front of crowds is not as bad now. Being a TA has increased my confidence when I speak at job interviews. TA-ing for this class especially has increased my knowledge as a black man in society. Some of the things that happen around me now I can put in perspective—such as the unemployment rate of black males, lack of responsibility for the kids brought into this world, drugs being pushed in the black community, etc. Knowledge of all these things has been intensified by the research I have done in this class as well as by the different opinions of the students. Also, my knowledge of black history developed through this class. I'm still in the dark about a lot of things, but I can say that I know more than I did before.

There are so many little positive aspects which I didn't mention, but it goes without saying that I enjoyed it a lot. Just the fact of teaching my peers something that I've learned makes me feel good as a person. It makes you feel like you are looked up to. This is a positive attitude to take with me in the workforce. If I had to mention anything [negative], it would have to be from a personal standpoint. For example, it is hard to keep up with your schoolwork and also prepare and deliver your lesson plans. It was extremely hard during test time because I didn't have enough time to do both like I wanted to. (Advice to future TAs would be: Try not to take 18 credits while doing this.)

Being allowed to assist with the African-American Culture and Society class has helped me greatly as a college student. As a communications major, speaking in front of my peers improved my public speaking ability. Also, dealing with students in the class allowed me to use and improve interpersonal skills acquired in college. The opportunity to be a teacher's assistant should be extended to all students, no matter what their major. Given this opportunity, students will be better prepared to communicate with others openly in the real world.

By having a chance to become a student assistant for your class, I have greatly increased my knowledge about my own people and have helped others learn as well. The assistantship has offered me a great opportunity that I would probably not have experienced at any other college. African-American courses here at UPJ are few and far between, and to have the opportunity to help lecture, answer questions, and correct tests is an even rarer phenomenon. Having this job was extremely important to me. I had the chance to "correctly" educate individuals about African-American culture and society. I'm extremely grateful to have had the chance.

Judging by the student evaluations, both the African-American and white students enrolled in the course appreciated the contributions of the two coteachers very much. I watched with great satisfaction how the African-American students embraced the course as *their* course, as a place where they could take charge of the material and where they were able to feel particularly confident and competent. This occurred even when the black students were a small minority in the class. On several occasions, other black students dropped in to participate in the class although they weren't even enrolled in it that semester!

For the white students, the experience was mixed. A few of them had some familiarity with African-American culture, and they were in general comfortable and enthusiastic about the opportunity to learn more. Others came with a genuine wish to learn but ended up feeling out of place, uncomfortable, or fearful that what they said would offend someone. A large proportion of the white students at UPJ come from almost totally white suburban neighborhoods or small towns. As we discussed African-American experiences of racism and interpretations of U.S history, some of the white students felt left out. The course was not about them. Some resisted what was being said, especially since many of the viewpoints were harshly critical of the country they had been taught to think of in completely uncritical terms. Others experienced feelings of guilt about the past. All, however, appreciated the fact that they had the opportunity to hear the perspectives and learn about the experiences of their African-American coteachers and peers.

The experiences of both the African-American students and the white students in this class provided many important lessons. What they were encouraged to think about was more than the course content presented in the texts, lectures, and discussions; they were encouraged to consider the importance of the setting in which learning takes place. In this regard, the contributions of the coteachers were crucial both in helping the black students become the "owners" of the course and in validating, by their own experiences, much of the information to the white students. I, as a white European woman, would have found it much more difficult to make the African-American students feel at home in the class and most likely would have been viewed by all the students as less believable than cultural insiders.

The discomfort felt by some of the white students, I believe, is also a necessary part of the learning experience. Many of them had to, for the first time in their lives, be confronted with highly charged issues in a situation where they were not the dominant party. Thus, they experienced, albeit in a temporary fashion, what it means to be marginalized and not be at the center of attention. Some of the most important lessons I have learned about race, class, gender, sexual orientation, and abilities and disabilities I have learned from people willing to engage in discussions about their experiences in an in-your-face manner, exposing their anger and frustration at not being heard, understood, or respected. These kinds of confrontations provided me with the greatest opportunities to examine my most deeply held, and often flawed, convictions.

Especially on relatively homogeneous campuses, all too often lessons on diversity are limited to feel-good sessions on tolerance, people of color's or women's contributions to society, or an appreciation of our differences. All too rarely does the dominant white student population (or faculty or staff, for that matter) have to confront their biases and superficial understandings of racially charged situations in circumstances where they are the minority. Providing a course setting where the usual structure was, however incompletely, reversed led to a more profound learning experience for all the student populations involved.

Unfortunately, I must end this essay on a negative note. My commitment to paying the coteachers a small stipend and the lack of sustained support from the university ultimately led me to a dead end. My insistence on paying the student coteachers (and invited speakers as well) was partially an issue of principle. It also was a matter of ensuring that any student who was interested in serving as a coteacher could afford to do so. When I was running out of funding sources, I taught the course once with one assistant who had agreed to work with me even without the assurance of a stipend. She was not sure whether she could return for another semester, however, as a result of a very precarious financial situation, which further convinced me of the necessity to provide at least some minimal material support.

Each of the times that the course was offered with student coteachers, I had to apply for approximately a total of $800 to $1,000, which included the minimum wage at the time and the cost of books and course materials, from various funding sources. None of these grants were designed to provide ongoing funding for the same project, however, and my efforts to secure continuous internal support were unsuccessful. This, I might add, occurred while the university was spending considerable amounts to try to improve the enrollment and retention rate of students of color and, specifically, African-American students. It was also a time when the black student population at UPJ was meeting with a great deal of hostility, including a violent attack, from some white students and was beginning to decline in numbers. One former top administrator went so far as to accuse me of placing the university at risk of a lawsuit without ever providing any evidence that paying student assistants for their work was indeed unlawful. The same individual also claimed that I could include black voices in my course by inviting African-Americans from the community to speak in the class. When I responded that this, too, would require funding for speakers fees, I was told that it would not be a problem as "*they* like to speak on campuses" and thus would do so for free.

No doubt, for a program like this one to be successful, it is important that the college or university administration be supportive of it and willing to set aside some $1,200 annually or biannually to ensure that the coteachers at least have enough money to buy the books for the course and receive the compensation they deserve for the many hours of additional work they perform. I strongly recommend the establishment of a fund for peer group teaching that includes a minority student support component and that is available to all teaching faculty. UPJ has taken a step in this direction by establishing the First Experiences in Teaching and the First Experiences in Research programs. However, at the present time, these programs do not include a minority component, and branch campus faculty are not eligible to apply for the funds.

49

Diversity and Multiculturalism in the Science Classroom

Lydia B. Daniels

At the University of Pittsburgh, biochemistry is a one-semester course that is required of all students majoring in the biological sciences and that is a technical elective for students majoring in chemistry, neuroscience, chemical engineering, and biomedical engineering. This course is designed to provide an introduction to the underlying chemical and physical principles governing living systems, such as biomolecular structure and function relationships, thermodynamics, membrane structure and function, intermediary metabolism, and nucleic acid chemistry. This course is offered during both 15-week terms of the academic year and during the 6-week summer term, which is when I teach it. Summer enrollment is variable, between 60 and 100 students, and includes students with various majors, nonmajors preparing for the MCAT exam, and visitors from other institutions.

So what does diversity mean within the context of biochemistry? Classically, a biochemistry class addresses issues of race and gender using a role model approach—highlighting contributions to the discipline by African-American and women investigators. Clearly, scientific exploration thrives because investigators of different ethnicities and both genders bring unique perspectives to the framing of experimental research. However, at this stage of their education, my students primarily need to develop a rich foundation of organizing concepts and key experimental approaches before they can appreciate the subtleties of how cultural perspectives drive the direction of scientific investigations. Two goals of my course are for students to develop a strong knowledge base of key structures and common experimental techniques and for them to learn how experimental results have led investigators to develop the current models for fundamental biochemical processes.

Developing a strong knowledge base is often hampered by differences in academic background, language and computational skills, and learning styles—issues that define the academic diversity within a classroom. Academic diversity cuts across all cultural and ethnic backgrounds and presents a serious barrier to success for many students. My approach to accommodating academic diversity has been to move toward a more learner-centered classroom wherein my role is primarily to model the process of scientific investigation and make time to practice, in class, how to use experimental results to build the models of biochemical processes.

Biochemical process models frequently emerge from studying metabolic variations revealed by altered functions of key enzymes or proteins as a result of genetic variation. This genetic diversity, often rooted in culture and ethnicity, provides a springboard for exploring biochemical concepts in personally relevant ways. Cystic fibrosis and sickle cell anemia provide insight into pathways of protein folding and protein-protein interactions. Lipid function can be taught by considering the dysfunction of Tay-Sachs disease. Teaching from genetic diversity can provide a powerful connection to students' cultural and ethnic backgrounds.

The implementation I describe here represents a work in progress. I have been addressing issues of academic diversity longer than I have used genetic diversity as a teaching approach. I will describe one approach to addressing academic diversity that I have found works well—an in-class activity about basic enzyme kinetics designed to accommodate differences in learning rates. I will then describe an approach I've tried using genetic diversity as a tool for teaching content information, a case study that includes ethnicity as a complicating issue in the diagnosis. This activity was not as useful as I had anticipated, and I offer some observations to describe why.

Implementation and Outcomes _____

Addressing Academic Diversity

Although most students bring to the course a qualitative understanding of reaction rate and enzyme specificity, developing a quantitative description of this process is one of the most challenging concepts my students face. For several years, I tried to teach the concepts of enzyme kinetics by showing graphical depictions of enzyme activity, deriving the Michaelis-Menten equation in class, and assigning a graded problem set requiring students to apply what they have seen in class. I found that most students could use mimicry to do well on the problem set but that exam performance showed they lacked a deep understanding of the concepts. In response, I developed an in-class activity to allow them to practice the graphical methods needed to solve the problem set. This exercise provided students with data from an experiment measuring enzyme activity as a function of substrate concentration and asked them to determine the affinity of the enzyme for its substrate (K_m) and the theoretical maximum rate of the reaction (V_{max}). I used the same lecture presentation as in previous years and then asked students to work together in small groups to do the graphical analysis of this data. As I moved from group to group, I found that every group was trying to solve the problem by plugging the enzyme activity data into the equation, which is a doomed approach because the only way to solve for the equation's constants (K_m and V_{max}) was by using the graphical method.

I was shocked—I had just demonstrated how to use the graphical method to solve the very problem given to the students. Why did they opt to try "plug and chug" instead? My response was to switch immediately to a guided whole-class activity. I asked them to describe the process of doing the double-reciprocal graph to me, which I demonstrated as they described the steps. I showed them how to draw the lines and how to find the constants from the intercepts, giving them time to do the same. I asked several groups to tell me the values they had determined for the constants and tabulated those values on an overhead so the class could see the range of responses. This exercise required almost 45 minutes, but each group of students did eventually work through the graphical analysis.

The following summer, I refined both the lecture and the activity. Using graphs, I first presented the most basic relationships among enzyme concentration, substrate concentration, and reaction rate. The class and I discussed the physical implications of the hyperbolic relationship between reaction rate and substrate concentration. Only after this qualitative discussion did I show the students how to describe these relationships algebraically using the Michaelis-Menten equation. I showed them how to manipulate this equation to find an equation for a straight line, which could be graphed. With this background, I provided the same data as the previous year and a premade graph for each group of students. I asked the students simply to graph the reaction rate versus substrate concentration data, which every group did without a problem. We determined the kinetic constants from the graph together.

In both years, I assigned a graded, out-of-class problem set involving the same graphical method demonstrated in class. Working the problem in class did modestly improve the scores on the problem set: Before using the in-class problem, the average score was 79%. Scores increased to 86% (year 1) and to 91% (year 2) after working a problem in class. In year 2, I used a short-answer question similar to the problem set on the exam to test students' grasp of this graphical method—the class averaged 8.4 out of 10 points on the problem. Spending time in class practicing how to graph data and how to manipulate the graphical analysis appears to help students grasp the concepts of enzyme kinetics. Furthermore, by devoting sufficient time to problem solving in class, every student had the time to work through the problem in the presence of someone (instructor or peer) who was able to provide guidance; every student was accommodated in his or her learning so that every student could be held accountable for this knowledge.

Genetic Diversity

One of the five problem sets I used in 2004 became a short case study presenting cultural diversity as an important factor in the case. The case involved an Asian child presenting with the symptoms of rickets. The root cause of rickets was a complex in-born error of metabolism preventing the production of active vitamin D; it was not lactose intolerance. I expected that the students would, at first, attribute the rickets to a lack of dietary calcium because of the cultural stereotype but that, once they had read the source paper, they would be able to describe the metabolic consequences of the genetic variation.

I don't know whether this problem set raised students' awareness about cultural stereotyping. I do know that most students found the genetics of the case confusing and were not able to explain why the dietary calcium issue was a red herring in the problem set. My effort to use genetic diversity as a teaching tool failed because I had assumed that all the students had an adequate background in genetics to understand the source paper; most did not. Thus, an academic diversity issue reduced the effectiveness of using genetic diversity as a teaching tool.

Another issue of academic diversity—variability in communication skills—interferes with the effectiveness of essay-based problem sets in general. Although I am more interested in the ideas students express than in how well they express those ideas, I find that it is almost impossible to determine whether a low-quality essay is the result of weak understanding or of weak writing skills. Although in the past I have allowed struggling students to revise and resubmit their essays, steadily increasing enrollments makes this an impractical solution.

Issues With Implementation

In my experience, the major barrier to implementing a diversity-sensitive curriculum is an ignorance of the degree of academic diversity within the classroom. I have had some success using one-minute papers (Angelo & Cross, 1993) to explore the breadth and depth of my students' background knowledge, but I need to survey student knowledge more often and be willing to adjust my presentation to build on their current knowledge base. A minor barrier to implementation is my reluctance to relinquish more control of the learning environment to the students. For example, rather than develop case studies myself, I should develop exercises wherein they research ethnicity-based genetic variations relevant to different lectures and have them describe for each other and me what this case tells us about metabolic functioning.

Conclusions _____

Although recruiting women and students of color to the sciences remains a challenge, I have focused on one question: Once they are in the classroom, how do we create a supportive environment that will encourage them to continue in their science studies? Ample evidence (National Research Council, 2000) shows that people are most motivated to learn information that has personal relevance, suggesting that using genetic diversity as a manifestation of cultural and ethnic diversity is a reasonable approach for engaging students with the course content. Sensitivity to academic diversity, by modeling and practicing the skills I desire the students to learn, addresses a barrier to student success that cuts across ethnic backgrounds. If we, as educators, agree that all students require a deep understanding of the core principles to advance in science, then it makes sense to enhance the content with culturally relevant examples and to change the pedagogy to be sensitive to our students' existing skills, attitudes, and beliefs to create learner-centered environments sensitive to diversity and multiculturalism.

Acknowledgments

The author would like to thank Dr. K. Curto and Ms. C. Berliner for their valuable advice during the preparation of this chapter.

References

Angelo, T. A., & Cross, K. P. (1993). *Classroom assessment techniques.* San Francisco, CA: Jossey-Bass.

National Research Council. (2000). *How people learn: Brain, mind, experience, and school.* Washington, DC: National Academies Press.

Resources

BiosciEdNet: www.biosciednet.org

BrighamRAD: http://brighamrad.harvard.edu/education/online/tcd/tcd.html

National Center for Case Study Teaching in Science: http://ublib.buffalo.edu/libraries/projects/cases/case.html

50

Integrating Diversity and Multicultural Education Into a Digital Library Course

Daqing He

Kitano (1997) defined diversity and multicultural education (DME) as the development of citizens for a more democratic society through provision of more accurate and comprehensive disciplinary knowledge and through enhancement of students' academic achievement and critical thinking applied to social problems. DME seeks to promote the value of diversity and equal opportunity for all people through understanding the contributions and perspectives of people of different races, ethnicities, cultures, languages, religions, genders, sexual orientations, and physical abilities and disabilities. Because of its focus, DME is often linked with courses in the social sciences, the political sciences, the humanities, languages, and other similar disciplines. Morey and Kitano (1997) demonstrate this type of connection. Technology-oriented courses—such as those about computer systems, programming languages, and digital libraries—are usually viewed as neutral in social, political, and cultural values and are therefore not usually a subject within the scope of DME. However, in this chapter, using the Digital Libraries course at the University of Pittsburgh as an example, I will demonstrate that technology-oriented courses can and should integrate diversity and multicultural (DM) issues into the course development.

Digital Libraries is a one-semester technology course that examines the conditions and factors that influence the development of digital library systems and services. The course focuses largely on technological and socioeconomic issues. The goal of the course is to enable students to develop a broad understanding of the technologies and services related to digital libraries, which include the techniques and standards for material digitization, collection construction, digital preservation, retrieval and access, and digital library resource management. Upon finishing this course, students should be able to evaluate the major components of digital libraries by considering their supporting technologies and socioeconomic factors, to review practical problems associated with digital libraries, and to develop valid solutions to solve those problems. This course contains the development of theoretical knowledge and practical understanding of digital libraries.

This course is taken by students who pursue a master's degree in library and information sciences. Traditionally, the majority of these students are from various disciplines in the humanities, the social sciences, or languages. They usually have a weak technology background, but most of them are aware of and are willing to take DME in the class.

Integration of Diversity and Multicultural Education_____

Digital libraries usually are viewed as the extension, and the future model, of traditional libraries. Borgman (2000) gives a two-part definition of a digital library. The first part examines the technology side of a digital library, which Borgman defines as a "set of electronic resources and associated technical capabilities for creating, searching and using information" (p. 42). The second part reviews the social and service side of a digital library; Borgman states that a digital library is "constructed—collected and organized—by [and for] a community of users, and the functional capabilities of a digital library support the information needs and uses of that community" (p. 42). Therefore, designing and developing a digital library involves many new technologies, but like many other services, it can be developed by and for a group of users. If such groups of users are in the minority or part of an underrepresented group, a digital library's systems and services can then be used for storing, preserving, and disseminating the knowledge, ideas, and voices of those groups. With the help of new infrastructures of computers and networks, the digital library approach of disseminating such groups' ideas and voices can be conducted much more easily than using traditional methods. Consequently, the dilemma is not whether DME should be integrated into digital library education but how the integration should happen. I think that the integration should be considered not only in the course's content but also in developing digital library systems and services to help minorities and underrepresented groups. In the remainder of this chapter, I will present how I made the changes to my digital library course to integrate DM-related issues.

The integration follows the scheme proposed by Kitano (1997), which involves four areas in course design: course content, instructional strategies and activities, assessment strategies, and classroom dynamics.

Course Content

The old syllabus of the Digital Libraries course did contain some social issues related to the application of digital libraries in modern society. However, those issues were taught at the end of the semester and were squeezed into the same session in which economic and legal issues were taught. In the redesigned syllabus of the course, I increased the emphasis on social issues and added an additional objective that, upon completing the course, students should be able to examine the social, economical, cultural, and political issues related to digital libraries and their services. To accomplish this objective, I first dedicated one whole class for social-related diversity and multicultural issues in digital library services. The major topics included universal access and the digital divide, minority voices in digital libraries, the impact of new subscription models to small and less-funded libraries, and different views of digital libraries. I then made changes in the instructional strategies, assessment strategies, and class dynamics to help students meet this new objective, the details of which are presented here.

Instructional Strategies and Activities

I think that DME deserves an early and universal introduction in the whole digital library course. Besides the discussion of a digital library as a technology, I introduced in the first class the view of the digital library as a service to communities. Then, whenever possible, I illustrated the value of digital libraries for DM issues by using related digital library systems and services. In addition, whenever appropriate, I requested that students review DM-related digital libraries in their assignments. This way, the students got a chance to interact with the diversity topics, and they became more prepared for their own DM-related digital library projects.

Assessment Strategies

To complete the coursework of my digital library class, students are required to work in a three-person team to design and develop a digital library system. To encourage students to work on DME-related topics, I require them to find real needs from real people and to develop digital library systems to provide services that are not yet available to those people. I developed a rubric for assessing the outcome of the team projects. The rubric is based on an analytical approach to present as clearly as possible the requirements for the team projects. The students are therefore pushed by the project requirements and pulled by the assessment strategies in the rubric to work on underdeveloped services for underrepresented groups of users in the digital world. This integrates more DM-related topics in students' term projects.

Classroom Dynamics

The integration of DME also includes the understanding that students are from different backgrounds and have different learning styles and personalities. To encourage as many students as possible to participate in class discussions, I require the students to hand in questions regarding the content of the reading assignments, from which I select the discussion topics for each class. This way, the students are more familiar with the class topics and are therefore more willing and likely to participate in the discussions. I also require students to tell me the most unclear points of the past class so that those points can be repeated in the next class. This helps me assess the delivery of the class topics and to identify the difficult topics that are worth repeating in the next class.

Outcomes

The integration of DME was applied to my Digital Libraries class in the 2005 fall semester. There were a total of 24 students, of whom 14 were female. The racial distributions were 14 whites, 2 African-Americans, 2 Latinos, and 6 Asians. Seven were international students.

I conducted a survey in the class to obtain feedback from the students about the integration of DME. The majority of students (21 out of 24 students) believed that DME should be included in the digital library curriculum, and most of them (17 out of those 21 students) liked the changes made to the course design to integrate DME. Interestingly, when the three remaining students who said that they did not believe in DME in the digital library curriculum were asked about their reasons, their responses were all DM related. Their reasons are 1) there should be more consideration of other cultures; 2) DME should be incorporated in all class lectures; and 3) there should be more international issues addressed in the course.

There were eight teams in the class. Half of the eight teams integrated DM considerations in their digital library projects. For example, one team rescued some important documents about Latin American culture and history from digital obsolescence and built a digital library for people to access those documents. Some of the important documents included in the collection were documents about slavery in Latin America and a grammar book about Nahuatl, the language of the ancient Aztec empire. Another team developed a digital library for Chinese minorities. To meet my requests for serving underrepresented groups, this team concentrated their collection on four minorities that were important in Chinese history but have not had adequate online presence yet, including Mongolian, Manchu, Miao, and Zhuang. The students in this group excluded Tibetan, which already has abundant online resources. Their collection contained a brief introduction; some multimedia presentations of each minority's culture, its language, its costumes, and its distribution throughout China. The third team built a digital library for Javanese Gamelan music, an influential music form in Indonesian and Southeastern Asian regions. (Gamelan music has some distinct features that are not presented in Western music.) This team's collection included images and videos about the Javanese culture, Gamelan music instruments and scripts, and recordings of Gamelan music. The digital library was built for a scholar in the music department of the University of Pittsburgh, and it has become a complementary instructional material for teaching undergraduate music majors about the Gamelan music.

The students were eager to make suggestions on further improvement to DME in teaching digital libraries, especially on the team projects. Some of their suggestions are to provide 1) more of a connection with local communities about their needs for building digital libraries; 2) more instructions about selecting items and documents related to DM issues; 3) some lectures on the cultural context of digital materials.

Conclusion

Diversity and multicultural education aims to promote the value of diversity and equal opportunity for all people of all races, ethnicities, cultures, languages, genders, sexual orientations, and physical abilities and disabilities. It has been associated with the courses in social sciences, political sciences, humanities, languages, and other similar disciplines. This chapter presents an exercise to integrate DME into technology-related courses. Through the discussion of the ideas, the practices, and some initial evaluation results of the integration I undertook, I hope that readers agree that DME can and should be integrated into the design of technology courses. In addition, the integration should not be limited to the course's content but should also be included in the instructional strategies, the assessment strategies, and the class dynamics. As society becomes more and more dependant on technology, it is important for students in technology-related disciplines to know that DME is part of their curriculum too.

References

Borgman, C. L. (2000). *From Gutenberg to the global information infrastructure: Access to information in the networked world.* Cambridge, MA: MIT Press.

Kitano, M. K. (1997). What a course will look like after multicultural change. In A. I. Morey & M. K. Kitano (Eds.), *Multicultural course transformation in higher education: A broader truth* (pp.18–34). Needham Heights, MA: Allyn & Bacon.

Morey, A. I., & Kitano, M. K. (1997). *Multicultural course transformation in higher education: A broader truth.* Needham Heights, MA: Allyn & Bacon.

51

Teaching Computer Skills Using Peer Tutoring

Dan P. Dewey

Technology in Foreign Language Education is a course at the University of Pittsburgh designed to teach foreign language educators how to use computers in their classrooms. As the instructor, the largest challenge I faced in teaching this course was how to deal with the students' broad range of experience with computers. During the semester under study, the course included doctoral students, master's students, and nondegree students seeking certification. Learners ranged in age from 22 to 58. Two students had recently left careers as computer programmers, and two others had been out of the workforce and home with their children for nearly 20 years. The two sections of the class included native speakers of Spanish, French, Italian, Arabic, Thai, Japanese, and Chinese. This international group made up approximately 30% of the participants.

Given the diversity of the student population in terms of technical expertise, native language, career goals, and so forth, during the semester I taught, I became overwhelmed with questions from students regarding everything from course procedures to the detailed how-tos of specific computer applications. By the end of each three-hour class, I usually felt frustrated that I had worked so hard and yet failed to meet the needs of many of the individuals in the class. Although a teaching assistant might have eliminated some of these frustrations, budgetary limitations did not allow for an assistant.

Implementation

Concerned about my inability to meet the class's needs, I decided to implement a peer tutoring system. At first I planned to use only individuals with considerable computer expertise as peer tutors, but I soon realized that by doing so I would be

303

sending the message that those not selected as peer tutors were not as capable. I therefore determined to have all students act as peer tutors, calling them Experts for the Week, twice during the semester. Students were encouraged to look over the syllabus and sign up to serve as experts during weeks when the content to be covered (e.g., creating PowerPoint presentations, editing images in Adobe Photoshop, creating movies using iMovie, etc.) was less familiar to them. This was done to encourage all students to engage in the task of learning new skills and teaching them to other students.

Experts for the Week (usually two to four people per week) were required to attend training with me outside class one week in advance of when their assigned material was to be covered. During this session, they were given an introduction to the skill or skills to be taught in the next class. These sessions typically lasted 10 to 20 minutes. Learners were able to watch me demonstrate the new skills and then practice briefly on their own and ask questions as needed. They then continued to practice on their own during the week and were able to contact me with questions as needed by email or telephone or by visiting during office hours.

During class, I would offer a brief introduction to a set of skills to all students, showing how to perform one or two small tasks using a computer whose image was projected to the front of the classroom. Following my introduction, learners worked on their own to fulfill short assignments using the tools introduced. Experts were asked to circulate and answer questions during this practice time. This process was repeated several times during each class. For the last hour of class, students were given larger assignments and were asked to experiment on their own and to work on these assignments during the remaining time with the guidance of me and the experts. As the Expert for the Week program evolved, some experts requested that I leave all the instruction to them. On these occasions, they gave their own unique introductions at the beginning of the class as a group and assigned activities they had designed by themselves to get learners to practice the tools they were teaching.

Outcomes

The first noticeable difference following implementation of the Expert for the Week program was a shift in my role. Although I had felt like a sage who was in great demand in previous years, through implementing the program, I began to feel more like a sideline coach supported by a capable set of assistant coaches. Students turned to each other more regularly, even for answers to questions related to course procedures. When linguistic barriers inhibited communication, learners asked each other, rather than me, for clarification. My assistance was needed only to guide the class in a general direction and to help individuals in the rare cases when experts were unable to provide help.

The second noteworthy change was that students took more ownership of the course. Two students commented that they felt that they had a real voice in the course—that they were able to help determine the direction of instruction. They also felt that they had some personal responsibility for the quality of weekly instruction. One student commented in a course evaluation:

> Dr. Dewey valued our expertise. He treated us like equals, and we were sometimes even able to teach him. I've never had a teacher let us be so involved in the instruction. If class wasn't good, it was our own fault.

On several occasions student experts made suggestions for redesigning activities before class that were implemented when they acted as experts in class.

A third change was the development of a strong group dynamic. Learners became more comfortable giving and receiving peer help. This group support was carried over to the class's electronic discussion board, where experts continued to offer help outside class and nonexperts also contributed advice and assistance when needed. Students reported in interviews and journal entries about being "more reliant on others," feeling "a strong feeling of cohort, largely from helping each other each week," and being "forced . . . to help each other more and rely on the instructor less."

Finally, learners developed a greater sense of self-confidence in their ability to use technology and implement it in their classrooms. One 58-year-old Hebrew teacher's comments illustrate this point:

> I was so afraid of being the expert. I didn't think I could learn any of this stuff, let alone teach it. But when I saw everyone else being experts and then got to sit down with Dr. Dewey and learn and ask questions beforehand, I understood that I could do it.

In class this learner showed great confidence as she acted as Expert for the Week, and she was able to provide useful support to other students. A 55-year-old Spanish teacher from Puerto Rico who had seldom used a computer before the course noted, "Being an expert made me realize I can do a lot more than I think if I just push myself." Another student who always labeled herself "the computer dummy of the class" commented that she was amazed that she was able to teach people how to become "real movie editors" when she didn't think she could ever be successful editing digital movies herself. Feeling more confident, students much more frequently reported taking initiative and learning additional skills beyond those required.

The results of peer tutoring described here are not unique to my experience. Ringstaff, Sandholtz, and Dwyer (1991) also found that having younger learners (elementary and secondary school students) tutor each other led to similar results, including 1) shifts in the teacher role from sage to guide, 2) a stronger group dynamic, and 3) increased individual self-confidence. Learners in that study also appreciated having a role in determining the course of instruction. Based on those authors' results and mine, it appears that these patterns may apply to learners at a variety of ages.

Finally, it should be noted that the Expert for the Week program was implemented in conjunction with two other measures that also helped contribute to the patterns described here. I asked learners either to write weekly journal entries and submit them by email or to participate in an electronic class discussion board. The purpose of the assignment design was to inform the instructor of learners' progress, questions, and concerns. The journal option accommodated learners who felt uncomfortable expressing questions or feelings in public. As the instructor, I was able to meet individuals' needs outside class by using these two forums to address student questions and concerns and therefore make class time more productive for the group as a whole. My own study (Dewey & Cannon, in press) indicates that the discussion board also helped build the group dynamic and that journal entries contributed significantly to self-confidence. Other research supports these findings, showing that discussion boards can be effective for promoting group dynamic (McFerrin, 1999) and that journals can be effective for increasing self-confidence (Ediger, 2001).

Peer tutoring can be applied to nearly every instructional setting (see Ringstaff et al., 1991; Reed, 1990; Phelps & Damon, 1989; Chesterfield & Chesterfield, 1985 for examples of uses in technology, writing, mathematics, reading, and foreign language instruction, respectively). Individuals need not start as experts to act as tutors. In my case, I prepared students in advance and outside class to become experts in the classroom. This approach allows even learners who might be typically labeled less capable to participate as leaders in the classroom environment. As other authors have also found (for elementary and secondary school students), peer tutoring can be especially useful for increasing the self-esteem, social status, motivation, and self-direction of learners—in particular those who might be labeled lower achieving (Maheady & Sainato, 1985; Ringstaff et al., 1991). Oakes (1990) notes that female and minority students benefit greatly from this type of collaborative learning.

References

Chesterfield, R. A., & Chesterfield, K. B. (1985). "Hoja's with the H": Spontaneous peer teaching in bilingual classrooms. *Bilingual Review, 12*(3), 198–208.

Dewey, D., & Cannon, A. (in press). Supporting technology instruction through peer tutoring, discussion boards and electronic journals. *IALLT Journal.*

Ediger, M. (2001). *Student journal writing in science.* Retrieved February 23, 2007, from http://eric.ed.gov/ERICDocs/data/ericdocs2/content_storage_01/0000000b/80/24/36/53 .pdf

Maheady, L., & Sainato, D. M. (1985). The effects of peer tutoring upon the social status and social interaction patterns of high and low status elementary school students. *Education and Treatment of Children, 8*(1), 51–65.

McFerrin, K. M. (1999). Incidental learning in a higher education asynchronous online distance education course. *Society for Information Technology & Teacher Education International Conference Proceedings, 10.* Charlottesville, VA: Association for the Advancement of Computing in Education.

Oakes, J. (1990). *Lost talent: The underparticipation of women, minorities and disabled persons in science.* Santa Monica, CA: RAND.

Phelps, E., & Damon, W. (1989). Problem solving with equals: Peer collaboration as a context for learning mathematics and special concepts. *Journal of Educational Psychology, 81*(4), 639–646.

Reed, S. (1990). The write team: Getting a foot in the door. *English Journal, 79*, 67–69.

Ringstaff, C., Sandholtz, J. H., & Dwyer, D. C. (1991). *Trading places: When teachers utilize student expertise in technology-intensive classrooms* (Research Rep. No. 15). Cupertino, CA: Apple Computer.

52

WISE Women: Women in Science and Engineering

Bonnie Shulman

Imagine a world where women make up 50% of the scientific community. Would the practice or content of science be different in such a world? WISE Women: Women in Science and Engineering examines the status of women in science through an exploration of the lives, times, and works of women scientists, past and present. In addition, it describes and analyzes the historical and contemporary barriers to women's full participation in science, engineering, and mathematics, drawing on recent scholarship in feminist science studies.

Introduction

In 1996, newly returned from a sabbatical in which I had immersed myself in feminist critiques of science, I created and taught this first-year seminar. At Bates College all first-year seminars share the goals of developing reasoning and writing skills and encouraging a participatory educational experience for students. In addition, they provide an opportunity for faculty to teach content that differs from existing courses. The WISE Women seminar is cross-listed with the program in women and gender studies, and, not surprisingly, only women have signed up for it. One year the women students actively tried (unsuccessfully) to recruit male peers. The women and I had a very lively and enlightening discussion of men's reasons for declining the invitation. However, since then, students have agreed that they appreciated having a women-only space in which to share and analyze their own and others' experiences as women in the sciences, engineering, and mathematics (SEM). Participation in this course raised their consciousness about the roles of gender norms and internalized stereotypes in explaining the small numbers of women in SEM. With increased confidence in their own abilities,

308

they, in turn, set out to raise the consciousness of their peers and challenged the chilly climate they began to acknowledge existed in some departments on campus. Ironically, over time, this effectively exclusive environment actually helped create a more welcoming and inclusive culture within these traditionally male-dominated disciplines.

Objectives

On the syllabus I list 10 objectives for the seminar. Four of them are elaborations on the common goals of developing critical reasoning and communication skills. The others are particular to this course: to become acquainted with women in SEM in history; to become acquainted with the experiences of younger, active women in SEM, including other students; to become acquainted with the names and achievements of some older living women in SEM; to study the social phenomena that have led to the small numbers of women in the SEM and technology professions; to explore sex differences research, comparing math ability in boys and girls; and to become involved in a project to raise the consciousness of the community about women in SEM.

Texts and Readings

To keep the course fresh, and because there are so many different options available that I want to explore, I use different texts each time I teach it. In addition, I hand out a list of suggested readings—including articles, audiovisual materials, and online sites—for students to use in their weekly assignments and projects. I continually update this list and have included some key resources in the Resources section at the end of this chapter.

Assignments

Although there are some differences in socioeconomic and ethnic backgrounds among Bates students in general, the greatest source of diversity in the population of students who sign up for this course is in their attitudes toward science and feminism. They span the spectrum from those planning to major in science or mathematics, to science haters and math avoiders. Although a few women identify themselves as feminists, many find this label objectionable, and some even see it as an outdated and superfluous concept. To get these differences on the table, the first assignment is an SEM autobiography ("SEM and Me") that instructs students to "describe your relationship to and feelings about science and mathematics." I include a list of guiding questions and encourage students to "be specific about your past and current sense of yourself in relation to science and math, and what has influenced that sense." For the second assignment

("Feminism and Me"), I ask students to "explain what 'feminism' means to you, both in your own life, and in your view of society." Again, I encourage them to be specific and examine "what and who have influenced your view of feminism."

Subsequent assignments prepare the class for writing a 7- to 10-page biography of a woman in an SEM field and introduce them to the resources of the library and other research skills. For the final project, I invite students to respond to the knowledge and experiences they have gained in the course. I ask them "to think of ways of bringing your new consciousness of stereotypes and awareness of the barriers faced by women to the larger community" and give them four choices: an essay responding to questions raised in the course description that cites readings and class discussions over the semester; an article or editorial for the student newspaper summarizing the current status of women in science on campus and advocating for actions to address problems they have documented; a brochure for middle school girls to raise awareness and increase their knowledge about women in SEM; or an interview with at least three women scientists, analyzing their stories in the context of what we have read and learned over the semester. The year I used *Nobel Prize Women in Science* as a text, I substituted a take-home essay exam for the final project. Because we spent most of the semester reading about individual women scientists, I asked students to pick three of the women and again gave them four choices: sets of questions that offered four different frameworks in which to compare and contrast the lives and experiences of their three women and the obstacles those scientists faced in the pursuit of science; the factors that sustained those scientists and enabled them to succeed; the difficult choices they had to negotiate between their career and personal lives; and the lessons to be learned from their lives.

Instructional Methods

Because of the diversity of attitudes, and because students' personal belief systems may very well be challenged, it is crucial to create an environment where they feel safe expressing their opinions. I have taken some cues from the literature on feminist pedagogy and incorporated teaching strategies designed to encourage and support frank discussion of controversial topics. The class and I introduce ourselves to each other on the first day and explain our reasons for taking (or, in my case, teaching) the course. Everyone is polite and friendly, and it is a good icebreaker. They hand in their first assignment (which they have received at an advising session before classes begin), and I present an overview lecture on four approaches to the field of gender and science: recover achievements of women in science; analyze history of women's participation in the institutions of science; examine how the sciences define the nature of women; and examine ways in which women's absence from the history of science may have distorted the very norms and methods of science. We end by brainstorming ground rules for discussion. I design the next two weeks of class to give us ample practice following these rules.

I work feverishly to read students' SEM autobiographies and create a summary of the responses including (anonymous) quotes from their essays, and I email this document to them to read in preparation for the second class. Students like seeing their words in print and having a chance to anticipate the range of opinions and viewpoints of their colleagues before engaging in face-to-face discussion. This approach also allows everyone to feel represented in the conversation. It also allows me to frame the discussion and move it in productive directions, all the while using the students' own words to support each framing statement. We laugh at the images we all have of scientists as mad old white men in lab coats and begin to examine where these images come from. We notice that the conflict between cultural images internalized early on, and subsequent experiences that contradict these stereotypes, can result in ambiguity and confusion. Finally, we look at the factors that can help us overcome restrictive gender roles and other societal norms or expectations that may be limiting. During the third week, we go through the same drill for the "Feminism and Me" essay. Although I assign short supplementary readings for each of these topics, the bulk of the content is determined by the students' own responses. Thus, by the end of the third week, we have established a rapport and trust and have developed a format—all of which will serve us well throughout the semester. For me, ensuring that this process of examining unquestioned (and often deeply cherished) beliefs with a group of peers is available for as many students as possible is at least as (if not more) important than any particular content I might impart.

Sample Responses

Here are some examples of student responses over the years. They demonstrate an evolution in thinking based on readings, discussions, and tools of analysis gained in the class.

> I had never truly thought about feminism before this. I have always felt that I am a feminist, on my own terms, but I never knew the accepted definition of feminism. I know now that feminism can mean a variety of different things and is represented by a variety of different people.

> As I learn more about feminism, my views continue to change; I am more willing to give up my stereotypes and be more open to the many concepts of feminism. Feminism does not play an important role in my life at this time, and I do not feel a strong urge to become a part of this movement. Perhaps as I am faced

with more of the barriers that feminism works to do away with, I will feel a need to make an effort in the movement of feminism.

As I had as a child, many children grow up with the image that a scientist is a male. As more and more women enter this field of study, this stereotype could change and, in turn, influence other girls to look up to these women and strive to be like them.

Even with my relatively broad exposure to SEM, I find it somewhat disheartening that the image of Albert Einstein still sometimes pops into my mind when someone mentions a scientist. I realize that Einstein was a genius and an important part of scientific history, but I think the importance of work by scientists like my aunt was overlooked by teachers as a result of his reputation.

These statements bring closure to what the class and I have been discussing over the course of the semester. We have discovered that the general concepts and ideas that we have learned about exist in the lives of the women with whom we spoke. The differences in all of these women's pasts have led them to hold diverse opinions on the current situation of women in scientific careers. We ourselves have not encountered obvious inequalities because of our gender. Through learning about others' experiences, however, we have become more conscious of the importance of recognizing the discrepancies that still exist between men and women today.

Resources

Books Used as Required Texts

Abir-Am, P. G., & Outram, D. (1989). *Uneasy careers and intimate lives: Women in science, 1789–1979.* New Brunswick, NJ: Rutgers University Press.

Ambrose, S. A., Dunkle, K. L., Lazarus, B. B., Nair, I., & Harkus, D. A. (1997). *Journeys of women in science and engineering: No universal constants.* Philadelphia, PA: Temple University Press.

Fort, D. C. (1993). *A hand up: Women mentoring women in science.* Washington, DC: Association for Women in Science.

McGrayne, S. B. (1998). *Nobel Prize women in science: Their lives, struggles and momentous discoveries* (2nd ed.). Secaucus, NJ: Carol Publishing Group.

McIlwee, J. S., & Robinson, G. R. (1992). *Women in engineering: Gender, power, and workplace culture.* Albany, NY: State University of New York Press.

Morse, M. (1995). *Women changing science: Voices from a field in transition.* New York, NY: Plenum Press.

Journal Articles and References

Amankwaa, L. A. (2000, October). Fear of feminism: An African-American woman's journey. *Women in Higher Education,* 40–41.

Benjamin, D. (2005). Women in science, mathematics, engineering, and technology: An experimental approach in an undergraduate course. *Feminist Teacher, 15*(2), 93–110.

Brush, S. G. (1991). Women in science and engineering. *American Scientist, 79,* 404–419.

Science and Technology [Special issue]. (1989, fall). *Sage: A Scholarly Journal on Black Women, 6*(2).

Weisner, J. (2004). Awakening teacher voice and student voice: The development of a feminist pedagogy. *Feminist Teacher, 15*(1), 34–47.

Women in Science [Special issue]. (1986, January). *Radical Teacher, 30.*

Women in Science '94: Comparisons across cultures [Special issue]. (1994, March). *Science, 263.*

Index